URBAN RAGE

URBAN RAGE

RAGE

THE REVOLT OF THE EXCLUDED

MUSTAFA DIKEÇ

YALE UNIVERSITY PRESS
NEW HAVEN AND LONDON

For information about this and other Yale University Press publications, please contact:

U.S. Office: sales.press@yale.edu   yalebooks.com
Europe Office: sales@yaleup.co.uk   yalebooks.co.uk

Set in Adobe Caslon Pro by IDSUK (DataConnection) Ltd
Printed in Great Britain by Gomer Press Ltd, Llandysul, Ceredigion, Wales

Library of Congress Cataloging-in-Publication Data

Names: Dikec, Mustafa, author.
Title: Urban rage : the revolt of the excluded / Mustafa Dikec.
Description: New Haven : Yale University Press, 2017.
Identifiers: LCCN 2017022056 | ISBN 9780300214949 (c1 : alk. paper)
Subjects: LCSH: Social conflict—Cross-cultural studies. |
   Equality—Cross-cultural studies. | Urban policy—Cross-cultural studies.
   | Urbanization—Social aspects—Cross-cultural studies. | Sociology,
   Urban—Cross-cultural studies.
Classification: LCC HN18.3 .D55 2017 | DDC 307.76—dc23
LC record available at https://lccn.loc.gov/2017022056

A catalogue record for this book is available from the British Library.

10 9 8 7 6 5 4 3 2 1

For Joakim, Elif and Félix

Contents

Acknowledgements

When I started working on this book, I was daunted by its scope; six countries is a tall order for a single researcher. Intensive research and reading helped, but the key to my understanding of these contexts was discussions with several activists, friends and colleagues: activists working with Megafonen in Sweden, participants of the Don't Shoot Coalition in St Louis, and community organizers in Over-the-Rhine, Yaşar Adanalı, Cihan Baysal, Gülnaz and Zeynep Bülbül, Erbatur Çavuşoğlu, Jonathan Diskin, Thomas Dutton, Patricia Ehrkamp, Sinan Erensü, Dave Featherstone, Tariq Jazeel, Roger Keil, Ute Lehrer, Gülçin Erdi Lelandais, Margit Mayer, Bonnie Neumeier, Jean-François Pérouse, Clémence Petit, Bahar Sakızlıoğlu, Ove Sernhede, Julia Strutz, Erik Swyngedouw, Mekonnen Tesfahuney, Catharina Thörn, Håkan Thörn, Hade Türkmen and Rebecca Wanzo. I thank them all for their generosity.

A special thanks goes to Mat Coleman and Mary Thomas for their hospitality in Columbus, Ohio, and again to Mat for joining me on the trip to St Louis and Cincinnati. The research visit to the US

ACKNOWLEDGEMENTS

was financed by my research unit in Paris, LATTS, and I thank them for their support.

I am grateful to a smaller group of friends and colleagues who took time out of their busy schedules to read and comment on chapters: Allan Cochrane, Mat Coleman, Kate Derickson, Lazaros Karaliotas, Ozan Karaman, Stefan Kipfer, Carina Listerborn, Don Mitchell, Irene Molina, Walter Nicholls, Steve Pile and Jonathan Rutherford. Thank you all for your generosity with your time and suggestions.

Another friend and colleague deserves a special mention. It was Florian Schui who first convinced me to write this book during a lunch in 2014. I was reluctant at first as I had just finished my space and politics book, wanted to rest a bit, and then get on with my historical research on nineteenth-century Paris. Having just published his *Austerity* with Yale University Press, Florian, a historian himself, convinced me that my historical project could wait. I had already been teaching, researching and writing about urban uprisings, so following his suggestion I approached Yale, and had the good fortune to work with Heather McCallum, who commissioned the book and supported the project from start to end. Rachael Lonsdale and Marika Lysandrou, again at Yale, helped me with their sharp comments and helpful suggestions during the preparation of the manuscript, and I had the pleasure of working with Melissa Bond and Charlotte Chapman during the copy-editing process. I am grateful to all of them, as well as to the anonymous colleagues who evaluated my book proposal and provided excellent comments for the manuscript. It has been a wonderful experience.

The final touches to the manuscript were made during a visiting professorship at Malmö University, where I enjoyed a pleasant working environment in one of the most exciting urban studies departments in Sweden. I thank my friends and colleagues there,

ACKNOWLEDGEMENTS

especially Guy Baeten, Sandra Jönsson, Carina Listerborn, Emil Pull and Per-Markku Ristilammi.

Without the benefit of a sabbatical or a fellowship to provide relief from teaching and afford uninterrupted time for writing, I had to make time within a busy schedule of work and family duties. Getting up at 5 a.m. every day to write is not always pleasant, but I have been lucky enough to be surrounded by a spirited group of supporters who ensured, sometimes despite my resistance, that I get a life. This book is for the members of this small group, my children, Joakim, Elif and Félix, with all my love.

Mustafa Dikeç
March 2017
Paris and Malmö

1

Rage in the Urban Age

The uprising that erupted in Cincinnati a year after the turn of the century was the largest in US cities since 1992 Los Angeles. It was quelled by the declaration of a state of emergency. A few years later, in 2005, French cities were on fire in the most extensive disruption the country had known since 1968. It lasted three weeks and led to the declaration of a state of emergency for the first time on mainland France. Athens was ablaze in 2008 in an uprising that was unique in its extent and intensity in Greece's recent history. London's uprising in 2011 was unprecedented since the Gordon Riots of 1780, Stockholm's in 2013 was unseen in Swedish cities since the food riots during the First World War, Istanbul's, again in 2013, was unique in the country's modern history. Ferguson, on the other side of the Atlantic, was on fire twice in 2014, Baltimore erupted in 2015, Milwaukee and Charlotte the following year – all of which led to the declaration of a state of emergency. Welcome to the era of urban rage.

We now live, as the UN-Habitat declared, in an 'urban age'; if the current trends continue, in a few years from now all future population increase will feed urban growth. But what has been heralded as the urban age turns out to be an era of urban rage as well. Since the turn of the century, a wave of urban anger has taken a global dimension. From Cincinnati to Istanbul and beyond, one city after another has gone up in flames, leaving in its wake death and injury, and fuelling more rage, which does not seem to be quenched either by the extent of the destruction or the severity of the repression.

Is this the prospect the urban age holds for us? Announced with much enthusiasm, the urban age signals, according to such bodies as the UN-Habitat, a chance of prosperity for the growing numbers of urbanites, with urban areas held up as being the 'engine-rooms of human development' that offer people the chance to realize their dreams and aspirations.[1] Yet we have constantly been reminded by the urban uprisings of the past two decades that congregations of people in cities are not to the benefit of all. Despite the dynamism and intense vitality of cities evident in such congregations, they are signs less of a fresh future taking shape than of a bleak one looming on the horizon, less clues of the prosperity of cities than warnings of the fractures in urban societies. As we will see, the so-called urban age is not only characterized by unprecedented levels of urbaniza-tion, but also by levels of inequality unseen since the early 1900s, and uprisings of unprecedented scale and intensity. Government responses to these incidents, with their repressive measures and inflammatory language, suggest that we are no longer in the engine room of human development, but in the waste management sector of troubled human behaviour and criminality. The rage that erupts into uprisings is the flip side of our urban age.[2]

In this book I seek to understand the sources of this urban rage by taking readers to cities in the United States, United Kingdom, France, Sweden, Greece and Turkey.[3] I have chosen to focus on the liberal democracies of the west with a history of giving democracy lessons to the rest of the world (leaving aside the question of where to place Turkey, which, furthermore, no longer looks like a democracy). If the cities of these mature democracies with relatively rich economies are mired with outbursts of rage, what does this tell us about our contemporary urban condition and the future of urban societies?

Urban rage is more widespread than my examples suggest, ranging from Cairo to São Paulo, Hong Kong to Madrid, Berlin to Tel Aviv. It takes different forms and expresses different grievances. Rising inequalities, bleak economic prospects, urban transformations, authoritarian governance, discriminatory policing and political corruption are among the main themes. I focus here on urban uprisings as one particular expression of urban rage. These are spontaneous insurrections, not planned events or organized movements, which are motivated by grievances that have to do with the everyday urban lives of those who revolt: those who live on the wrong side of town fearing a brush with the police might put an end to their lives; those who are on the right side of town but have the wrong skin colour; those who find the wrong side of town where they live is now becoming the right side of it, squeezing them out; those, in general, whose everyday urban lives are marked by reminders of their exclusion from the wealth, rights and privileges available to other urban dwellers. Urban rage that erupts in uprisings is the revolt of the excluded, overtaking urban spaces through unruly practices and defying the order of things.[4]

Exclusion and Inequality

No social scientist is able to say on this day or that day, at this hour or that hour, X or Y will trigger off social unrest, but it will follow, as night follows day, that such an excluded population with a deep sense of social injustice will sooner or later explode.

– Stuart Hall, 1987

The urban uprisings of the past decades were unprecedented not only in terms of their intensity, but also in their geography. They occurred more in liberal democratic countries than in dictatorships, and were all repressed by increasingly militarized measures. Although severe material conditions mark the context for most, exclusion is key to understanding them. The exceptional rise of urban uprisings in our urban age is thus a symptom of the failure of liberal democracies to address exclusion. This suggests that contemporary urban processes produce discontent and dissent that the established institutions of liberal democracies cannot accommodate in non-coercive ways. We will see for each case what delimits and delegitimizes liberal democratic processes in precisely the spaces they are most meant to work.

Liberal democracies do not guarantee equality in terms of wealth or social status. Indeed, it is one of the basic assumptions of such political orders that a democratic political life can be organized despite social and economic inequalities.[5] There are two implications of such inequalities. First, they produce political inequality by excluding or marginalizing the voice and influence of subordinate groups. Second, these two forms of inequality reinforce each other, which means that formally democratic procedures and processes, when they operate under conditions of structural social and economic inequality, work to the advantage of dominant groups, perpetuating relations of privilege, domination and oppression.[6] Liberal democracies are thus prone to disparities of power, which undermines their democratic commitment to the political equality and equal respect of their members. The tension created by the discrepancy between this image of equality and the empirical reality of inequality and exclusion fuels the rage that erupts in urban uprisings and other expressions of discontent. The concentration cities allow has many advantages, but it also means that those excluded from the rights and privileges that others enjoy are reminded of their deprivation on a daily basis in their everyday urban lives.

4

Exclusion, as I use the term here, does not imply the actual exclusion of some groups from society, but their exclusion from enjoying the rights, opportunities and privileges within it as much as others do. This was the case in Ferguson, for example, where the city's poor and black residents were concentrated in a segregated area, and were subject to discriminatory and aggressive policing. In Cincinnati, it was again the poor and black residents who bore the burden of downtown regeneration policies and aggressive policing that accompanied them. Similar discriminatory practices enraged youth in the stigmatized suburbs of Paris and Stockholm, immigrant youth in Athens, and ethnic and religious minorities that faced displacement because of urban transformation policies in Istanbul. In the chapters that follow, we will see diverse reasons for and forms of exclusion as sources of urban rage.

Think, for example, about the widening income gap in the past three decades or so: a growing share of income is going to top earners, where the richest 10 per cent reap the largest gains, while the rest find themselves with fewer resources, in precarious jobs and with lower incomes.[7] Those who do not belong to the richest few have good reason to believe that they are excluded from something, and poverty amid plenty is a powerful source of resentment, especially when coupled with the aggressive policing of those excluded from the privileges of urban life around them.[8] We have seen various examples of this in recent years, with protests and revolts in several countries, drawing in not only the poorest populations, but the increasingly squeezed middle classes as well. As we will see in the following chapters, urban uprisings do not always occur in the context of poverty and those who participate are not always the usual suspects of 'the excluded', as this term is understood in the Euro-technocratic language (referring, that is, to immigrants and unemployed youth of immigrant origin).

Therefore, I use exclusion as an entry point to understand sources of urban rage, rather than throwing it as an abstract blanket over the incidents to explain them away. In each case, as we shall see, exclusion takes several forms (segregation, concentrated poverty, displacement, targeted policing), feeds on particular histories of oppression (slavery, colonialism), and is legitimized by different political ideologies (neoliberalism, republicanism, political Islam). Despite differences, however, it never fails, in its various forms, to undermine the democratic ideal of political equality; it is highly corrosive, gnawing away at the confidence of marginalized groups in the established institutions of society. As a result urban uprisings can be seen to carry with them a call for redress, for equality and justice; they can be seen as a reaction to police violence in particular but also to the forms of exclusion noted above. This brings us to the question of the political element in urban uprisings. What political significance do they carry?

From the Pathological to the Political

None, nineteenth-century observers of such incidents thought. They saw in revolts signs of human pathology rather than symptoms of social problems. Within their framework – which I call 'the pathological framework' – such mass behaviour came to distinguish the normal from the pathological, marginal and irrational. The rioting crowds were, for them, the collective signs of irrationality, marginality, uncontrolled and violent emotions and lack of moral sense. This pathological framework, then, sought to explain such incidents in terms of human behaviour.[9]

You may think this pathological framework is now a thing of the past, a century-old sociological fallacy that no longer finds any purchase. I am afraid, however, that the pathological framework is still very much alive, and it has come back with a vengeance during the urban uprisings of the twenty-first century. References to 'scum', 'criminals', 'feral youth', 'people with a twisted moral code' and 'marauders and marginals' were repeatedly made by politicians in power during the uprisings of late in France, the United States, the United Kingdom and Turkey. However, the pathological framework leads to an ethical dead end because it attributes urban unrest to flawed individuals and in so doing encourages a limited and punitive approach. Attributing the source of riots to human nature also fails to explain the where and when of such incidents: why do they occur here and now rather than there and then? Why don't they occur all the time and everywhere since in a given society, if we follow the logic of the pathological framework, there will always be individuals who deviate from norms (however defined) and who are, by definition, incapable of self-control. And this is the logical dead end of the pathological framework.

I propose, therefore, a shift away from this pathological framework to a political one. Urban uprisings are political in that they expose patterns, dynamics and structures of exclusion and oppression that have become routine and normalized. As eruptions of accumulated grievances, they bring into sharp relief the fault lines and exclusions in our cities. They are like 'a revealing flash of lightning', as Alain Locke described the 1935 Harlem riot, not only disrupting, but also exposing routinized injustices. As Don Mitchell puts it, they 'arise out of the very social and physical structure of the city, and when they do, they suddenly illuminate it', bringing to light 'the structure and exercise of power' in cities.[10] The occurrence of burning and looting, unfortunate as it is, does not render urban uprisings less or not political at all. As a show of indignation about unequal treatment of groups and other forms of injustice, these revolts are calls for justice and equality, even when these are not always expressed explicitly.

As we will see with our examples, urban uprisings never start as gratuitous burning and looting. They follow some form of oppression, and perhaps also some inflammatory remark that adds insult to injury. They are triggered by a specific, usually tragic, incident that symbolizes the sufferings and hardship of certain populations. The triggering incidents, however, are not random or one-off occurrences, but part of systematic injustices. In other words, the incident that triggers an uprising is neither rare nor unprecedented, but perhaps one that has gone awry and finally 'overflowed the unimaginably bitter cup', as James Baldwin put it in 1966.[11] And sometimes it takes unruly practices to expose injustices and change the terms of the debate – just think about how the Ferguson uprising revealed the exploitation and criminalization of blacks (more on this in the following chapter).

The political element in urban uprisings is this exposure of injustices and grievances. Focusing on the looting and the burning to negate the political significance of uprisings is to confound the unfolding of an event with its causes. The forms of exclusion that build rage up, the triggering incident that sets the spark and the immediate response of authorities are crucial in understanding the political significance of uprisings. Once the rage erupts, the event takes on a dynamic of its own and unfolds in ways that the participants, who have different motives and engage in different actions, could not have planned in advance and can no longer control.[12] There is, therefore, an element of the unexpected in these incidents once they start unfolding. As Marcus Knox-Hooke, the man charged with instigating the 2011 London uprising by smashing up a police car, put it: 'I was not expecting it to turn out the way it turned out. . . . I was in a rage. . . It just escalated.'[13]

This does not imply, however, that the participants are irrational and unable to measure the consequences of their actions, as the pathological framework would have us believe. But once caught up in the fury of the moment and with the sense of empowerment that comes with taking over urban spaces, some participants in urban uprisings do things they probably would not have done under other circumstances – and some, benefiting from the cover of disorder, do things they would have done anyway. As Pauline Pearce, who earned the nickname 'Hackney Heroine' for standing up to rioters in London 2011, put it: 'These are people who got carried away in the moment. You've got 100 people and 98 are smashing the shit out of everything. Are you going to be the only two to stand there? In a place like Pembury [estate] you'd be accused of being an informer.'[14]

Although uprisings are impossible to predict, there are patterns that suggest that specific conditions are more prone to eruption; the places where they occur, the people who participate and the triggering incidents share some common features. These eruptions, we will see, are not signs of defective human nature, but of justified rage with interrelated economic, social and political causes.

The Wires

Imagine a birdcage with a bird in it. If you get close to the cage and focus on a single wire, you would be puzzled about the behaviour of the caged animal. You would discover nothing about the nature of that single wire that could possibly prevent the bird from flying away to its freedom. But if you stopped looking at the individual wire, stepped back and looked at the cage, it would become obvious why the bird does not – cannot – fly away. The seemingly harmless single wires, when coming together in a certain way, become as solid as a wall in confining what is inside. The 'cageness' of the birdcage does not derive from some property of the individual wires, but from the way they intertwine; from, in other words, their systematic relations, which form an oppressive structure.[15] So, rather than trying to pin down one precise reason behind urban uprisings, what we need, it seems to me, is more of a birdcage method that allows multiple stories of resentment to emerge.

I do not offer this as some fancy metaphor. A central finding of urban inequality research, for example, is that this is a systematic phenomenon produced by various interrelated elements such as changes in labour markets, educational failure, political neglect, incarceration policy and policing practices, to name a few. These interrelated elements – economic, social, political processes – have 'concentration effects', which means that they work together to produce concentrated poverty with severe disadvantages in certain neighbourhoods.[16] Therefore, urban inequality is not produced merely by educational failure, social attitudes, economic changes or institutional practices. It is the product of an ensemble of economic changes (e.g. deindustrialization), institutional practices (e.g. police brutality), social attitudes (e.g. discrimination) and policies (e.g. reduced social provision) that make up the birdcage. This is why the problems of urban inequality and concentration of poverty cannot be resolved simply by neighbourhood renovation or demolition programmes; the former, renovation, focuses on a single wire, while the latter, demolition, moves the cage somewhere else without addressing the broader dynamics that produced the problem in the first place.

We should, however, note the limits of the birdcage metaphor. The sources of grievances, of rage that erupts in urban uprisings, vary from context to context, both geographically and historically. After all, Ferguson is not Istanbul is not Clichy-sous-Bois. The London uprisings of the 1980s are different from London 2011, both in their context and unfolding, as Los Angeles 1965 is from Los Angeles 1992. Nevertheless, as we will see in the following chapters, these uprisings are all outcomes of deep-rooted grievances, of long histories of exclusion of and violence perpetrated against particular populations. They are not reactions to isolated incidents, but to injustices that have become routine and normalized. There are structural reasons, not individual pathologies, behind urban rage – reasons that have to do with the routine workings of our cities. As Sharlen Moore put it, a resident of Sherman Park, Milwaukee, where an uprising erupted in August 2016 after the police shot a black man to death:

'This isn't just, "Oh, my gosh, all of a sudden this happened." It's a series of things that has happened over a period of time. And right now you shake a soda bottle and you open the top and it explodes, and this is what it is.' Milwaukee is one of the most segregated cities in the United States, with some of the highest incarceration and unemployment rates for black men in the country.[17] Urban rage is not about isolated cases of bad practice. It is rage against systematic, sustained oppression with many sources – not an individual wire, but intertwined wires.

Understanding urban rage requires an approach that takes into consideration these intertwined wires. It is the interrelated economic, political and urban transformations since especially the 1970s that set the context for our era of urban rage. These transformations vary among and within the countries we will explore in this book. It seems to me, however, that the following capture their nature: economic restructuring and rising inequalities, changes in urban policy, increased stigmatization of minority groups, decreasing civil liberties, and an increasing crisis of legitimacy. Let us briefly look at each before moving on to our examples, which will show how these set the context for urban rage.

The first transformation involves economic restructuring and rising inequalities. Most of the rich economies considered in this book have gone through a process of deindustrialization and deregulation, becoming less reliant on manufacturing and more on finance and services, and shrinking the prospects for stable jobs. The changes in the economy not only increased unemployment and job precariousness among the working classes, but also left many middle-class families in difficulty, especially if they belonged to historically oppressed minorities. This new economic context favoured owners of capital more than wage earners, and has contributed to rising inequalities, which are more visible in cities with their concentration of wealth as well as poverty.

11

This increase in inequalities was not only the product of increasing incomes at the high end: it appears that we are not far from what David Harvey calls 'accumulation by dispossession'.[18] Harvey uses this term to refer to wealth accumulation by dispossessing people of their resources – their water through privatization, their neighbourhood through urban transformation projects, their public spaces through commodified use of urban space, their houses through predatory mortgages. Accumulation by dispossession occurs when the wealth and power of the few derive from the dispossession of the many of their resources, in the name not of the common good, but for profit.

These changes set the stage for a related, second transformation. With the changing nature of urban economies and government policies, city governments were forced to seek other revenue sources. This search led to the increasing popularity of urban regeneration projects, conceived to generate revenue by attracting better-off residents to cities with prestigious commercial and housing projects. Urban land and property development became important areas of investment and profit, and the exchange value of urban space took priority over the common good, even over democratic procedures, as we will see in some of our examples. Gentrification of old neighbourhoods led to displacement and escalating tensions, as we will see with the Istanbul uprising, especially when coupled with aggressive policing aimed at clearing the streets, as the Cincinnati uprising will show. Cities with little or no prospect of attracting profitable commercial and housing projects found more creative ways to generate revenue, as we will see with Ferguson.

A third component that set the stage for contemporary urban rage is the increasing stigmatization of minority groups. This is not a new phenomenon, but western military interventions and a series of tragic events associated with the rise of Islamist terrorism have aggravated this problem. There are certainly differences among the countries we will study in terms of who is stigmatized and why, but we will see that continued or increasing stigmatization of minority groups is a major source of resentment behind urban uprisings.

Related to this, a fourth component is decreasing civil liberties, often justified with references to the threat of terrorism. Within this context, state responses to protest have become more repressive and ever more militarized. I do not mean to overstate this last point; after all, state responses to protest have never involved open arms and flowers. Interventions to repress protest, however, have become more military in style with the increasing use of army gear, a trend that Stephen Graham defined as 'the new military urbanism'.[19]

The fifth element that sets the context of our era of urban rage is a crisis of legitimacy, marked by decreasing confidence in the political elite and liberal democratic systems of representation. This, again, is not an entirely new phenomenon, but we cannot ignore the legacy of the financial crisis of 2008 and government responses to it, which left millions of people wondering whom their governments were serving. Not all the countries we explore in this book were affected to the same extent by the crisis. We will see, however, that they are all marked by incidents that undermine trust in the political elite, and the effective representation of the voices of common people in the political system is a major source of grievance.

For ordinary citizens, especially if they belong to historically stigmatized groups, the economic context set by these transformations is not one of advantage, but of difficulty; the social context is not one of peace, but of increased tension; the political context is not one of empowerment and equality, but of disenfranchisement and widening inequalities of voice, power and influence. For the many left behind, these transformations do not signal a 'fresh future taking shape' in cities, as the UN-Habitat report states, but more hardship to come. The prospect of an 'urban age' is marked by sharply widening inequalities, increasing material difficulties and social tension, decreasing civil liberties and, to top it all, more repression.

I am painting a bleak picture, and some readers may wonder why we don't have uprisings all the time. These incidents, as we will see with our examples, are not planned in advance. They erupt spontaneously, usually following a tragic event in a context of simmering anger. While media images focus on the spectacular aspects, revolting is not always fun and games, as anyone who has faced the riot police would agree. Uprisings are risky and destructive, often destroying the participants' own neighbourhoods, not something you engage in at the slightest frustration. They are also painful for the participants to the extent that they are outcomes of rage. It is unjust, political philosopher Judith Shklar wrote, to 'cause rage by arousing a sense of injustice'. But what is unjust, she noted, is not only the material deprivation that gives rise to this sense of injustice. It is equally unjust to make people 'feel the fury and resentment' for 'nothing is more painful or soul-destroying than rage'.[20] Rage that erupts in uprisings is not necessarily emancipatory; it is destructive, sometimes unjustifiably so. But it is not necessarily pathological either. We will see with our examples how injustices lead to urban rage, erupting in uprisings that reveal and disrupt them, if only temporarily.

It is best, therefore, not to trivialize such outbursts of rage by assuming that people will simply revolt when the conditions are dire. There is no sure-fire formula since uprisings are never dependent on a single factor – an individual wire – that we can neatly isolate. Many people live in conditions of material difficulty and suffer daily discrimination, but none of this automatically leads to revolt. At some point, however, something will overflow the unimaginably bitter cup, and lead to a destructive outburst of rage. In order to understand why this happens, how urban rage builds up, we will look at the context of these incidents in detail. For each country, I will start with the urban uprisings of the past decade, then trace them back to earlier uprisings in order to understand the context and see historical continuities or differences. Based on patterns that emerge from this exploration, I will argue that urban uprisings are products of violence inflicted on excluded urban citizens. They expose forms of exclusion and the violence suffered, and are thus political events.

If our cities are to absorb all future population growth, as estimated, then it is crucial to understand the underlying reasons behind urban uprisings. But is rioting the correct way to express discontent, readers may ask, as a television reporter did during the 2011 London uprising.[21] 'Yes,' said the young Londoner to whom the question was addressed. 'You wouldn't be talking to me now if we didn't riot, would you?'

2

Fatal Encounters in US Cities

Black Lives Matter. That this even needs pointing out is telling about twenty-first-century America. The grievances had been accumulating over decades, but it took yet another uprising to put them once again on the public agenda as an appeal to justice, equality and accountability. In a democratic country like the United States, such an appeal does not have to take the destructive form it did – twice – in Ferguson in 2014. The fact that it did showed whose lives did not matter and whose voices did not count. The fact that it did, however, also showed those lives do matter.

The Ferguson uprising began on 10 August 2014, the day after a white police officer, Darren Wilson, shot several times and killed an unarmed black teenager, Michael Brown. For about two weeks, peaceful protests as well as arson, looting and clashes with the police kept Ferguson in the headlines, both national and international. The uprising was repressed by police officers equipped with military-grade weapons and the National Guard, who referred to the protestors as 'enemy forces'. A state of emergency was declared – an extreme measure that was also taken in April 2015 during the Baltimore uprising triggered by another black life lost during police custody, in Milwaukee in August 2016 and in Charlotte a month later.[1] In Ferguson, another week of protests and clashes followed in November 2014, after a grand jury decided not to indict Wilson, and protests on a smaller scale took place on the anniversary of Brown's killing.

Violence visited upon black lives by white police officers has long been a trigger for revolt – for example, in Cincinnati in 2001, Los Angeles in 1992, Miami in 1980 and others during the turbulent 1960s.[2] It would be a mistake, however, to see these as isolated or random instances of brutality committed by some bad cops. As Ferguson, and others before and after, showed, rage builds up over time through systematic, not occasional, oppression of certain groups and their exclusion from the rights and privileges enjoyed by others. Racist police officers do exist and do horrible things, but as we will see with Ferguson, Los Angeles, Cincinnati and Baltimore, urban uprisings cannot be explained away by a focus on the individual perpetrators of violence. In other words, the sources of urban rage are structural rather than individual. This may be getting a bit too abstract, so perhaps it is time we paid a visit to Ferguson, an inner suburb of St Louis, Missouri.

Who Loves Ferguson?

'I kept thinking, They're coloured and I'm white but the same things have happened, really the *same* things, and how can I make them know that?'

'But they didn't', she said, 'happen to you *because* you were white. They just happened. But what happens up here . . . happens *because* they are coloured. And that makes a difference.'

– James Baldwin, *Another Country*

If you arrived in Ferguson by South Florissant Road, you would probably find it difficult to match it to the image that made Ferguson's name both nationally and internationally. Ferguson, you would see, has its wine bar, cigar lounge, local brewery and Italian bakery, all conveniently located along this commercial road – not quite the image of a run-down city devastated by riots; more of a quaint suburban community. You might think, as I did, that either they fixed everything up very quickly, or else it was just a big fuss over nothing, all the while wondering where the black citizens of Ferguson were.

Walking north on South Florissant, you would start seeing signs of the incidents once you have passed the building that houses both Ferguson's police department and its municipal court. Signs of damage, however, are not many. There are few boarded-up businesses, and one of these is a law firm that specializes in traffic law. Once we have understood the workings of the police department and the municipal court, we will see that this was not a random choice.

Across the street from the police department and the municipal court is a curious store called 'I Love Ferguson', with black letters and a red heart instead of 'love'. This is where you buy your 'I Love Ferguson' memorabilia – hats, T-shirts, coffee mugs and signs that you also see displayed on many of the shopfronts on South Florissant Road. If you are a foreigner, a push pin marks your country on the world map hanging above the guestbook. As the lady keeping the store explains, the store was set up after the uprisings, and the revenue it generates goes to businesses that suffered damage during the incidents. When asked why people revolted, her smile gives way to a concerned look, and she says, nodding with her chin, 'Well, they put all the Section 8 housing there.'

There are, it turns out, two Fergusons, and the other one is farther east. This second Ferguson feels more contained and compact, and it is clearly separated from the first one by West Florissant Avenue, a commercial strip that bore the brunt during the uprisings. The houses in this part of Ferguson are of two kinds: single family houses and apartment complexes. The gardens are well kept, houses are maintained; you can see it is not a particularly wealthy neighbourhood, but not a run-down one either. The area with the apartment complexes is where Michael Brown was killed. It is one of the most concentrated areas of poverty in the region, because these apartment complexes are home to Section 8 renters, recipients of rent aid vouchers who are by definition poor. Northwinds Apartments, where Brown lived, has 438 housing units, and it is one of the largest in the region. It is followed by Park Ridge with 336 units. There are also Canfield Green Apartments, Versailles Apartments and Oakmont Townhomes, all concentrated in this eastern tip of Ferguson, where the population is practically all black.

The Section 8 voucher system allows people to choose where they want to live by providing rent subsidies rather than units in designated projects. In theory, this system could reduce segregation and concentration of poverty by increasing the options available to the poor by allowing them to rent in the private housing market. In practice, however, voucher users get concentrated in certain areas for four reasons. First, the federal government sets an upper limit for rent, which also limits the areas for the use of vouchers. Better areas have higher rents, which prevents the use of vouchers in these areas and pushes Section 8 renters to less desirable neighbourhoods where rents are lower. Second, housing provision for vouchers is scant as landlords do not want to deal with poor tenants and the bureaucracy that comes with the voucher system. Third, landlords who are willing to have Section 8 renters offer units in poorer areas, which aggravates the problem of concentrated poverty. And finally, zoning laws that deliberately restrict rental housing, as we find in St Louis and elsewhere, further reduce opportunities for these tenants. The majority of Section 8 renters are thus highly concentrated and segregated in low-income neighbourhoods like this eastern tip of Ferguson.[3]

St Louis is among the most segregated metropolitan areas in the United States, not least because of its history of racially segregative public policies, ranging from zoning decisions to public housing projects. Although blacks were the majority in its inner-city neighbourhoods for decades, the suburban colour line began to shift after 1970. Whites, who had already left the inner city, started fleeing the inner suburbs as well. This process, bluntly referred to as 'ghetto spillover' by a local observer in 1981, changed the population dynamics in inner suburbs such as Ferguson. Until the mid-1960s, Ferguson was a 'sundown town': blacks came in during the day to work as housekeepers and nannies, but were banned from the city after dark. The city even barricaded through streets and made sure most of the others dead-ended before reaching Kinloch to the west, a neighbouring all-black suburb, then quite exceptional in St Louis.[4]

But the demographics of Ferguson changed in the following decades. While the black population increased from 25 per cent in 1990 to 67 per cent in 2010, the white population decreased from 74 per cent to 29 per cent – a change, as we will see, that has not been reflected in the city's administration and police force. Increasing poverty that hit other metropolitan areas hit St Louis and its suburbs as well, and Ferguson saw its poor population double between 2000 and 2012. One in four Ferguson residents lived below the poverty line in 2012. This suburbanization of poverty was not unique to St Louis. During the 2000s, suburban poverty not only increased, but also concentrated in certain neighbourhoods in almost every major US metropolitan area. This partly had to do with the dismantling of public housing projects and the shift to the voucher system.[5] Coupled with a trend in inner-city revival and gentrification, as we will see with Cincinnati below, these shifts pushed inner-city poor out to the suburbs.

Ferguson's economic problems reflect broader transformations that negatively affect American society. One of these transformations, as we have seen in the previous chapter, is rising inequalities. American post-war growth and reductions in inequality came to an end in the mid-1970s. After that, inequality in the US rose steadily;

wealth concentrated more at the top, while poverty engulfed even greater proportions of the population. From 2000 to 2010, fifteen million more people fell below the poverty line, bringing the proportion of Americans living in poverty to over 15 per cent. In 2012, one in six Americans lived below the poverty line, one in four American children lived in poverty, and six million people had no cash income, relying exclusively on charity and food stamps.[6]

The largest number of the poor is still white. But poverty disproportionately affects certain non-white minorities, who were particularly hard hit by the economic transformations of the past four decades. Nearly half of black children who began their lives in middle-class families in the late 1960s, just before the economy started its downward shift, ended up in the bottom fifth as adults. The rate is 16 per cent for white children.[7] The increasing income inequality of the past decades has also led to increased polarization and residential isolation. Black–white segregation is still high for historical reasons and due to the persistence of discrimination in the housing market.[8]

One particular aspect of this growing poverty is geographical: American poverty is expanding and moving from the inner city to the suburbs. In 2000, most of the poor lived in the country's major cities. By 2008, suburbs had overtaken cities and become 'home to the largest and fastest-growing poor population in the country', housing almost one-third of America's poor. In other words, suburbs, rather than cities, have absorbed the growing number of poor since 2000. St Louis was no exception. Between 2000 and 2008, the share of the population living below the poverty line decreased from 24.6 per cent to 22.9 per cent in the cities of St Louis metropolitan area, but it increased from 7.9 per cent to 9.6 per cent in its suburbs. In 2000, St Louis metropolitan area was second (after Atlanta) nationwide in the share of metropolitan poor living in the suburbs, with 69 per cent of its poor in suburbs. In 2008, the ranking remained the same, but St Louis's share of metropolitan poor living in suburbs went from 69 per cent to 75 per cent. In

2008, in other words, three-quarters of its metropolitan poor lived in suburbs.[9] Inner-city revival projects displaced the poor, while housing vouchers concentrated poor families in already segregated areas like the apartment complexes in the second Ferguson. This new geography of American poverty, then, is not merely a product of private prejudice or preference, but of public policies, from the local to the federal. Ferguson is not some aberrant case, but a product of policy choices that have been transforming the economy and cities over the past decades. The formation of segregated and concentrated areas of poverty like the second Ferguson is a result of urban policies that eliminated affordable housing in inner cities and concentrated recipients of rental aid – who are poor by definition – in the inner suburbs.[10]

This broader context allows us to understand why we have two Fergusons. When he was stopped by a white police officer, Michael Brown was walking back to Northwinds, one of the Section 8 apartment complexes in the area. Northwinds has been owned by the Maine-based Eagle Point Companies since 2005. As the president of the company said, there is 'a lot of turnover', and some of their residents cannot pay the rent.[11] An investigation of law enforcement practices in Ferguson may explain why they could not afford the rent, or, even if they could, why they would be tempted to leave. No one, it seems, loves Ferguson in this part of the city, not enough at least to display a sign of affection. There is not a single 'I love Ferguson' sign in the second Ferguson, but plenty that read 'We must stop killing each other'. Let us see how law was enforced in Ferguson, the self-affirmed 'community of choice'.

Getting Blood from a Turnip

Municipal Court gross revenue for calendar year 2012 passed the $2,000,000 mark for the first time in history, reaching $2,066,050 (not including red light photo enforcement).

Awesome! Thanks!
– Email exchange between Ferguson's police chief and city
manager, 2013

Failure to perform *can* result in disciplinary action not just a bad
evaluation.
– Ferguson Captain of the Patrol Division to patrol supervisors,
2012

The Department of Justice (DoJ) report following the investigation
of Ferguson police department and municipal court was categorical:
'Ferguson's law enforcement practices are shaped by the City's focus
on revenue rather than by public safety needs.'[12] This emphasis on
revenue generation led to unconstitutional policing and irregular
practices at the municipal court, both of which reflected and exacerbated racial stereotypes and discrimination. The investigation found
that the police and the court disproportionately targeted blacks. The
uprising of 2014 was not a reaction to an isolated incident; it was a
response to years of institutionalized racism, oppression and exploitation. The City of Ferguson had put in place a 'business model' that
used the police and the municipal court to generate revenue by
preying on blacks, who were also less likely to be able to pay extravagant fines.

'How can you get blood from a turnip?' asked one member of the
Ferguson police when questioned by the DoJ. Another said it would
have been better for public safety to allow residents to use their
limited income to fix equipment violations (such as a broken tail
light) rather than force them to pay fines to the city, which could
eventually lead to an arrest warrant and still leave the equipment
unfixed. But such views were not shared by the majority of police
officers, and certainly not by the senior management. A culture of
'productivity' prevailed over Ferguson's police department and

municipal court, a culture so internalized that it dissociated law enforcement from public safety, and turned it into the city's second largest source of revenue.

In this context, the number of citations issued by police officers became indicators of their productivity, and played an important role in officer evaluations and promotions. Indeed, every month the municipal court provided the police department with a list of the number of tickets issued by each officer. Officers wrote up to six, eight and, in one instance, fourteen citations during a single encounter. What had been happening in Ferguson for years went beyond occasional abuse by some bad apples. It was a systematic and deliberate exploitation of the poor and black population through the coordinated efforts of the city's police department and municipal court, pushed by the city management. Here is how it worked.

Municipal fines and fees are the second largest source of income for Ferguson. Over the years, the city has been increasing their part in the budget, pressuring the police and court staff to deliver, whose performance it closely monitored. In the five years leading up to the uprisings, the share of fines and fees in Ferguson's municipal revenue increased from 8 per cent to over 13 per cent. In the year before the uprisings, the court generated more than $2.5 million through municipal fines and fees.[13] Once this pattern was exposed by the uprisings, however, the revenue from this source was cut in half, and its share in the city's revenue decreased to 6 per cent.[14]

The DoJ investigation found that city officials routinely urged the police chief to generate more revenue. In March 2000, for example, the city's finance director contacted the police chief to express his concern about the expected sales tax shortfall and to ask him to offset this through fines. 'Unless ticket writing ramps up significantly before the end of the year,' he wrote, 'it will be hard to significantly raise collections next year.' The police chief responded that the city would see an increase in fines and that he could target the $1.5

million forecast once more officers were hired. He also said he was considering a different shift schedule to have more officers on the street to increase traffic enforcement. Shortly after this exchange, the Ferguson police switched to a twelve-hour shift schedule, which is less conducive to community policing but more effective in generating revenue through enforcement. This was not an isolated incident. In the year leading up to the uprisings, in March 2013, the finance director wrote the following to the city manager: 'Court fees are anticipated to rise about 7.5 per cent. I did ask the [police] Chief if he thought the PD [police department] could deliver 10 per cent increase. He indicated they could try.'[15]

Data also show certain municipal charges applied almost exclusively to blacks. The five most common charges brought against blacks were also the ones that gave the widest discretion to police officers: Manner of Walking in Roadway, Failure to Comply, Resisting Arrest, Peace Disturbance, and Failure to Obey. Between 2011 and 2013, blacks accounted for 95 per cent of Manner of Walking in Roadway charges, and 94 per cent of Failure to Comply charges.[16] A similar pattern also emerged for speeding charges. The DoJ investigation showed that when citations were issued based on the officer's visual assessment, rather than on radar readings, blacks were disproportionately charged.

This racial bias was accompanied by illegal police practices. Ferguson police officers stopped, searched, arrested and used force in ways that went beyond their legal authority. They targeted blacks, and when citizens cited their rights or asked for a cause, they responded by retaliation, fining or arresting them for talking back. One typical example of this was traffic stops. Ferguson police officers routinely asked for identification from all passengers, and if they refused, they cited and arrested them under the municipal Failure to Comply charge. This is unconstitutional. Passengers are in their right to refuse to provide identification, and this is protected under the

Fourth Amendment. Talking back to officers or recording their activities are protected by the First Amendment. Even verbal expressions of disrespect, including the use of foul language, cannot constitutionally be a basis for arrest. Yet, Ferguson police officers regularly used arrest to retaliate against disrespect, usually charged as Failure to Comply, Disorderly Conduct, Interference with Officer or Resisting Arrest. Such constitutional violations were also evident during the protests outside Ferguson's police department in February 2015 to mark the six-month anniversary of Michael Brown's death. Peaceful protesters were menaced by jail: one man recording arrests and another in a wheelchair live-streaming the events from the sidewalk were threatened that they would be arrested on the grounds of Manner of Walking.

The DoJ investigation also revealed a pattern of excessive force use. Ferguson police officers routinely used excessive force in violation of the Fourth Amendment, again disproportionately targeting blacks, who accounted for about 90 per cent of the cases. The DoJ's conclusion was that use of excessive force by Ferguson police officers was racially biased, punitive and retaliatory rather than necessary (for example, to counter a physical threat). Ferguson police regularly used Tasers and dogs against unarmed individuals, people with mental problems and even juvenile students. In 2011, for example, a mentally troubled man claiming to be God died after officers Tasered him multiple times. In another, during the year leading up to the uprisings, a fourteen-year-old black student was Tasered and arrested in the classroom after refusing to leave following an argument with a fellow student. Taser use was routine, including on people in handcuffs. Dogs were also used unnecessarily, deployed even to bite unarmed children. And Ferguson police dogs bit only blacks – not a single incident reported a police dog biting a white person.

There is also evidence of police harassment in the area with the apartment complexes. For example, a few months before the uprisings, in December 2013, police officers stopped and searched people in this area with no reasonable suspicion. This was not an isolated incident but, as the DoJ report put it, part of a 'consistent . . . pattern of suspicionless, legally unsupportable stops' that targeted blacks. The following month, in the same area, the police arrested a young black man at the home of his girlfriend's grandparents for trespassing, even though the young man was there upon invitation. When he resisted arrest, seven officers repeatedly hit and Tasered him, causing significant injuries. 'Partly as a consequence of City and FPD [Ferguson Police Department] priorities,' the DoJ report stated, 'many officers appear to see some residents, especially those who live in Ferguson's predominantly African-American neighbourhoods, less as constituents to be protected than as potential offenders and sources of revenue.'

There are several examples in the report, but perhaps the following one shows best the legally arbitrary, racially targeted and revenue-driven nature of policing in Ferguson. In the summer of 2012, an officer pulled up behind a thirty-two-year-old black man's car. The man had just finished a game of basketball in a public park, and was cooling off in his parked car. The officer asked him for his social security number and identification. Then, pointing at the presence of children in the public park, he accused the man of being a paedo-phile, and ordered him out for a search. The man cited his constitu-tional rights, which led to his arrest. The officer then charged him with eight violations of Ferguson's municipal code, including one for making a false declaration (he said his name was 'Mike', whereas it was 'Michael' in reality), one for not wearing a seat belt, one for having an expired driver's licence, and one for not having one.

To put it bluntly, Ferguson police preyed upon blacks to generate revenue for the city until one encounter went awry with the killing of Michael Brown. The police, however, were only one part of Ferguson's revenue-generating mechanism. Officers might issue as many citations as they could, but there has to be something else to force people to pay fines and fees. This was the role of Ferguson's municipal court.

The Court as Cash Machine

Each month we are setting new all-time records in fines and forfeitures.

– Ferguson City Manager, January 2013

Ferguson Municipal Court did not act as a neutral arbiter of the law, but as a cash machine. It used its judicial authority to collect outstanding fees, and worked in a way that particularly harmed blacks, violating the Fourth Amendment's requirements of due process and equal protection. Thus, rather than promoting public safety, it undermined, just like Ferguson's police did, the legitimacy of law enforcement, creating a deep mistrust among black citizens.

Ferguson Municipal Court is in the same building as the police station. It operates as part of the police department, and is supervised by the chief of police, to whom the court staff directly reports. The judge, court clerk, prosecuting attorney and assistant court clerks were all white at the time of the DoJ investigation. The residents of Ferguson are not involved in the election of court staff. The judge is nominated by the city manager and appointed by the city council. It is a two-year position subject to reappointment, and judge Ronald Brockmeyer worked as Ferguson's municipal judge for eleven years until he had to resign following the DoJ investigation. The court clerk, supervised by the police chief, has broad authority according to Ferguson's municipal code. As the DoJ investigation found, Mary Ann Twitty, the court clerk at the time, played the most significant role and exercised wide discretion in the everyday workings of the court. One area where she used her authority and discretion was discarding charges brought against friends. She was fired over racist emails revealed by the investigation, including one with a photo of Ronald Reagan feeding a baby chimpanzee. The caption read 'Rare photo of Ronald Reagan babysitting Barack Obama in early 1962.'

The court, like the police, worked in a legally arbitrary, racially targeted and revenue-driven way. On the one hand, it routinely helped many city officials – including the judge, court clerk and several high-ranking police officers – and their friends by removing their fines and fees. On the other, the court fined blacks more heavily than others. For example, the fifty-three Failure to Obey charges brought during 2013 not only involved a majority of blacks (forty-four), but also resulted in higher fines for them: an average of $206, whereas others were fined an average of $147 for the same offence.

In order to force people to pay fines and fees, the court issued arrest warrants. These warrants, however, were not issued out of concern for public safety, but to secure collection. They were the court's routine response to pending fine payments and missed court appearances. This city of 21,000 issued warrants for the arrest of 9,000 people for 33,000 offences in 2013 alone. This would amount to twenty-five arrest warrants a day if the court worked every single day during the year. The municipal judge, however, only worked a grand total of twelve hours per month. The rate of arrest warrants impressed even Ferguson police officers, who called it 'staggering' in internal emails. With so many arrest warrants to go around, police officers regularly made unlawful stops, not because of a reasonable suspicion, but to catch individuals with pending arrest warrants. As noted, the police deliberately and disproportionately targeted blacks: 85 per cent of vehicle stops and practically all pedestrian stops involved blacks. Blacks also accounted for 90 per cent of citations, 93 per cent of arrests, 92 per cent of cases with arrest warrants, about 90 per cent of cases of use of force, and all police-dog bites.

Most of the arrest warrants issued by Ferguson Municipal Court originated from minor violations for which jail time is far too severe a penalty (parking infractions, traffic tickets or housing code violations). But because Ferguson used its court to generate revenue, minor violations resulted in arrests, jail time and payments that well exceeded the original fine. The following case of a black woman shows how minor infractions turn into crippling debts and unduly harsh penalties. This woman parked her car illegally in 2007, and received two citations, a $151 fine, plus fees. Because of financial difficulties and periods of homelessness, she missed court dates and fine payments, which led the court to charge her with seven Failure to Appear offences over the years. The court also issued an arrest warrant, and new fines and fees for each Failure to Appear offence. Thus, what started in 2007 as a minor parking infraction led over the years to two arrests, six days in jail and a debilitating debt despite the considerable amount she had already paid. As of December 2014, she had already paid the city $550, but still owed $541.

Moreover, Ferguson Municipal Court often failed to provide clear and accurate information about the charges and obligations. There is also evidence that Ferguson police officers frequently provided incorrect information about the date and time of court sessions to the people they cited, potentially leading to additional charges and fines under Failure to Appear, as well as an arrest warrant. The court issued arrest warrants when a second court date was missed, but did not confirm that the notice of the second court date had been safely received by those concerned. Indeed, in many cases individuals did not even know that an arrest warrant was issued against them since the court had stopped sending warrant notices in 2012 to save money on the cost of warrant cards and postage.

Although Ferguson city officials blamed lack of responsibility for certain groups of the population, the DoJ investigation found strong evidence of racial bias among Ferguson police and court staff. Indeed, even the lack of personal responsibility explanation used by city officials reflected such racial bias and stereotyping, which was also evident in emails between senior police officers and court staff that included overtly racist jokes about blacks associated with laziness, irresponsibility and criminality.

The Ferguson police are authorized to issue citations under both the municipal code and state law. Most charges, however, are filed as municipal offences, because pursuing municipal rather than state charges benefits Ferguson financially. The city has a comprehensive municipal code that leaves few areas of civic life untouched – housing, height and removal of grass and weeds, use of the city's trash service, animal control and walking. Compared to other municipalities in the region, its fines are high, 'at or near the top of the list', as the city's finance director noted approvingly in a 2011 report. For example, a parking fine in Ferguson was $102, whereas it ranged between $5 and $100 in other municipalities; Weeds/Tall Grass charge was as low as $5 in one municipality, whereas Ferguson set it between $77 and $102. Ferguson charges $375 for Failing to Provide Proof of Insurance, more than twice the average fine for this offence in the region's seventy municipalities. This allowed Ferguson to collect $286,000 in fines for this offence in 2013 alone, exceeding all but the Failure to Appear fines.

These high fees, coupled with Ferguson police officers' routine practice of issuing multiple citations in a single encounter, amount to sums that people in poverty cannot pay. In order to resolve a municipal code violation, the offender must have the means to hire an attorney and pay fines. Even for a simple speeding ticket, the defendant must pay $50–$100 to the attorney, and $150–$200 to the municipality in fines and court fees.[17] These are not negligible amounts, especially for the poor. The situation is aggravated by Ferguson Municipal Court's tendency to inflate fines and charge, for example, $302 for Manner of Walking, $427 for Peace Disturbance,

$531 for High Grass and Weeds, $777 for Resisting Arrest, $792 for Failure to Obey and $527 for Failure to Comply. These are colossal amounts, especially for people living in poverty, and disproportionately high for minor violations.

Between July 2010 and June 2014, about 90,000 citations and summonses were issued for Ferguson municipal code violations – 22,500 citations and summonses a year in a city with a population of 21,000. In 2014, during the year leading up to the uprisings, nearly 50 per cent more citations were issued compared to those issued during 2010. This suggests a deliberate attempt to generate more revenue through fines and fees, which is also indicated in email exchanges between city officials (as we have seen, the share of fines and fees revenue in Ferguson's municipal budget has constantly increased over the years). The DoJ investigation established that this upsurge was not driven by a rise in serious crime; indeed, serious crime (assault, stealing, driving while intoxicated) has remained constant or declined in Ferguson over the last ten years.

There was a similar rise in municipal court cases: 16,178 new cases were filed, and 8,727 were resolved during the fiscal year 2009. During the year leading up to the uprisings, the number of new cases had increased by 50 per cent to 24,256, and the cases resolved to 10,975. The judge, it might be imagined, must have been working hard. But municipal court judge is a part-time position, and the incumbent does not need to be a resident of the municipality. Municipal judges may hold positions in multiple jurisdictions, as Ferguson's did. The court holds three or four sessions each month, each lasting no more than three hours. It is not uncommon for the court to see as many as 500 people in a single session, and given that police officers issue as many citations as they possibly can, usually 1,200 to 1,500 offences are considered in each three-hour period (which may even, as it has in the past, surpass 2,000 offences in one sitting). The court's efficiency did not escape the city manager, who noted in January 2013 that 'each month we are setting new all-time records in fines and forfeitures'.

The hand-picked judge was under pressure to generate revenue for the municipality, and he delivered with great zeal, which had allowed him to keep his office since his first appointment in 2003. As the city's finance director reported to the city council in 2011, Judge Brockmeyer had been 'successful in significantly increasing court collections over the years' – though it turns out he was less successful with his own finances and owed over $170,000 to the government in unpaid taxes.[18] His productivity was due partly to the creation of additional fees, which were deemed abusive and possibly unlawful by the DoJ. He also managed to see hundreds of cases in a single three-hour session, as we saw above.

These dubious practices did not go unnoticed. In 2012, a member of the city council wrote to other city officials to oppose reappointing the judge. Brockmeyer was so efficient because he did not listen to the testimony, did not review the reports or the criminal history of the defendants and also did not let all the relevant witnesses testify. Although a change of judge would probably result in less revenue, the member of the city council argued, it was more important to handle the cases properly and fairly. Proper and fair, however, were not among the priorities of the city manager, who stated that Ferguson could not afford any decrease in its revenue from the court, and called for the judge to be reappointed, which he was.

The revolting Ferguson residents were well aware that their actions were disrupting the city's business model based on the exploitation and criminalization of black people. DeAndre Smith, a black resident of Ferguson, was present during the incidents that led to the looting and burning of QuikTrip, a convenience store that later became a gathering point for protestors. Two days into the uprisings, in an interview on television, he said: 'This is how they eat here. This is how they receive money. The businesses, the taxes, police stopping

33

people, giving them tickets, taking them to court, locking them up
... So, when you stop their flow of income. When you stop their
whole ... everything ... their business.'[19]

At the site of QuikTrip where Smith was interviewed, there is
writing on the burnt-out shell of a petrol pump. It lists several uprisings, starting with 'Spain 36' and ending with 'Ferguson 14'. Brixton,
Paris and Cairo are on the list, so are 'Watts 65', 'L.A. 92' and 'Cincy
01'. We saw that racist, oppressive and abusive law enforcement practices in Ferguson were not occasional incidents, but part of the regular
workings of the city. Let us now take a look at urban uprisings in Los
Angeles, Cincinnati and Baltimore to see that the Ferguson uprisings
were not aberrational, but a justified response to urban rage. The
sources of resentment that led to the Ferguson uprisings were also
behind those of Los Angeles, Cincinnati and Baltimore, although
Ferguson's business model remains unique among those. As long as
the sources of resentment remain unaddressed, these examples suggest,
recurrent uprisings will be part of our urban futures.

Careful Police Work

This is not some orgy of violence. This is careful police work.
   – Defence attorney in the 1992 Rodney King beating trial

There's a black person up our street and we say 'Hi' like he's a
normal person.
   – A resident of Simi Valley, home of Rodney King beating trial,
                                       1992

One warm summer night, on 1 August 1988, officers from the Los
Angeles Police Department (LAPD) stormed two buildings in the
area known as South Central, searching for drugs. While helicopters
hovered over the area, the eighty-eight police officers on the ground

were engaged in a demolition job in the apartments: they punched holes in the walls, destroyed furniture and appliances, hammered toilets, poured bleach over clothes and emptied refrigerators. Some even left graffiti that read 'LAPD rules'. The damage to the apartments was so great that the operation left ten adults and twelve minors homeless, leading to their being offered help by the Red Cross. Residents from the two buildings and others from the neighbourhood were rounded up, humiliated, insulted with racist epithets, punched, kicked and choked by police officers, though none was charged with a crime. The result of this massive raid was the successful seizure of less than six ounces of marijuana and less than an ounce of cocaine, plus $4 million in court fees and damages paid to the residents, property owners, and to those rounded up during the operation.[20]

South Central was the epicentre of the 1992 Los Angeles uprising. In terms of its geographical extent, ethnic diversity, violence and destruction, the Los Angeles uprising remains the most devastating in US urban history. Like the Watts uprising of 1965 in the same area, the 1992 uprising took place at a time of economic difficulties and in a context marked by racism, involuntary segregation and police brutality. The Watts and other uprisings of the 1960s had all occurred at times of economic recession.[21] The 1992 Los Angeles uprising took place during the worst recession southern California had experienced since the 1930s. Income inequality and proportion of the poor increased steadily in Los Angeles between the 1965 and 1992 uprisings. In 1990, one in four young black men in South Central was unemployed.

The context was set by policy decisions. The federal government's economic policies since the early 1980s contributed to rising unemployment. Dismantling of social safety nets, attacks on anti-discrimination and affirmative action agendas meant more hardship for the poor and racialized minorities. Cutting the funds for community-based organizations had devastating effects in places like South Central since these organizations worked with disadvantaged populations in inner cities. On top of all these issues, growing reliance on the criminal justice system doubled the prison population in the decade from 1980 to 1990. The racialized poor were hit by every single one of these policy decisions. Wealth continued to concentrate at the top, while the poor saw their prospects shrink, and became increasingly subject to aggressive policing and incarceration. Mass incarceration further reduced the prospects for the racialized poor. As a 2014 report put it, the United States saw a 'historically unprecedented and internationally unique' growth in incarceration rates since the mid-1970s. One quarter of all prisoners in the world are behind bars in the United States, which today has a prison population of 2.2 million. Almost 60 per cent of them are blacks and Latinos, although these groups make up only about a quarter of the US population.[22]

Economic difficulties do not automatically lead to unrest, but when they are compounded by discrimination and police brutality in everyday urban life, eventually something has to give. As one of the participants in the 1965 Watts uprising put it: 'We've been holding out for a long time, a long time; giving the white man a chance.'[23] The 1992 Los Angeles uprising showed, however, that this was not just an issue of black and white. Unlike the incidents in 1965, which were confined to the Watts area of Los Angeles where the majority of the city's black population was pushed to live, the 1992 uprising covered a much larger area, expanding especially north from South Central to Hollywood. Unlike Watts, the participants in the 1992 uprising were not overwhelmingly black. Latinos, who had been at the receiving end of Los Angeles police's discriminatory practices, also participated widely. Not everyone had the same purpose; the participants' motivations ranged from outrage at the Rodney King verdict, which triggered the incidents, to simple opportunism, from resentment built up by discrimination to securing necessities for their families by looting stores.

The Los Angeles uprising started on 29 April 1992 following the announcement of the not-guilty verdict in the trial of four white police officers. They were filmed beating Rodney King, an unarmed black man aged twenty-five, in the early hours of 3 March 1991. The video showed King lying on the ground after a car chase, with twenty-three LAPD officers at the scene, four of them beating him with batons and kicks. After fifty-six baton blows, six kicks and two Taser shots, King was left with injuries 'of a minor nature', according to the report of the sergeant involved in the beating. The medical report showed something else: King's skull and cheekbone were fractured, lip split, face partly paralysed, one eye socket shattered and one leg broken. Three surgeons had to operate for five hours on his battered body.

Broadcast the next day, the video – which President Bush called 'sickening' – became a national and international sensation, and led to the trial of the four police officers. The trial should have taken place in Los Angeles County with a jury selected from there, because that is where the incident took place. The defence asked for a change of venue, but this was denied by the trial judge, Bernard Kamins. After the California Court of Appeals replaced Judge Kamins with Judge Stanley Weisberg, the new judge changed the trial venue to Simi Valley in Ventura County, arguing that this would avoid unfair treatment of the police officers due to adverse publicity around the incident. Home of the Ronald Reagan Presidential Library, Simi Valley, and Ventura County in general, was known for its conservative politics and strong law and order stance. With its overwhelming white majority – 80 per cent white and only 2 per cent black – Simi Valley was home to a large number of LAPD officers and retirees. Indeed, about a quarter of LAPD officers lived in Simi Valley.[24]

In the end, there was not a single black person among the twelve members of the jury, which was made up of six white men, four white women, a Hispanic woman and an Asian woman. Eight of the jury members had either served in the army or had spouses who had served in the military. Three had relatives in the police. Five of them were gun owners, of whom two were National Rifle Association members. Where many saw a repeated beating of a black man offering no resistance, the jury saw a black man threatening police officers who only hit him in self-defence. The defence attorneys had broken the video down into stills, and used them for raising questions about restraining suspects. Thus, the repeated beating of King was reduced to disjointed stills to be analysed in isolation by restraint experts. This strategy allowed the defence to argue that what the jury had before their eyes was 'not some orgy of violence [but] careful police work'. The jury was convinced, and they acquitted the police officers.

Following the announcement of the verdict, unrest started in the South Central area in the late afternoon of 29 April. This is also when the barbaric beatings of Reginald Denny, a white truck driver, and Fidel Lopez, a construction worker from Guatemala, occurred. Despite the contentious nature and publicity of the trial, the LAPD had not taken any precautions, and was unable to respond effectively once the incidents started. The unrest turned into full-scale rioting the following day, moving north towards Hollywood. Koreatown was on the way, but police forces were deployed to protect downtown Los Angeles, Beverly Hills and West Hollywood. This left Koreatown and South Central without protection, which would prove disastrous for Korean businesses.

Less than two weeks after the Rodney King beating, Latasha Harlins, a black teenager, was murdered by a Korean shopkeeper, who shot her in the back of the head while she was walking away from her store after an altercation over a carton of orange juice. The shopkeeper was convicted of voluntary manslaughter, but was only sentenced to five years of probation and some community service. The demographic transformation of South Central had already put blacks, Latinos and Koreans in competition over housing and jobs.[25]

Both the murder and what many felt was an unfairly light sentence further strained the relations between blacks and Koreans, making Korean businesses, not least the one where Harlins was murdered, targets of choice during the riots.

The incidents continued with increasing intensity, which first led to the deployment of the National Guard, then of army troops. California Governor Wilson declared a state of emergency, Mayor Bradley imposed a curfew, and on 2 May, President Bush declared Los Angeles a disaster area. Thus ended one of the most devastating urban uprisings in American history, leaving in its wake fifty-three people dead and more than 2,000 injured. The number of arrestees went over 10,000, about half of whom were Latino and 38 per cent of whom were black. These figures almost doubled those of the Watts uprising that had started in the same area in 1965, leaving thirty-four people dead and about a thousand injured. Let us now take a closer look at Watts in 1965 to see how it differed from or resembled the 1992 uprising.

From 'Monkeys in the Zoo' to 'Gorillas in the Mist'

One person threw a rock and then, like monkeys in the zoo, others started throwing rocks.
– William Parker, LAPD police chief, on the Watts uprisings, 1965

. . . right out of 'Gorillas in the Mist'.
– Police officer Powell, shortly before the King beating, 1992

Unlike in 1992, the Watts area in 1965 was predominantly black. Nearby industrial jobs and public transit access to downtown had made Watts relatively attractive earlier, but by 1965 both were gone. After the war, many factories closed or moved out, and many black workers were laid off. The construction of the elevated north–south

Harbor Freeway (Interstate 110) in the 1950s separated the run-down Watts area to the east and the slightly better-off areas to the west (including South Central).[26] Thus, Watts became separated by this physical barrier from the rest of the city. The disappearance of jobs and public transit left little chance for upward mobility for its residents.

The barriers that confined blacks to Watts were not only physical. In a state-wide referendum held a year before the 1965 uprising, two-thirds of California voters supported Proposition 14. Led by the real estate sector, Proposition 14 was a response to the Rumford Fair Housing Act passed in 1963, which prohibited discrimination in the private housing market. Promoted with the slogan 'A man's home is his castle', Proposition 14 nullified the Rumford Fair Housing Act by amending the California Constitution, and turned discrimination into a constitutional right. Property owners had the right to refuse to sell or let property to people on the basis of their race, religion or ethnicity.[27] Watts was already home to more than 80 per cent of the black population of Los Angeles. Proposition 14 meant they were stuck there.

Unlike the other uprisings we study in this book, the Watts uprising of 1965 did not follow from a dramatic incident. It was triggered by police action, but a trivial one compared to others we will see. There was no beating, as in Los Angeles in 1992, or killing, as in Cincinnati in 2001, Ferguson 2014 or Baltimore 2015. The uprising in Watts followed an arrest for drunken driving, and there was no evidence of excessive use of force. Blacks in Los Angeles, however, had been victims of police brutality for such a long time that a minor arrest quickly triggered a full-scale uprising. For six days, between 11 and 16 August, Watts was the scene of clashes with police, arson and looting. The uprising left thirty-one civilians dead, all killed by law-enforcement officers. There were also three fatalities among officers and firefighters, but none was killed by the participants in the revolts:

a firefighter died when a wall collapsed, a deputy sheriff was killed by friendly fire, and a policeman was shot by his own gun when the person he was threatening instinctively raised his arm in self defence, which was later judged an accident. It took a curfew, 1,000 police officers and 13,000 National Guard soldiers to quell the uprising. About 4,000 people were arrested, mostly for theft and curfew violations, but many were either acquitted or had their cases dismissed.[28]

Unlike in 1992, the Watts uprising led to an official inquiry by the so-called McCone Commission, led by John A. McCone, a prominent businessman and former director of the CIA. The findings of the commission were widely discredited by social science research at the time. When the archives related to the inquiry became public, further research revealed that the commission had come to conclusions about matters on which no research had been carried out, and had deliberately neglected unsavoury evidence collected during the investigation.[29] The McCone Commission report had explained the uprising by the so-called 'riffraff theory', an example of the pathological framework we discussed in the previous chapter. Contrary to the commission's assertions, however, researchers found that the participants in the Watts uprising were not a marginal group of deviants and criminals – the riffraff – but were representative of, not marginal to, the black population of Los Angeles. Their actions were popular even among blacks who had not participated in the uprising. These findings were supported by the records of the hearings and testimonies in the commission's archives, but they did not find their way into the official report on the Watts uprising.

What was common to both the 1965 and 1992 uprisings in Los Angeles (and also to those later in Cincinnati, Ferguson and Baltimore) was where they started. All of these urban uprisings erupted in areas that were home to poor and racially defined groups who disproportionately found themselves on the receiving end of police brutality and harassment. By the time of the 1992 uprising, the Watts district had equal black and Hispanic populations, as well as a small minority of Asians. Central Americans were newcomers to the area in 1992, just as blacks had been earlier. Jewish ghetto merchants were replaced by Koreans. But the area still remained a poor neighbourhood of racially defined groups, and was subject to racially biased police practices. The racial bias in policing, however, was not a matter of a few rogue police officers. Just like Ferguson, there was a well-documented pattern of racially biased police violence, ranging from patrol officers all the way up to police chiefs.

The context leading up to the 1992 uprising shows the discriminatory, systematic and targeted nature of police violence in Los Angeles. Several reports demonstrate Los Angeles police officers regularly using excessive force, in particular against blacks and Latinos. Although complaints were discouraged (as it happened, for example, when King's brother tried to file one) or covered by supervisors, the city of Los Angeles still had to pay millions of dollars to settle complaints and lawsuits by the victims of LAPD abuse, a pattern we will also see with Baltimore later on. Blacks and Latinos suffered disproportionately. One particular issue was the use of chokeholds by the police, which claimed eighteen lives during the 1980s. Sixteen of those victims were black, a disproportionality explained by the LAPD police chief Daryl Gates in a most peculiar manner. It was probably, he argued, because their 'veins and arteries do not open up as fast as on normal people'. Gates was the controversial police chief of Los Angeles from 1978 until he was forced to resign in 1992 following the uprising. The legacy of his paramilitary style of policing included the creation of SWAT teams in the 1960s, and Operation Hammer starting in 1987. The latter turned South Central and East Los Angeles into occupied territories saturated by police forces operating with a war mentality, produced the police raid that opens the previous section, and largely contributed to the growing resentment that ended up erupting in 1992.[30]

When placed within this context, even the Rodney King beating does not look exceptional; what set it apart was that it was caught on video. King's beating was part of a broader pattern of police abuse in Los Angeles. Like Ferguson's police department, LAPD's practices showed racial bias, and its officers, like Ferguson's, did not refrain from using excessive force and racial epithets. A commission investigation found, for example, that two of the officers who beat King had sent a computer message shortly before the incident about a domestic dispute of a black couple, referring to it as something 'right out of "Gorillas in the Mist"'. After the beating, one of them – Officer Powell, who alone struck King over forty times – sent a message stating he hadn't 'beaten anyone this bad in a long time'. Powell had a history of violence that was well known in the LAPD. The same officers accompanied King to the hospital, where they openly joked and bragged about the beating, as the nurses reported.[31]

The commission investigation revealed that the use of excessive force, aggravated by racism, was a deeply entrenched problem within the LAPD. A significant number of LAPD police officers with a well-known pattern of violence were not only not disciplined, but rewarded with positive evaluations and promotions. Racist remarks were recurrent in the messages officers sent, which were not monitored and sanctioned by their supervisors. Indeed, the commission found that the supervisors themselves frequently made racist remarks. Racist abuse, however, went beyond messages within the department. There was also evidence of verbal harassment of blacks and Latinos, who were frequently subjected to humiliating practices and unnecessary use of force, as well as to dog attacks. Just like in Ferguson, dogs were frequently used in minority neighbourhoods, particularly in South Central where the uprising started. Between 1986 and 1989, 71 per cent of all LAPD dog searches, 70 per cent of all arrests using dogs and 70 per cent of all reported police-dog bites took place in South Central. The commission also heard complaints about LAPD officers having dogs attack minority youth already in custody or not calling the dogs off even after the suspect was restrained.

Another report by Amnesty International supported these findings.[32] There was clear evidence that LAPD officers used excessive force for years, mostly in black and Latino neighbourhoods, leading to serious injuries and death. The use of force by officers reached such levels that Amnesty International claimed it amounted at times to torture. The findings were not all that different then from now: use of force that exceeded guidelines and was not justified by circumstances, shooting victims several times even after they had been disabled, use of Tasers, setting dogs on unarmed people or suspects who had already surrendered, even on those in custody – practices all concentrated in black and Latino neighbourhoods. Dogs were deployed predominantly in areas with large minority populations, and among dog-bite victims, less than 2 per cent were identified as white, whereas 70 per cent were Latino and 20 per cent black.

A similar pattern of targeted police violence was also an important factor behind the 2014 Ferguson uprising, as we saw, but also behind those of Cincinnati in 2001 (the largest urban unrest since the 1992 Los Angeles uprising) and the 2015 uprising in Baltimore. Let us now take a look at these two cities to see what else related them to or differentiated them from Ferguson and Los Angeles.

From Feast to Famine

Plastic baggies in hand, the recipients headed back out into the cold – four blocks, and a world away, from the bright lights of Main.

– Michelle Cottle on post-riot Cincinnati, 2001

You go feast to famine in a matter of blocks.

– David Bramble, developer in Baltimore, 2015

The Main Street with its bright lights mentioned in the first epigraph is the one in Over-the-Rhine (OTR) neighbourhood, the epicentre of the 2001 uprisings in Cincinnati. It runs parallel to Vine, another street with vibrant commercial activity four blocks to the east. The shops here speak to the extent and nature of the city's attempt to transform the area, starting from 12th Street. If you walk north on Vine Street from 12th, you find, for example, a store selling organic pet food, a 'movement studio' (aka gym), or a company specializing in 'brainstorming and business coaching', in addition to your regular cafes, trattorias and restaurants. Once you have passed Kroger super-market and hit 15th Street, however, the pretty shops and refurbished historical houses give way to boarded-up stores and derelict build-ings. The contrast reaches its starkest with a food bank located some-where between Vine and Main streets. You have gone from feast to famine in a matter of blocks.

OTR had a mostly white population of about 30,000 in the 1950s, which went down to about 7,500, mainly black, by the turn of the century. OTR first attracted black residents from the adjacent West End, a historically black neighbourhood. After the war, like many other inner-city black neighbourhoods at the time, West End became the target of urban renewal projects. The old housing stock was razed and Interstate 75 tore right through it, resulting in the displacement of its residents, some to the neighbouring OTR. The displacement process now at work in OTR is more subtle. Although no bulldozers are involved, the forces of change are strong, and we must first under-stand the profit potential of this area to get a sense of the stakes.

Downtown Cincinnati is bordered by Interstate 71 to the east, Interstate 75 to the west, the Ohio River and Kentucky state border to the south. This leaves only north for downtown Cincinnati to expand, which is where OTR is. So this 'pocket of poverty', long forgotten by the city, is now among Cincinnati's most valuable land. The economic potential of OTR was recognized in the 1980s, which led to its designation as a historic district in 1983. The neighbourhood has since been the object of fierce struggles between developers and community activists, notably the Over-the-Rhine People's Movement. Perhaps the struggle over the area can be illustrated by this 1996 *Cincinnati Enquirer* headline reporting the murder of Buddy Gray, the influential leader of the People's Movement: 'Over-the-Rhine now up for grabs'.

At the time of the 2001 uprising, three-quarters of OTR residents were black, most living below the poverty line. About one-third of the housing units in the area were vacant. It was, however, a time of economic revival as the city had been investing for a decade in this area. It had refurbished the Main Street entertainment district with jazz clubs and art galleries, and managed to attract wealthier white populations. The patrons of the new facilities had to be protected, so the city also invested in measures to have greater police presence and vigilance in the area. In a city already marked with racism and in an area with sharp inequalities, this increased vigilance quickly translated into police harassment of black youth. What was seen as a revival by the city officials and the new patrons of the area was seen as an assault by the residents.[33]

Cecil Thomas, a black Cincinnati police officer, observed a pattern of aggressive policing emerge during the 1990s. In his expert report for the 2001 case on racial discrimination in Cincinnati police, Thomas wrote that blacks were disproportionately subject to arbitrary searches, undue detention, improper use of handcuffs, use of force and guns, as well as retaliation if they asked badge numbers and names of police officers. They were also disproportionately subjects of discretionary offences such as jaywalking, just like in Ferguson. Aggressive policing, even when it violated civil rights, was rewarded by the city, rather than supervised and disciplined. The case was settled by a court-supervised collaborative agreement between the citizens, the city of Cincinnati and the Fraternal Order of Police to reform police practices and improve police–community relations.[34]

In addition to the more serious allegations of disproportionate use of excessive or deadly force against blacks, Cincinnati police officers were also accused of routine harassment, targeting blacks for multiple traffic citations, again as in Ferguson. This was one of the important factors in the eruption of simmering anger when Timothy Thomas, a nineteen-year-old black man, was shot and killed by a white police officer after a chase in an OTR alley, shortly after 2 a.m. on Saturday, 7 April 2001. Thomas was unarmed and had no history of violent crime, but had fourteen outstanding warrants, twelve of which were for traffic violations. He was the fifteenth black man killed by Cincinnati police in the previous six years, and the fourth in the previous six months, including the high-profile death of Roger Owensby, Jr, an unarmed black man who died of asphyxiation in police custody on 7 November 2000. Already a month before Thomas's death, the American Civil Liberties Union and the Cincinnati Black United Front had filed the federal lawsuit mentioned above against racial bias in Cincinnati policing.

Thus, the tension created by the prospect of displacement and resentment over the perceived occupation of OTR by a police eager to protect the visitors from the residents reached a critical point. Yet, the incidents did not start immediately. On 9 April, Thomas's mother, joined by protestors, confronted the mayor in the City Hall and asked for an explanation, but received none. The uprising started only then. Dozens of protesters broke City Hall windows and gathered outside the police headquarters that night. The next day, 10 April, there was a protest march through OTR towards downtown. The events escalated when the police started using tear gas and shooting rubber bullets at protestors and bystanders. That night protests turned violent with clashes, arson, looting and property destruction in OTR. The following day, 11 April, unrest went beyond OTR, with rioting in mainly black and poor neighbourhoods, notably Avondale, Bond Hill, Evanston, Madisonville, Walnut Hills and

Westwood. It was on the evening of 11 April that someone shot a police officer in OTR, who was spared injury by his belt buckle and bulletproof vest. On 12 April the mayor declared a state of emergency and imposed a citywide curfew, which brought the uprising to an end.[35] Although social workers in the area who had also been through the urban uprisings of the 1960s thought what happened in 2001 did not really call for a curfew, the mayor likened the situation in OTR to Beirut, which on all counts was a stretch of the imagination.[36]

As community activist Thomas Dutton observed, although uprisings are readily lamented as unreasonable violence, violence takes many forms. In Cincinnati, the problem was not merely police–community relations, but many interrelated forms of violence that have been affecting black inner-city residents for a long time. Unlike the episodic violence of the uprising, these other forms of violence – unemployment, poverty, displacement, police harassment and brutality – were systematic. As City Councilwoman Alicia Reece put it: 'This situation has been festering for over five years. It is a time bomb that has exploded.' At the time of the uprising, Cincinnati was the most segregated city in the country, and OTR was its poorest neighbourhood, with about 77 per cent of its residents black (Cincinnati was 43 per cent black). The city invested in OTR to turn it into a marketable area, but the investment led to the displacement of existing OTR residents, who were not provided with alternatives.[37]

After the incidents, the mayor asked the Department of Justice to review Cincinnati Police Department's use of force. The preliminary findings of the investigation were outlined in an October 2001 letter.[38] There was evidence of excessive use of force by Cincinnati police officers, regarding, in particular, the use of chemical irritants and dogs. Police officers used chemical irritants at close range, sprayed them up people's noses or down their throats, and emptied entire canisters on single individuals. The canine unit used a 'find and bite' – rather than 'find and bark' – policy. The use of force was under-reported, and police officers were too willing to draw their guns and point them at citizens even for minor traffic violations. Finally, as we have already seen with Ferguson and Los Angeles police departments, there were concerns about the complaints procedure, which discouraged the filing of complaints and prevented effective monitoring.

Even the mayor admitted that 'the protest shows there is a huge outcry in the community about legitimate frustrations between police and African-American residents'.[39] The day after the mayor uttered these words, Cincinnati police provided one more reason to be frustrated. On 14 April, following Timothy Thomas's funeral, hundreds marched peacefully through OTR. Suddenly, however, two police cars stopped, eight police officers, six from Cincinnati's SWAT team, got out with shotguns to shoulders, and fired, unprovoked and without warning, on the crowd with beanbag rounds. Four people, two of them children, were injured. Cincinnati's police chief defended the officers, who, he said, were 'damn good people'. The injured thought otherwise.

'We cannot deny,' the mayor had said the previous day, 'that we have a serious racial divide.' At the time the Cincinnati police force was three-quarters white. But urban rage still erupted in cities where blacks were in a majority in the police and the government, as the recent uprising in Baltimore showed. On 12 April 2015, Freddie Gray, a twenty-five-year-old black man, was arrested for no apparent reason and put into a police van in Sandtown-Winchester, one of the most deprived neighbourhoods in the already quite deprived and 96 per cent black West Baltimore area. Gray was conscious when he entered the van, but when he came out, less than an hour later, his spinal cord was nearly severed. He died in hospital a week later. The six officers involved in his arrest, three of them black, were later indicted on charges including second-degree murder.[40]

Starting from 18 April, peaceful protests were organized for about a week. There was some escalation of violence during a downtown protest on 25 April, but it was only on the evening of 27 April, soon after Gray's funeral, that rage erupted in the streets of West Baltimore. Fearing incidents after the funeral, riot police in full gear arrived in the early afternoon, and cordoned off Mondawmin Mall to the north of Sandtown. The presence of riot police in full gear was provocative, but things only got worse when the police also blocked access to Mondawmin station next to the mall, which is a main transportation hub with an underground station and stops for several bus routes. This prevented the students of nearby Frederick Douglass High School from getting home after school.[41] Sandtown was on fire by the evening. Police cars and various stores were set ablaze. The next day the mayor declared a curfew, and a 2,500-strong National Guard contingent arrived. Incidents continued the following day, but calm returned gradually. The curfew was lifted on 3 May, and the National Guard withdrew the following day.

We saw with our earlier examples that urban uprisings are triggered not by some isolated police action, but by police practices that have long become routine. Baltimore 2015 was no exception. The police action that cost Gray his life was part of an established pattern of police brutality. An investigation by the *Baltimore Sun* revealed that between 2011 and 2014, the city had to pay about $6 million in settlements to more than 100 victims of police violence, most often blacks, including a twenty-six-year-old pregnant woman and an eighty-seven-year-old grandmother. Injuries inflicted by police officers ranged from broken bones to organ failure, and led to death in some cases.

Serious injuries during police van rides were not unprecedented either. Baltimore police had an established practice of going for 'a rough ride' – driving to harm handcuffed but unbuckled detainees in the back of the police van – which had already left several people paralysed by fracturing their necks.[42] Just as we saw with the police departments of Ferguson, Los Angeles and Cincinnati, Baltimore police department has a long history of brutality and misconduct. Until the *Baltimore Sun*'s investigation in 2014, the city did not even keep track of its police officers who faced multiple lawsuits because of brutality, and police officers with a history of violence were promoted, and some even became supervisors.

What sets Baltimore apart from our other examples is that blacks hold prominent positions in both city government and police department. The city is 63 per cent black, the mayor is black, her police chief is black, the majority of the city council, including its president, is black, the top prosecutor is black, and practically half the police force is black too. This suggests that class, not just 'race', plays an important role. As we saw in chapter 1, our era of urban rage is marked by sharp inequalities unmatched since the nineteenth century, and cities are places where inequalities are at their starkest and most obvious.

Sandtown, where Freddie Gray grew up, is a neighbourhood with a long history of problems, including mass unemployment, poverty, vacant buildings and crime. More than one-third of the houses are abandoned, more than one-third of the residents do not have a high school diploma, more than 20 per cent of working-age residents are unemployed (twice the city average), and more than a third of the families live below the poverty line. Gray suffered lead poisoning – another unflattering feature of the area – as a little boy, leading to educational problems later on.

Sandtown, like the rest of West Baltimore where it is located, is a racially segregated neighbourhood. Baltimore has a long history of racial segregation. It was the first American city to legalize it in 1911 through a racially restrictive zoning law. Racial segregation and concentrated poverty still mark Baltimore's urban landscape. West Baltimore residents are excluded from the privileges enjoyed by others, such as waterfront homes, restaurants and bars – or simply good schools, jobs, a safe environment and a living wage. There are, as a *Washington Post* article suggested, 'two Baltimores, one affluent and predominantly white, the other impoverished and largely black'. As David Bramble, a black developer, put it, it is possible to go from 'feast to famine in a matter of blocks' in Baltimore, just like in parts of Cincinnati.[43]

Material difficulties were aggravated by heavy-handed policing that targeted poor and stigmatized neighbourhoods. In Baltimore, the seeds of rage that erupted after Gray's death were partly sowed during the previous mayor Martin O'Malley's term, marked by the targeting of poor and black neighbourhoods with a zero-tolerance approach. Hundreds of thousands were arrested, though not necessarily charged, even for minor offences such as loitering and littering – referred to as 'quality of life' arrests. This policy got so out of control that in a single year the Baltimore police arrested practically one in six people in the city: in 2005, more than 100,000 arrests were made in this city of about 640,000. More than 23,000 were released without charge, which means that the police arrested 23,000 Baltimore residents for nothing. This policy of mass arrest was eventually challenged with a lawsuit filed in 2006, and Baltimore agreed to pay an $870,000 settlement.[44]

The effects of this policy on the poor and black population of the city have been devastating. Arrest records make it very difficult to get a job or qualify for housing. Moreover, this mass arrest policy turned residents of areas like Sandtown into criminal suspects in the eyes of the police, who, just like in Ferguson, were under pressure to perform. 'It ain't cops against robbers,' as Brandon Ross, godbrother of Freddie Gray put it. 'It's cops against the community.' Targeting stigmatized areas with aggressive policing – just as in Watts, South Central, Over-the-Rhine and the 'second' Ferguson – created only more resentment among residents who already had to face economic hardship and discrimination. Arbitrary arrests and brutality did not help. Even the police officers who arrested Freddie Gray could not provide an account suggesting Gray was involved in any wrongdoing. Why did he run then when he saw the police? Perhaps he knew better, as Timothy Thomas of Over-the-Rhine did, although it ended badly for both. As Thomas's mother had said at the time: 'They keep asking me why did my son run. If you are an African male, you will run.'[45]

As the differences between the two Los Angeles uprisings show, exclusion and oppression are not uniquely black experiences, although blacks in the United States have always had to face unique challenges. The Baltimore uprising suggests that class plays an important role as well. Urban uprisings are marked by 'race', class and rage, as Mike Davis observed after Los Angeles burned in 1992. The context for the uprisings in each case we have explored was prepared by inequalities, poverty, and aggressive and discriminatory policing. These were, we have seen, results of policy choices that hit racially stigmatized groups the hardest, rather than outcomes of inevitable trends, cultural peculiarities or individual pathologies.

This brings us to a central argument of this book. Urban rage builds up from systematic exclusion and oppression, which go beyond police violence and expand to all areas of urban life, including housing, employment, social encounters and political worth. It would be a mistake to let the spectacular character of police violence detract from this larger picture. Although police brutality is usually the triggering incident of uprisings, a narrow focus on policing distracts from the historical and structural sources of urban rage. Government policies, private developers, urban renewal programmes and real estate firms all play their role in the formation of areas of concentrated poverty, which then become targets for aggressive and discriminatory policing. 'This is not a rogue officer problem,' as Charles M. Blow put it, 'this is a rogue society problem.'[46] Urban uprisings, then, are not signs of individual flaws or cultural traits, but manifestations of grievances that expose such problems and defy the normalized workings of the established order. If the examples of Ferguson, Los Angeles, Cincinnati and Baltimore have not sufficed to dispel doubts about this, or if this looks like an American eccentricity, perhaps examples from across the Atlantic may help.

3

Of Seditions and Troubles in the UK

'For if there be fuel prepared,' Francis Bacon wrote in his essay on seditions and troubles, 'it is hard to tell whence the spark shall come that shall set it on fire.' The spark in London, the most unequal western city, came in August 2011. It did not come, however, when an unarmed black man, Mark Duggan, was shot to death by the police. Rage erupted when the police failed to clarify the circumstances of his death, transforming a peaceful protest into what was to become the most extensive and intense uprising in the capital's history since the Gordon Riots of 1780. What started in London spread to other cities, hitting in particular Birmingham, Liverpool, Manchester and Nottingham.

The 2011 London uprising was similar to that of 1992 in Los Angeles in many ways. It was the most devastating in the city's modern history, could not be reduced to a uniquely black phenomenon and, despite its extent, no official inquiry into its causes was conducted. It was not, however, unprecedented; similar waves of urban unrest had occurred in English cities, especially from the 1980s onwards, all in a context of exclusion and police violence, as we will see. While the similarities with the previous uprisings point to the persistence of grievances waiting for a spark, the differences are significant. The consensual response of politicians to the 2011 uprising reduced it to a pathological framework, denying all political significance. That it occurred at all, especially with such intensity, is reason enough, it seems to me, to be concerned about the state of things rather than seeking individual pathologies behind it. That it occurred in the world's sixth richest country, with a mature democracy, might have come as a surprise, but probably not the fact that it started in the city that leads cities of the 'developed' world in terms of wealth inequalities. The 2011 London uprising exposed, like others before, traces of grievances, ranging from racist policing to inequality and exclusion.

What made it unique was that, unlike others, it was not a sign of localized disenfranchisement, but of widespread deprivation, exclusion and anger that went beyond individual neighbourhoods. Urban uprisings of the 1980s in London were largely confined to specific sites, which became iconic places of conflict, such as Brixton and the Broadwater Farm estate. The participants in the 2011 uprising were more mobile, something that was attributed by commentators to mobile phone technology. This, however, can be relativized. Although mobile phone technology undoubtedly facilitated communication, it cannot alone account for the expansion of uprisings. Before Facebook and smartphones, it was television that was blamed for the spread of riots in the 1980s (and in 1992 in Los Angeles). Before that, it was the telephone – not the sort you now carry in your pocket, but the hefty one that comes attached to a cable. The 1980 uprising in St Pauls, Bristol, for example, was orchestrated by people phoning each other before the unrest started, as a local councillor explained, who were then joined by others arriving in buses from Coventry and Birmingham.[1]

The 2011 London uprising went beyond the limits of stigmatized areas associated with earlier uprisings. Nationally sixty-six local authority areas experienced incidents in August 2011. In London, twenty-two boroughs out of thirty-two had scenes of unrest. One of the distinguishing features of the 2011 uprising, then, was its spatial expansion. It was also ethnically heterogeneous, as we will see, despite some peculiar claims to the contrary.

All Blacks

The whites have become black.
> – Historian David Starkey, 2011

Politically they were all black.
> – Witness to the St Pauls uprising, Bristol, 1980

The Home Office published data on the ethnicity of some 4,000 people arrested for offences related to the 2011 uprising. If this data can be used as a proxy for those who participated in the incidents, then 40 per cent of them were white, 39 per cent black, 11 per cent mixed, 8 per cent Asian and the rest 'unspecified others'. Compared to the 1981 uprisings, the participation of whites overall was less pronounced (again, to the extent that arrest figures can be taken as a proxy). The police then had also rounded up some 4,000 people, two-thirds of whom were white, although there were significant geographical variations: two-thirds of those arrested in Brixton and Southall were non-white compared to only one-third in Toxteth and Moss Side.[2]

None of these figures suggests the uprisings were simply a black or white issue. I wish I had something as original, if not as delirious, as Starkey to say about the reasons behind them. But as bland as this may sound, we have been here before. Many of the grievances that led to the eruption of British cities in the 1980s were also the fuel that set them on fire in 2011. These were not 'race riots', although racial discrimination was a substantial factor in the accumulation of anger. Economic deprivation and aggressive policing were common to both. What distinguished the latter, as I have already noted, was its intensity, duration and geographical scope, which suggests that things have only got worse. Indeed, with five days of unrest in two-thirds of its boroughs, London had not experienced such extended disorder since the eighteenth century. Perhaps this was why the government subscribed to a pathological framework, and decided there would be no official inquiry into the causes – another distinguishing feature of the 2011 uprising compared to that of 1981, which had fed into a more dynamic and less consensual political context.

Starkey and the witness to the St Pauls incidents illustrate two distinct approaches: the former an empirically inaccurate cultural explanation with racist undertones, the latter, which I share, a political explanation that emphasizes resonance. What resonates across diverse groups participating in these incidents is the experience of exclusion. The killing of a black man was probably not something many of the participants could directly relate to, but it resonated with their problems that had to do with their relations with the police, and, more broadly, with how they saw their place and future in the society. As a woman involved in the incidents in north London put it:

> I think some people were there for justice for that boy who got killed. And the rest of them because of what's happening. The cuts, the government not doing the right thing. No job, no money. And the young these days needs to be heard. It's got to be justice for them.[3]

Injustice was a recurrent theme in the interviews with those involved in the uprising, as the *Guardian*/LSE study, *Reading the Riots* documented. The majority of those interviewed – 270 people from London, Birmingham, Manchester, Salford, Liverpool and Nottingham – were moved by a sense of injustice and inequality:

> They expressed it in different ways, but at heart what the rioters talked about was a pervasive sense of injustice. For some this was economic – the lack of a job, money or opportunity. For others it was more broadly social, not just the absence of material things, but how they felt they were treated compared with others. . . [W]hat a great many shared, and talked animatedly about, was injustice and inequality.[4]

This certainly does not imply that whites have become black and rioted, but that urban uprisings are marked by a profound sense of exclusion – not enjoying the privileges others do, and being reminded of it on a daily basis. I am not trying to suggest, however, that the experiences of all those who participated in the incidents are the same. We will see, especially with the stop and search practices of the police, that if you have a darker skin, discrimination will more likely be part of your everyday urban life. But discriminatory police stops have a broader implication. They are a sign of arbitrary and intrusive use of power by the police. And that speaks to all groups, disenfranchised youth in particular, regardless of their skin colour. 'The police is the biggest gang out there,' was another recurrent remark in the *Guardian*/LSE interviews. But I am getting ahead of myself. Let us first take a look at the context leading up to the 2011 uprising, and trace it back to similar incidents in the 1980s to see the continuities as well as differences.

Research into the 2011 uprising suggests that it was to do with 'a pervasive sense of injustice', the sources of which lay mainly in deprivation and discriminatory police practices.[5] Data provided by the Ministry of Justice show that practically two-thirds (64 per cent) of the young people brought to court for participating in riots were from the twenty most deprived areas in the country. These were areas with high levels of youth unemployment and child poverty, and low levels of educational attainment.[6] Economic deprivation was a shared experience for most of the participants. The economic context of the 2011 uprising was one of unemployment, poverty and increasing polarization between rich and poor.

A report published in *The Guardian* in December 2011 found that unemployment had hit a seventeen-year high following public sector layoffs in the tens of thousands. Youth unemployment had also reached a record high with more than one million unemployed. It is important to note that these job losses were the outcomes of the government's austerity policies. The Office for National Statistics data show that during the June–September 2011 period, employment in the private sector had increased by 5,000, whereas public sector employment had decreased by 67,000. Unemployment was on the rise during the years leading up to the uprising for all groups, but some were hit harder. As a 2010 report showed, the unemployment rate for blacks had increased by 13 per cent since 2008, compared with 8 per cent for whites, and 6 per cent among Asians. This gap between minority ethnic and white unemployment rates was greatest in London.[7]

Poverty has also increased constantly. Between 2010 and 2013, about nineteen million people in the UK – one-third of the population – experienced poverty in at least one year. Compared to other EU countries, the UK, the world's sixth richest country, is in the top three after Greece and Latvia in terms of the proportion of its poor. Oxfam estimates that one in five people in the UK lives below the official poverty line. Another study by the Poverty and Social Exclusion (PSE) research project found that almost half of the population of the UK, over 30 million people, suffer from financial insecurity, which makes it even harder to comprehend the government's decision to cut social security benefits. With more people experiencing financial insecurity in a context of diminished safety nets, no wonder the number of food banks has soared in recent years. Food banks provide food to people in acute need. Their use has been rising steadily since 2005, and dramatically since 2013 following the government's cuts and changes to the social security system.[8]

One-third of people in the UK suffer significant economic difficulties, and one in four people has 'an unacceptably low standard of living', according to PSE researchers. The PSE researchers also compared figures from earlier surveys, and found that the situation is worse today than it has been since the early 1980s, when the number of people living below minimum standards was half of what it is today. What makes this increase in poverty even more alarming is that it took place in a context of economic growth. The UK is a wealthier country now than it was in the early 1980s. Its economy has doubled since 1983, but so has its population living below minimum standards. Increases in wealth went to the richest, making the country much more economically polarized. The recession hurt, but post-recession recovery made the rich only richer, allowing Britain's billionaires to more than double their worth. In 2009, the richest thousand families in Britain had assets worth £258 billion, which went up to £547 billion in 2015, a 112 per cent increase. Average household incomes, on the other hand, were 2 per cent below their 2009 peak.[9]

Therefore, the rise in poverty in the UK is accompanied by an increased concentration of wealth in the top end. This increasing polarization can be illustrated by the shrinking of the middle class. Two-thirds (66 per cent) of households were in the middle in the early 1980s, which fell to 48 per cent in 2010. This means that more households are now concentrated at the poor and wealthy ends, a sign of growing economic polarization. This polarization has been more pronounced in London, the epicentre of the 2011 uprising. The proportion of both poor and wealthy households came close to doubling their 1980 values in 2010. In 1980 middle-class households comprised 65 per cent of London's households, which had fallen to 37 per cent by 2010. In the same period, the proportion of poor households rose from 20 per cent to 36 per cent, and that of the wealthy went up from 15 per cent to 27 per cent. More than one-third of London's households live in poverty, meaning they cannot afford at least three or more necessities in their everyday lives.[10]

The disintegration of neighbourhoods because of gentrification and the selling off of social housing stock without providing alternatives increased tensions, especially in areas where economic deprivation is coupled with racial discrimination. 'It's blatantly clear they want to ethnically cleanse us,' said one resident of Haringey, a borough with a significant black population, and home to the Broadwater Farm estate where Mark Duggan lived. The neighbouring Hackney is also under pressure from similar processes that drive people out, and the racial tension is evident. As Pauline Pearce, 'Hackney Heroine', recently put it: 'The authorities want to ethnically cleanse Hackney, get rid of its grassroots. By doing so they are getting rid of its culture, the diversity we celebrate here.' Large-scale regeneration projects, like the one for Tottenham, continue building tension as they are seen by locals as projects conceived to bring in wealthier residents rather than improving their own lot. As one resident of the Broadwater Farm estate, now in his late fifties, put it, recalling earlier riots in the area: 'The riot in 1985 was about food, water, basic needs. Now it's about having a stake in society, the chance to be someone. You have all these developments springing up, incomers with money and we're left looking on, wondering if we feature in the future blueprint.'[11]

As noted in chapter 1, as urban land has become an important source of profit, economically disadvantaged residents have suffered the consequences, bearing the burden of urban transformations without benefiting from their advantages – especially in rapidly gentrifying cities like London. Such transformations give little, if any, voice to affected residents, and leave them feeling powerless in the face of urban change. This was an important aspect of the context for the 2011 uprising. Another was austerity policies and their effects on youth, as illustrated by a July 2011 *Guardian* video on youth club closures in Haringey, the borough where Tottenham, the epicentre of the 2011 uprising, is. Haringey Council had to close eight of its thirteen youth clubs because of the withdrawal of state funding. As a young woman from the area, Erika Lopez, commented: 'The cuts are affecting the young people a lot, but the government doesn't realize what they are doing to us.' Chavez Campbell, an eighteen-year old, was more categorical: 'There'll be riots,' he said, 'there'll be riots.' Indeed, just six days after he made this prediction, riots erupted in London, starting in Haringey. Later reflecting back on the video, Campbell said:

> I did see the riots coming and the government should have seen it coming, too. Jobs are hard to get and, when they do become available, youths don't get the jobs. There is nothing to do, they are closing youth clubs so the streets are just crazy. They are full of people who have no ambitions, or have ambitions but can't fulfil them.[12]

But the years leading up to the 2011 uprising were not only marked by the steady ramping up of unemployment, financial insecurity, austerity, poverty and polarization – signs not of a broken society, but of a 'broken state';[13] it was a context also marked by major scandals, such as the financial crisis and the bank bail-outs, the parliamentiary expenses scandal (more on this later) and police involvement in the phone-hacking scandal. These all undermined confidence in the political elite and the police. In the previous winter, there were major protests over the tripling of university tuition fees and cuts to educational maintenance allowance that helped students from poor families. London, especially, saw several major protests, which adds another layer to the story. Almost all the London protests during the years leading up to the 2011 uprisings delivered two messages to the broader public: that their government would ignore their demands, and that it would resort to violence to intimidate, disperse and punish protestors. From May Day 2001 to the 'Not in my name' anti-war rally in 2003, from the G20 protest in 2009 to student protests against tuition fee hikes a year later, and to the anti-cuts protests the following year, both messages were received loud and clear. Increased police violence against protestors and the deteriorating image of the police led Her Majesty's Inspectorate of Constabulary to prepare a report in 2009, which recommended a set of principles to keep police violence in control and within the limits of the law.[14] As we will see, however, police violence and illegal police practices continued, not just during protests, but in everyday urban encounters as well.

This, then, was part of the context that prepared the fuel for the 2011 uprising: more people living in poverty, the poor getting poorer while the rich got richer, the prospects for higher education and secure jobs shrinking dramatically for the less well-off, the prospect of displacement looming on the horizon, the banks looting, members of Parliament looting, youth clubs closing, the police corrupt and violent, and a government deaf to its citizens' protests. The anger had been simmering, rage building up, especially among those who, on top of everything else, had to put up with abusive policing. So let us now take a look at the incident that led to the uprising to explore this aspect of the incendiary context. We will see that what happened then was not exceptional, but part of a pattern that non-whites, in particular, will recognize all too well.

The Writing on the Wall

when yu jack mi up gainst de wall
ha didn't bawl

but I did warn yu
now yu si fire burning in mi eye
smell badness pan mi breat
feel vialence, vialence
burstin outta mi
look out!
it too late now
I did warn yu

– From Linton Kwesi Johnson, *Time Come*, 1979

I find what has happened deeply tragic and worrying. The fires which were started in Birmingham and London lit up for us a portrait of our inner cities that we cannot allow to fade from our mind. We must not forget what happened, because it could happen again.

– Douglas Hurd, home secretary, 1985

What is deeply tragic and worrying is that it did happen again, only on a broader scale. The home secretary said these words in the wake of the 1985 uprising that started in Tottenham, north London, which was also the epicentre of the 2011 uprising.[15] Both were triggered by police action that resulted in the deaths of black people in one of the most ethnically diverse and also one of the poorest areas of London. Yet in both cases, the government refused to call for a judicial inquiry. What could have happened?

Shortly after 6 p.m. on Thursday, 4 August 2011, firearms officers stopped a minicab in Tottenham. The passenger was Mark Duggan, a twenty-nine-year old black man, whom they were following on the suspicion that he was carrying an unregistered gun. Within seconds of getting out of the car, Duggan was shot twice and killed. There was no gun on him, but a sock discovered on the grass some five metres away from his body had one in it.

When the police kill or seriously wound someone, the Independent Police Complaints Commission (IPCC) is called to investigate. Thus, the IPCC started an investigation, and made its first public statement towards 11 p.m. the same day. It reported that an officer had been shot and taken to hospital, but did not mention Duggan's killing. The IPCC then issued another statement: 'Having reviewed the information the IPCC received and gave out during the very early hours of the unfolding incidents, before any documentation had been received, it seems possible that we may have verbally led journalists to believe that shots were exchanged.'[16] Translation: we did not tell the truth in our first public statement.

Two days later, still not given information about the fatal shooting, Duggan's family and friends marched from Broadwater Farm estate to Tottenham police station in the afternoon, but the police refused to speak to them. By the evening the crowd had grown to about 300 people. Feelings ran high, and when the rumours of the police beating a black teenager spread, a police car was set alight. That rumour has not been confirmed, but it is significant that the crowds believed in the likelihood of a policeman beating a black teenager during a peaceful protest. Things only escalated from then onwards. The 2011 uprising was set in motion.

As noted, the uprising did not start as an immediate reaction to Duggan's death, but to the way the police treated his family and friends. It is not merely a matter of courtesy, but a requirement to inform the family of the dead when the police kill someone. The Metropolitan Police failed to do so (and were eventually forced to issue a public apology). 'There was some confusion in terms of who was going to tell Mr Duggan's family,' said Tom Godwin, then acting commissioner of the Metropolitan Police, which, he added, they 'deeply regret'. But the codes of professional practice are unmistakeably clear on this: 'Following a death after police contact, the police will always deploy a Family Liaison Officer [FLO] to the family/next of kin of the deceased.'[17]

Duggan's family heard through the news, not from the police, that he had been killed. Moreover, they heard that he was killed in a shoot-out with the police. The police thus not only failed to inform Duggan's family of his death, but also diffused misleading public information – no shoot-out had taken place. Regarding the diffusion of misleading information about the circumstances surrounding Mark Duggan's killing, the IPCC deputy chair Deborah Glass admitted that one of their staff had made a mistake, which they only realized a week later: 'We realised we had made that mistake the following week we admitted it and we apologised.'[18] But the damage was done. This was a lesson the police could have learned from the 1985 uprising in Tottenham. After the news was received of the death of Cynthia Jarrett, a black woman, during a police raid, community leaders first held a meeting with the police at Tottenham Police Station. What escalated matters then was that, despite requests, the deputy commissioner refused to suspend the four police officers involved in the incident. Revolts erupted the next day.

The IPCC's competence and impartiality were tested by the Duggan killing, and it failed on both counts. As the Home Affairs Committee put it: 'The public do not fully trust the IPCC and without faith in the Commission, the damaged public opinion of the police cannot be restored. Unfortunately, too often the work of the Commission seems to exacerbate public mistrust, rather than mend it.' The committee found that the main reason for public mistrust was the perception that the police were 'getting away with misconduct and criminality'. This had to do with three factors: complaints were often investigated by the police force about which they had been made; one-third of investigators working for IPCC were former police officers; and the police often did not interview officers involved in death or serious injury, which is standard procedure for civilians.[19] It also appeared that the government itself did not care much about the IPCC, for which it failed to appoint a permanent chair for almost two years between 2010 and 2012.

The IPCC, as you may have guessed, cleared the officers involved in the killing of Mark Duggan of any wrongdoing. The IPCC's pedigree leaves little to the imagination about the diligence of the investigation. As the coroner's report showed, it was marred with limitations and irregularities. First, the coroner noted in his report, the whole operation seemed ill conceived. The police had not devised a strategy to seize the guns from the provider, who was known to be storing them, but waited until one was collected by Duggan (though, as we will see, whether Duggan had a gun with him or not is unclear). Given that the whole operation was aimed at getting guns off the streets, the coroner was also concerned by the fact that it was abandoned once Duggan was killed.

Regarding the investigation that followed, the coroner criticized the failure to record the scene of the shooting, even though equipment and staff to do so were available. This was especially important given that there was major concern about how the gun that was found in the bushes had ended up in that location, some five metres away from Duggan's body. The coroner also noted several irregularities at the investigation scene that compromised the evidence. The seats of the minicab and the box found in it were moved around before being examined. The minicab itself was removed from its location, brought back, then removed again and taken to a car pound before a full forensic examination was conducted. The location of Duggan's mobile phone, key evidence at the scene, was not even recorded. 'Much of what happened at the scene was less than ideal,' the coroner wrote. 'I was left with an impression of some uncertainty about precisely what was being investigated, on whose behalf, for what purpose, and by what means.'

The irregularities did not end here. The coroner noted that comprehensive accounts were not taken from police witnesses as soon as possible after the shooting. The involved officers' initial accounts were 'universally bland and uninformative', failing to record relevant detail (none of the officers, for example, noted how many shots they had heard, but stuck with the vague 'a number of shots'). The fact that the police officers, following a recommendation by the Association of Chief Police Officers, were given at least forty-eight hours before being asked to give a full statement was also troubling. 'A civilian who uses lethal force in defence of himself or another would not be given 48 hours to compose himself prior to being questioned by the police,' the coroner wrote, 'and it is not immediately obvious why a trained firearms officer should require what a civilian is not given.' Not only were the police officers given ample time before preparing their statements (which they only did three days after the shooting), but they were also allowed to compile them in a room together. The coroner observed that 'there was considerable scope for conferring before any account was given', and noted his concern that 'fatal police shootings are not as rigorously examined as they could be'.[20]

The anomalies of the investigation were also noted by Stafford Scott.[21] Scott was one of the three community members working with the IPCC on Duggan's shooting, but he resigned because of what he saw as the IPCC's 'flawed and in all probability tainted' investigation of this case. His account points to two major irregularities: compromise of evidence (as the coroner's report details) and disappearance of witness statements. The commission, Scott maintains, was initially told that there were at least three police officers who had given statements about witnessing another officer throwing away the gun in the sock that was later discovered in the grass away from Duggan's body. When the community members sought to identify who these officers were, they were told such a statement was never given.

There is little here to inspire confidence. Such blunders invite suspicion not only of incompetence but of misconduct as well, especially when placed in the context of long-standing police discrimination against non-whites. The IPCC's solid track record of clearing police officers does not help either: 'The IPCC has investigated 460 deaths following police contact; these investigations have led – astonishingly – to zero convictions of officers.'[22] Even the home secretary had to admit that 'there were very real concerns about the work of the IPCC and its perceived independence'.[23] No wonder one in three people thinks the police are corrupt, as a government study found.[24]

The perceived corruption and impunity of the police result also from several deaths in police custody. According to data collected by INQUEST, 999 people died in police custody or shortly afterwards between 1990 and 2015 in England and Wales. Another fifty-five were shot and killed by the police. There has, however, not been a single successful prosecution. Although there have been a few cases where an inquest jury has concluded that death was caused by gross negligence, manslaughter or the use of excessive force, and delivered unlawful killing verdicts, no officer has ever been convicted. Deaths in police custody undermine public trust in the police, especially when the data show a strong racial disproportionality. This seeming impunity of police officers and the racial aspect of police custody deaths were also noted by the Home Affairs Committee:

> There is ongoing concern about racism in the police and the IPCC. Black people account for 2.9% of the population, but 20% of those who die in custody. Over 33% of cases in which a black detainee had died occurred in circumstances in which police actions may have been a factor, compared with only 4% of cases where the detainee was white. In 2008 black and minority ethnic communities deaths accounted for 32% of all deaths in police custody, a figure which is broadly consistent with other recent years.[25]

Among police custody or shooting deaths, the ones with non-white victims have been the most controversial. Despite more than a thousand deaths since 1990, only thirteen unlawful killing verdicts have been delivered. Twelve of the victims were non-white. As noted above, none of these led to convictions. Tottenham, where Mark Duggan lived and was killed, has a particularly sad history of deaths or life-changing injuries following police action. As David Lammy, Member of Parliament for Tottenham put it:

> Clearly, the death of Mark Duggan is significant in relation to Tottenham. This Committee will understand that the death of any individual, but a young, black man in open air, on a busy Thursday evening in Tottenham, was of tremendous concern. Sadly, Tottenham has a history – Joy Gardner, Cynthia Jarrett, Roger Sylvester – of deaths, in police custody particularly, that have been difficult events and indeed have led to other unrest.[26]

Roger Sylvester collapsed and died in 1999 after being restrained by eight police officers. An inquest jury ruled in 2003 that he was unlawfully killed. This verdict was quashed a year later by a High Court judge. Cynthia Jarrett collapsed and died in 1985 during a police search at her home in 1985, triggering an uprising in Broadwater Farm, Tottenham, which cost the life of police officer Keith Blakelock. Just a week before, another black woman, Dorothy 'Cherry' Groce, was shot and paralysed by the police during a home raid, sparking the 1985 Brixton uprising. Joy Gardner was another black woman killed by the police. In 1993 the police raided her home in north London to deport her, but she collapsed and died after being restrained. Gardner, a Jamaican mother, was put in a 'body-belt' – a leather belt with handcuffs and chains attached, similar to slave manacles – and wrapped with 13-foot adhesive tape, including around her head, which led to her death by cutting oxygen to the brain. The three police officers involved in Gardner's killing stood trial for manslaughter, but were acquitted.

The resentment that builds over such deaths, especially when they go unpunished, is a major ingredient of urban rage. Not all deaths or life-changing injuries trigger revolts, but when we look at the ones that do, we see that they are not just one-off incidents. Mark Duggan was the third black man to die at the hands of the police that year. About four months before Duggan's death, two high-profile deaths occurred in suspicious circumstances that implicated the police. On 15 March 2011 the British reggae singer Smiley Culture died during a police raid at his house. According to the police version, he had stabbed himself while making tea in his kitchen. The four police officers involved were not suspended. The IPCC investigated the incident, but found no wrongdoing. Two weeks after Smiley Culture's death, Kingsley Burrell, a black father from Birmingham, died after being restrained by the police. Again, the four police officers involved were not suspended. After four years of legal battle, an inquest jury found that Burrell's death was caused by the use of excessive force and negligence: after brutalizing him, the police officers had left Burrell handcuffed on the floor, his face covered with a blanket.

We saw a similar pattern in the previous chapter, and we will see more in the following chapters. A long history of police violence, if not always killing, is a major source of urban rage. This, however, is an issue that governments have been unwilling to address, even when the evidence is abundant, confirmed by independent researchers as well as governments' own. But police killings and deaths in police custody are relatively rare, even though 1,504 deaths in twenty-five years is an alarmingly high figure. What I mean is that although the likelihood of death in police custody is not negligible, especially for non-whites, police custody is not a regular part of most people's everyday lives. But for some people, stop and search is.

Stop and Think

I felt alright before I was stopped, I felt like this is my country, I was born here and there are so many parts of me that are all London... After the second time I was stopped I started to feel like people see what they want to see... There's no such thing as democracy, no human rights. How would you feel?
– A young British-Pakistani male, 2009

And you are not the guy and still you fit the description because there is only one guy who is always the guy fitting the description.
– Claudia Rankine, *Citizen: An American Lyric*

The 2011 uprising made some government officials stop and think about a routinized police practice called 'stop and search'. This is an intrusive practice that harms the relationship between the community, youth in particular, and the police. Furthermore, there is no legal basis for its widespread and routine use. It is an investigative power that should be used for crime detection and prevention, justified by reasonable suspicion. In practice, however, stop and search is widely and routinely used by the police to gain intelligence, to disperse groups of youths and, more broadly, for social control.[27]

In a 2013 report, Her Majesty's Inspectorate of Constabulary recognized the relationship between unrest and the inappropriate use of stop and search by the police: 'Thirty years after the riots in Brixton, concerns about how the police use stop and search powers were raised again following the riots in England in August 2011.'[28] The *Guardian*/LSE study found that stop and search was a major source of resentment. Almost three-quarters (73 per cent) of those interviewed had been stopped and searched at least once in the past year, and they felt it to be an arbitrary, discriminatory and aggressive practice.

There was no need, however, to wait for thirty years and for another series of uprisings to realize that this practice was a main source of urban rage. The 1981 Brixton uprising had already given enough reason to stop and think about it. A major source of resentment that contributed to the 1981 uprising was 'sus', a shorthand for 'suspected person'. Under Section 4 of the Vagrancy Act 1824, the police had the power to stop and search any person they suspected of planning to commit a crime. This was a controversial power not only because it gave wide discretion to the police about whom to stop and search, but also because it set a very low bar for the burden of proof. A person arrested under sus could be convicted if two officers gave corroborative evidence. They needed to present neither a potential victim nor an independent witness.[29]

There is ample evidence that 'sus' was focused on particular groups, black youth in particular, and on specific areas of the city, including Brixton. In the years leading up to the Brixton uprising, London topped the list with more than half of 'sus' charges in the country. Government researchers found that in 1975, 40 per cent of 'sus' arrests in London involved blacks.[30] This is disproportionate given that only 12 per cent of all arrests were of blacks and, especially, that blacks then made up about only 4 per cent of the city's population. Blacks, the researchers found, were fifteen times more likely than whites to be arrested for 'sus'. This disproportionality led to complaints about racial discrimination, but not a single complaint was upheld by the Metropolitan Police's complaints procedure between 1973 and 1978.

On Friday, 3 April 1981, a week before the outbreak of unrest, the police raided several premises in Brixton with search warrants and arrested twenty-two people. This raid came just before a police operation scheduled for 6–11 April. Insensitively called 'Swamp 81', this operation targeted Brixton with the aim of curbing street crime through substantial police presence and extensive use of 'sus', which was already a source of tension between the community and the police. The written instructions defined the nature of this operation as follows:

> The purpose of this Operation is to flood identified areas ... to detect and arrest burglars and robbers. The essence of the exercise is therefore to ensure that all officers remain on the streets and success will depend on a concentrated effort of 'stops', based on powers of surveillance and suspicion proceeded by persistent and astute questioning.[31]

During the five days that preceded the uprising, the police stopped 943 people, slightly more than half of whom were black. Only seventy-five charges followed, of which only one was for robbery, one for attempted burglary, and twenty for theft or attempted theft. We do not know how many people were eventually tried and found guilty, but it is unlikely that all seventy-five were. For five days leading up to the uprising, then, the police harassed close to 900 residents of Brixton for nothing.

The efficacy of such 'street saturation' operations is doubtful, Scarman noted in his report on the Brixton uprising, as the figures cited above also suggest. Moreover, they aggravate tensions between the community and the police. The situation was already tense in Brixton, which had been subject to such policing practices for over a decade.[32] Had the police consulted with local leaders before launching Swamp 81, Scarman noted, the operation would not have been authorized. But the community leaders were not even told about it, let alone consulted. Tension grew as the police carried on with the operation. Then on Friday, 10 April 1981, the first incidents broke out. At about 6 p.m., police officers came under attack while they were attending to the wound of a bleeding black youth, apparently stabbed. A crowd gathered, suspicious of what the police were doing to the injured man. By the time the clashes came to an end an hour and a half later, six people had been arrested, six police officers injured and four police vehicles damaged. Operation Swamp 81, however, would carry on as planned.

The decision to continue with the operation was 'unwise', as Scarman put it. It was, indeed, an arrest by two officers from the operation that set off the major revolt on Saturday. While the officers were questioning a black cab driver, who was stopped and searched on suspicion of drug possession, a hostile crowd gathered. The pieces of paper that the police saw the driver placing in his socks, which they suspected were drugs, turned out to be money, put in the socks for safe-keeping. The officers, however, decided to carry on with their search. Tension grew, and one of them ended up arresting a young man in the crowd. The spark to the fuel was set.

What prepared the fuel was not only resentment of the police. Like the one in 2011, the urban uprisings of the 1980s took place in a context of growing economic difficulties. It was a context marked by economic recession, deindustrialization and major job losses, which hit inner-city residents, especially black youth, hardest. Whereas 400,000 people were unemployed in Britain in the mid-1960s, this figure had more than tripled by 1979, with 1.4 million unemployed. By 1982, the number of unemployed had increased to over three million.[33] As a Policy Studies Institute survey carried out in 1982 found, the rate of unemployment was much higher for black and Asian minorities than among white people: about twice as high for West Indians and about 1.5 times as high for Asians. Among men included in the survey, the unemployment rates were 13 per cent for whites, 25 per cent for West Indians and 20 per cent for Asians (though with variations in the latter group). Young West Indian men were particularly hard hit by unemployment, with almost half affected – 46 per cent of youth aged sixteen to nineteen and 42 per cent of those aged twenty to twenty-four. Unemployment levels in the inner cities of London, Birmingham and Manchester were higher than for the rest of these cities and the rest of the country. Here again West Indian men were hit hardest with an overall unemployment rate of 29 per cent.[34]

Racism was also part of the picture, and the months leading up to the 1981 Brixton uprising were particularly tense. In January 1981, a fire – arson, according to many local residents – in New Cross Road, Deptford had killed thirteen black youths. A New Cross Massacre Action Committee was formed, and a demonstration was organized (Black People's Day of Action) on 2 March to protest against the police handling of the investigation. When the 15,000-strong demonstration arrived in central London, some shop windows were smashed and violence broke out, ending with twenty-three arrests. This incident, which took place about a month before the Brixton uprisings, was once again a sign of tension with the police, who were accused of interrupting the march and precipitating the violent conflict.[35] The Deptford fire and the conflict it generated angered black people, haunted the police, and gave rise to many racist jokes within the police force, the most unsavoury of which was probably the following:

Police officer 1: Do you know that they've renamed Deptford?
Police officer 2: No, what have they renamed it?
Police officer 1: Blackfriars.[36]

This, then, was the context for the urban uprisings of the 1980s, and the similarities with the context of the 2011 uprising are remarkable. This context, let us note once again, was not set by some irreversible process. The economic changes that left millions unemployed in a few years were products of policy decisions. Perhaps those decisions increased overall wealth, but we saw above in the economic context leading to the 2011 uprisings how unequally it was distributed. Saturation policing targeting certain neighbourhoods was also a policy decision, so was not tackling discriminatory and racist police practices, which, as we will see, continued.

Plus ça change ...

How does an experienced policeman decide who to stop? Well, the one that you stop is often wearing a woolly hat, he is dark in complexion, he has thick lips and he usually has dark fuzzy hair.

– Senior policeman, 1983

Police officer Daley [the journalist]: If you were walking down the road, and you see [bleep] what are you immediately thinking?
Police officer Hall: Stopping him.
Daley: Why?
Hall: Searching him, cos he's black, cos he's Asian ... because most Asians carry knives. And I'd fucking search him ... plus he's a fucking, he's a Paki I'm searching him. It's fucking proactive policing yeah innit? He's a Paki and I'm stopping him – cause I'm fucking English [laughter].

– From the BBC documentary *The Secret Policeman*, 2003

The 'sus' was scrapped after the 1981 Brixton uprising.[37] Stop and search, however, continued within other legal frameworks, of which the following three are the most frequently used: Section 1 of the Police and Criminal Evidence Act of 1984 (PACE); Section 60 of the Criminal Justice and Public Order Act of 1994; and Section 44 of the Terrorism Act 2000.

Section 1 requires police officers to have 'reasonable suspicion' that the person to be stopped and searched is involved in a crime. Section 60 is controversial, because it does not require police officers to have reasonable suspicion to stop and search someone, thus giving them wide discretion. It does require, however, authorization from a senior officer to be used in a defined area and at a specific time (twenty-four hours that can be extended for another twenty-four hours). In other words, the police are free to stop and search any person or vehicle they want within the defined place and during the defined time. Even more controversial is – or was – Section 44, an anti-terrorism power that does not require reasonable suspicion to stop and search a person or a vehicle, giving the police the widest possible discretion. Following the terrorist attacks in London in 2005, there was an increase in the use of this power, especially for stopping and searching British Asian males. Section 44 was scrapped after the European Court of Human Rights ruled it unlawful in 2010. Section 47A was put in place, but has not been used since 2011.[38]

Perhaps the debate around Section 44 might help to emphasize my point that what happens on the street is not merely the result of police officers behaving badly, but of higher-level policy decisions. The former Labour MP Hazel Blears's comments are revealing here. As the minister responsible for counter-terrorism, speaking at the Commons Home Affairs Committee inquiry in 2005, she said that Muslims would have to accept as a 'reality' that they would be stopped and searched more often than others. It is also important to remember that this is not an issue of left-wing progressives versus right-wing bigots, and Blears's remarks testify to that. When Conservative home secretary Theresa May announced the scrapping of Section 44 anti-terror stop and search powers following the ruling of the European Court of Human Rights, she was attacked by a former Labour home secretary, Alan Johnson, who was worried about restricting the powers of the police.[39]

Police stop and searches cause resentment not only because they are intrusive, but also because they are seen to be arbitrary and discriminatory. Both anecdotal and statistical evidence supports this perception. The epigraphs that open this section are good examples. The first is from a senior policeman preparing a talk for the trainee's street duties course in 1983. The second is from a 2003 documentary where a journalist joined Greater Manchester Police and secretly filmed some of his fellow recruits during his training. Here is Officer Hall again, this time giving some practical advice to Daley:

> I would never say this in class, if you did not discriminate and you did not bring out your prejudices you would be a shit copper, do you know that? If you was on the street Mark and you wouldn't stop anyone because of their colour, because of their race, because of how they dress because of how they thingy you'd be a shit copper. We used to drive down the road and say he looks a dodgy c*** let's stop him. That is practical policing. It is mate. And nine times out of ten you are right. But in a training environment you can't be seen to do it because it's discrimination – it's against equal opportunities but when you're on the street you will fucking pick it up.[40]

You may think this was just some dirty journalistic trick and that Officer Hall fell for it. Here, then, is Chief Constable John Newing, former president of the Association of Chief Police Officers, who was invited in 1999 to give evidence to the Lawrence Inquiry:

> In the police service there is a distinct tendency for officers to stereotype people. That creates problems in a number of areas, but particularly in the way officers deal with black people. Discrimination and unfairness are the result. I know because as a young police officer I was guilty of such behaviour.[41]

Such remarks might be judged to be exceptional and thus not generalizable. So let us take a look at some figures to get a sense of the broader picture. I hope you will bear with me as I go through some statistics again.

The 2000 British Crime Survey found that black people had the highest rate of foot and vehicle stops. In 1999, almost one-third

(32 per cent) of black males on foot aged between sixteen and twenty-five were stopped by the police, compared to 21 per cent of white males in the same age group. They were also subjected to the highest number of recurrent stops, with 18 per cent stopped five or more times. The rate was even higher for vehicle stops: almost two in five (39 per cent) black males aged sixteen to twenty-nine were stopped in a car by the police compared to one-quarter of white males, and 14 per cent of them were stopped five or more times (4 per cent for white males of the same age group).[42] In another 2000 report, Home Office researchers put it in clear terms: 'Being black means that you get stopped and searched more often.' They also found evidence that 'stops and searches were targeted at some areas where there were disproportionate numbers of those from minority ethnic backgrounds, yet where the local crime rates did not appear to justify this attention'.[43]

These findings were confirmed again in a 2004 report by the Metropolitan Police Authority, which found 'compelling statistical evidence of stop and search practice in London show[ing] that minorities are disproportionately targeted by the police'. They put their concern in even clearer terms: 'The current increases in disproportionate stop and search rates has raised community concerns about a return to uglier periods in London's history when overt racism was common police practice.' A year after this report, another Home Office report made the same point: 'One of the main problems with stop and search has been its disproportionate use against black and minority ethnic communities. This has damaged police relations with many of these communities.' The same message was delivered again a couple of years later by yet another government report: 'Our witnesses made clear that in some cases, the benefits of stop and search might be outweighed by the negative consequences in terms of the willingness of young people to communicate with and trust the police. Stop and search is not a notably productive means of tackling crime.'[44]

None of these reports suggests that stop and search is an effective way of fighting crime. The one message they all deliver is that it is practised in a discriminative manner, damaging police–community relations. Many stop and searches are based on stereotypes, but this goes beyond bad police practice. The law is conceived to give perhaps unacceptably wide discretionary powers to the police in this domain, and we could ask, as legal scholars Bowling and Phillips suggest, 'whether the police in a democracy should *ever* have the power to stop and search citizens without any suspicion of wrongdoing'.[45]

Government data show that in the years leading up to the 2011 uprising, the number of stop and searches increased steadily, peaking in 2009 for all searches.[46] During the year before the uprisings, Section 1 searches peaked with more than 1.2 million people stopped and searched, close to half in London only. This is a dramatic increase compared to 100,000 in 1986. Section 60 stop and searches went up from fewer than 3,000 in 1995 to more than 150,000 in 2009. Under Section 44, the number of stop and searches increased five times in a period of two years, from 2007 to 2009, when they surpassed 200,000 – a twenty-fold increase from 2002.

These are colossal figures, especially in a mature democracy. Moreover, ethnic data of those stopped and searched show a clear and consistent pattern: blacks and Asians are stopped and searched disproportionately. As a 2013 report by the Ministry of Justice puts it, blacks are six times more likely than whites to be stopped and searched under Section 1, and Asians or mixed ethnic groups over twice more likely, even though the arrest rates are the same for whites and blacks, and lower for Asians.[47]

Section 60 searches are even more biased. Remember that Section 60 searches do not require reasonable suspicion, as Section 1 searches do, thus give more discretion to police officers. Under these powers, black people are searched at about twenty-nine times the rate of whites, and Asians at about six times. In 2012/13, more than half the people stopped and searched in London under Section 60 were black (53 per cent). However, the arrest rates in these searches over the past couple of years have never gone above 5 per cent (except for whites in 2012/13). We must remember, furthermore, that arrest rate does not necessarily imply that the person arrested will be charged; what is recorded as an arrest might eventually lead to an unlawful arrest decision, so this rate is not a perfect representation of effective police activity. But even if we assume that the 5 per cent arrest rate recorded in 2013 and 2014 is unproblematic, this still means that nineteen out of twenty people were stopped and searched unnecessarily – and indeed some of them illegally, as even home secretary Theresa May admitted.[48]

Let us focus on the period leading up to the 2011 uprising. During the financial year 2010/11 (April 2010 to April 2011), the police conducted more than 1.2 million stop and searches. Of those stopped and searched, 16 per cent were black and 11 per cent were Asian. This is disproportionate given the proportion of blacks (3.3 per cent) and Asians (7.5 per cent) in the population. The disproportionality was even higher in stop and searches under Section 60 powers – 37 per cent of those stopped and searched were black (up from 33 per cent the previous year) and 20 per cent Asian (up from 16 per cent the previous year) – which, as we have seen above, gives more discretion to the police, thus increasing the likelihood of stops based on stereotypes and prejudices. In London, out of five people stopped and searched under Section 60 powers, two were black and one Asian.

Some readers might now be thinking that perhaps this is a necessary evil to catch criminals, so stopping and searching more than a million people a year should be permitted in a democracy, and that this is a good and effective use of police time and resources. They might also be thinking that if non-white ethnic groups are searched disproportionately, this is probably because of their disproportionate involvement in crime.

In the two years leading up to the 2011 uprisings, the police stopped and searched more than 2.5 million people, but the arrest rate remained between 8 per cent and 9 per cent – not even one in ten people. Nearly half of all stop and searches were conducted in London, where the arrest rates were even lower (6 per cent for 2009/10 and 7 per cent for the following financial year). Stop and searches conducted under Section 60 powers yielded an even lower arrest rate of 2 per cent. These low arrest rates raise questions about the efficacy of this intrusive and controversial police practice. What about the ethnic dimension then? Did these powers enable the police to catch non-white criminals, justifying the disproportionate police pressure on non-white populations? Not really. In those two years, the arrest rate for whites following a stop and search was higher than it was for blacks and Asians (9 per cent in 2009/10 compared to 7 per cent and 5 per cent for blacks and Asians; 10 per cent in 2010/11 compared to 8 per cent and 6 per cent respectively).

Arbitrary stop and search alienates not just non-whites, but all groups of youths subjected to this practice, especially when it is used for social control and harassing groups of young people. Since the 'sus' in the 1980s, stop and search continued under different legislative frameworks, and remained both an ineffective tool to fight crime and a highly effective way to damage police–community relations. As government reports recognized, it was a major – and legitimate – source of resentment that led to unrest both in the 1980s and in 2011. One important difference, however, is that the anger was much more widespread in 2011 than it was in the 1980s. So how did the government respond?

Fever Pitch

Why have our police been dispersing these hoods so that they can riot in other vicinities, instead of rounding them up? Does the

Prime Minister remember that in 1971, at the peak of the opposition to the Vietnam war in the United States, the US Government brought 16,000 troops into Washington, in addition to the police, who rounded up and arrested the rioters and put 40,000 of them in the DC stadium in one morning? Has he any plans to make Wembley stadium available for similar use?
– Sir Peter Tapsell, Member of Parliament, 11 August 2011

Sir Peter has an astonishing memory when it comes to numbers. David Cameron had no such plans, fortunately, and decided to keep Wembley stadium 'available for great sporting events' rather than for locking people in.[49] But he offered perhaps the best example of the pathological framework in his so-called 'fight back' speech as a response to the 2011 uprising. 'These riots were not about race,' he said. 'These riots were not about government cuts . . . And these riots were not about poverty. . . No, this was about behaviour, people showing indifference to right and wrong, people with a twisted moral code, people with a complete absence of self-restraint.'[50]

Now I wonder. . . If this is about behaviour, how then can we explain what made 15,000 individuals with behavioural problems come together and revolt for several days? If English cities are home to tens of thousands of people of this pathological disposition, why didn't they do it before? Why don't they do it *all* the time? After all, if we are to believe Cameron, they are not capable of self-restraint.

Ironically, the pathological framework explains the parliamentary expenses scandal better than it explains urban uprisings. As we learned in 2009, several MPs – people in a position of political power who do not experience economic hardship and intrusive police stop and searches – had used taxpayers' money to buy plasma TV screens and dog food, to have duck houses built in their gardens, to have their pianos tuned, and even to claim the £5 given to a church charity. Now, *that* is 'about behaviour, people showing indifference to right and wrong, people with a twisted moral code, people with a complete absence of self-restraint' – to quote Cameron again.

This pathological framework with its emphasis on criminality is not credible. Nor is it very original. The uprisings of the 1980s were also condemned as 'mindless violence', and Thatcher referred to them as 'a spree of naked greed', though her home secretary at least admitted that there was a serious unemployment problem.[51] Who then were the criminals involved in these acts? The lack of imagination between the 1980s and 2011 is perhaps most striking here. The Left was a target of choice for the media and the Conservatives in the 1980s, and the descriptions were somewhat more colourful. Let us take a look at a couple of media examples that echo the parliamentary debates after the 1985 uprising in Tottenham. The *Daily Express* blamed 'crazed Left-wing extremists' and 'street-fighting experts trained in Moscow and Libya'. The *Daily Telegraph* cast a wider net:

> Trotskyites, socialist extremists, Revolutionary Communists, marxists and black militants from as far away as Toxteth descended on Tottenham yesterday... They cheered speakers who declared: 'This war is just beginning', and supported calls for the police to be put under the control of the local community... White, bearded men in sandals, many accompanied by girls, rubbed shoulders with the local black people and supported calls for more violence.[52]

Crucially there were no women in the list (perhaps the men in sandals were the girls' parents?). I realize that the image of white, bearded men in sandals might send cold shivers up one's spine, but today they are more likely to be benign hipsters than rioters. The Left, Blair made sure, is nothing to be scared of for the Conservatives. And Libya is in shambles after revolts that were praised by the very David Cameron who deemed those revolting at home criminals.

That leaves us with gangs. Gangs were mentioned in the earlier uprisings as well, but the government's assertions in 2011 were original, if not always accurate. The home secretary was categorical: 'It is obvious that gangs were involved.' This echoed Prime Minister Cameron's earlier claim that '[a]t the heart of all the violence sits the issue of the street gangs'.[53] It turns out, however, that the earlier figures released by the Metropolitan Police were inaccurate; 19 per cent (and not 28 per cent, as it was initially claimed) of those arrested in London were 'estimated' gang members. Home Office data also showed that overall only 13 per cent of those arrested were estimated to be 'affiliated to a gang' – a classification that the Home Affairs Committee found not only vague, but also unhelpful as evidence to conclude that gangs had organized the incidents. The *Guardian/ LSE* research also found that although gang members were present during the incidents, there was 'little indication that they were orchestrating the riots'.[54]

Other data mobilized to support these claims are the previous criminal records of those involved in the incidents. The Ministry of Justice data suggest that 76 per cent of those arrested had a previous caution or conviction, whereas among the *Reading the Riots* interviewees (the majority of whom were not arrested), this rate is 68 per cent. This suggests that the police might have rounded up those with criminal records because they would be easier to identify – a possibility admitted by the police themselves: 'the ones that you know are going to be arrested first'.[55] There is, overall, little to indicate that the 2011 uprising was orchestrated by gangs and was the product of pure criminality.

But the looting – surely that was criminal? Looting was not a distinguishing feature of the 2011 uprising. There was looting in the 1980s, as there was looting during the Gordon Riots of 1780. As I argued in chapter 1, urban uprisings present opportunities to those who want to benefit from the breakdown of order. Looting during disorder may be opportunistic behaviour not to be condoned, but the fact that it happens does not make the uprising an affair of 'people with a twisted moral code', and should not 'displace the fact that an unarmed man was shot to death'.[56] Looting was extensive during the London uprising, but the media focus on the looting of businesses obscured the fact that many public buildings, including police stations and municipal institutions, were among the targets. More importantly, the police were the first and constant target of the participants during the uprising.[57] Looting, moreover, is also an act of defiance, which is what such uprisings are about.

So far I have argued that despite the government's claims, there is little to warrant reducing the 2011 uprising to criminality, gangs and looting. It would have been very helpful if a full official inquiry had been conducted. On 11 August, at the House of Commons, Cameron was asked if the scale of the incidents did not call for a detailed and independent inquiry like Scarman's into the 1981 Brixton uprising. 'Of course one should not jump to conclusions,' Cameron said,

> but I think everyone is clear on the differences between what we have seen in the last three days and what we saw in 1981. This was not political protest, or a riot about protest or politics – it was common or garden thieving, robbing and looting, and we do not need an inquiry to tell us that.[58]

Cameron is misleading us here. Not everyone in the government thought the 1981 Brixton uprising was political and thus merited an inquiry. There was resistance to an inquiry at that time as well. During debates in the House of Commons on 13 April 1981, the Conservative William Benyon had asked, using exactly the same line of reasoning as Cameron: 'What can the inquiry tell us that we do not know already?' And he added: 'Does not the inquiry itself appear to make the violence worth while?'[59]

It appears that the memory of Scarman haunted the government. His was an independent inquiry, and he was certainly not one to mince his words. His report on the 1981 Brixton uprising did not remain yet another dust-gathering government document; it became something of a sensation, going beyond the local context it was investigating and becoming a topic of broader debate about urban deprivation, racial disadvantage and police harassment. This did not sit very well with the government. 'I'm afraid the report seems highly critical of the police,' read a handwritten note by Thatcher to her home secretary Whitelaw.[60]

When the next series of urban uprisings erupted in 1985, in Brixton again and then in Tottenham, home secretary Douglas Hurd firmly resisted calling for a judicial inquiry. He explained that unlike 1981, the uprisings of 1985 were 'triggered by specific action by police officers', by which he meant police officers shooting and paralysing a black woman at her home in Brixton and, a week later, the death of another black woman during a police raid on her home in Tottenham. A judicial inquiry like Scarman's, he reasoned, would have to investigate these incidents, and would thus 'prejudice completely the possibility of criminal proceedings'.[61] The British police, as we saw, have a record of impunity regarding its officers implicated in civilian deaths, and the 1985 incidents were no exception. What the home secretary wanted to avoid was the questioning of the officers implicated.

The government does its best to avoid official inquiries when uprisings are triggered by civilian deaths in the hands of the police. Only under pressure did the government agree to an inquiry after the 2011 uprising, but made sure that it would not be a full public inquiry operated under the Inquiries Act. Inquiries conducted under this act are led by a judge (like the Scarman inquiry), who has the powers to call witnesses, and require them to give evidence and to provide any documents relevant to the case.[62] But as we saw above with the aftermath of the Mark Duggan killing and others, police officers implicated in deaths are often not even interviewed.

A major official inquiry was thus avoided, and the task was given to the Riots Communities and Victims Panel to produce a report, which it did in 2012 with a photograph of broom cleaners, volunteers armed with brooms to clean up the riot damage, on its cover. The cover photograph and the opening sentence set the tone of the report: 'Residents in communities where riots took place last summer want rioters – many of whom had long criminal records – appropriately punished.'[63] Crime and punishment, then.

That is what the government did. 'This is criminality, pure and simple,' Cameron claimed. 'Wanton criminality' was the diagnosis of London's mayor. When asked by the Home Affairs Committee why she thought the uprising had occurred, the home secretary Theresa May replied: 'I think there are a number of issues here that we can only properly assess when we have a proper analysis of the people who were involved in the riots. . . But I am absolutely clear that what underlay it was criminality.'[64] Need 'a proper analysis', yet already 'absolutely clear'? Cameron was right; the government really did not need an inquiry.

Punishment followed. This was yet another difference from the 1981 uprising. As a Home Office study found, the sentence most used was a fine in 1981.[65] In 2011, the government used exemplary sentences, the most notorious of which involved two young people punished for trying to 'incite' revolts through Facebook. They were sentenced to four years in jail even though their actions had produced nothing. Research into sentences given to the participants in incidents showed that they had been subjected to much harsher punishment than they would have been had they committed similar offences in other circumstances. The severity of the punishments was reflected in higher immediate custody rates and longer sentences. The participants in the uprising were three times more likely to be placed in immediate custody compared to sentences given for similar offences in the previous year. Their sentences were also two months longer on average.[66]

As we have seen, the sources of grievances remained the same: deprivation, increasing inequalities and economic insecurity, discrimination and police harassment, which accumulated like fuel over the years. The urban uprisings of 2011 were similar to the uprisings of the 1980s in terms of their causes, but their expanding geography is worrying as it suggests widespread deprivation, exclusion and resentment, which was met by the government with a crime and punishment approach. These trends – an expanding geography of uprisings and increasingly repressive government responses – are not unique to the UK. Let us now cross to the other side of the Channel, where the ghost of British urban uprisings haunted an allegedly 'one and indivisible' Republic.

4

The Algerian War is Not Over in France

'The Algerian War is not over in France.' Abdel made this remark while we were talking about the relationship between the police and youth of immigrant origin – a politically correct way of saying non-white youth in France – in 2002 in Vaulx-en-Velin, a *banlieue* to the east of Lyon.[1] Just as in the US and the UK, the police in France are a persistent source of grievance for non-white youth, especially those living in the social housing estates on the peripheries of cities – the *banlieues* – which also happen to be the areas where most of the uprisings occur.

In France, state policies and inner-city property market dynamics led to the formation of deprived neighbourhoods in these peripheral areas in the second half of the twentieth century. The issues around French *banlieues* have wider resonance, with connotations ranging from threats to French identity to Islamist terrorism. The term *banlieue* is commonly used in political and media discourses to evoke such issues as immigration, insecurity, ethnic separatism and Islam. This image, however, hides from view the grievances of inhabitants, including mass unemployment, discrimination, stigmatization and police violence – all of which suggest that if the *banlieues* are revolting, it is because the conditions are revolting.

Although the term *banlieue* is commonly used to refer to a certain form of housing (social housing estates) associated with certain kinds of populations (immigrants and non-white French), *banlieue* designates a geographical area surrounding the city, not specific forms of housing or certain groups of the population. The peripheral status of the *banlieues* suggests an image of exclusion, but the term is not necessarily negative, and not all *banlieues* are poor. Indeed, there is a rich variety of them, including wealthy and exclusive ones such as Neuilly-sur-Seine to the west of Paris, the political base of Nicolas Sarkozy, the former president whose political rhetoric resembles that of the extreme Right.

Yet the dominant and stereotypical image of *banlieues* is one of social housing estates in the peripheral areas of cities – 'badlands' that do not quite fit in the French Republic. This image, we will see, is fed by France's colonial past, as well as the dystopian images of American ghettos, which is why the main groups associated with this 'badlands' image are Arabs and blacks, even when they are born and raised in France. The fear of the formation of ethnic communities and ghettos – incompatible with France's image of itself as a 'one and indivisible' Republic – makes the poorer and more ethnically diverse *banlieues* objects of much policy and debate, even though the concentration of ethnic communities is stronger among the white French than the non-white. It is, however, the latter's concentration that seems to pose problems.

Despite the alarmist discourses, French *banlieues* are not ethnically homogeneous and large enough to function as self-contained ghettos. Many of the *banlieues* referred to as ghettos today are the products of France's post-Second World War period of intense industrialization, economic growth and urbanization – the so-called *trente glorieuses*, thirty glorious years of growth that ended with the economic crisis of the 1970s. These settlements were built in the peripheries of cities where land was available and cheap, and they involved large housing estates (*grands ensembles*), which were a quick and economical response to the housing shortage that had emerged as a result of rapid urbanization. Initially, these estates improved the lives of many by eradicating shantytowns and providing affordable dwellings, though they were by no means accommodation just for the poor. Once the economic crisis hit in the 1970s, however, problems started to emerge. Middle-class families left the estates following the housing finance reform of 1977 that sought to encourage owner-occupied housing. Thus the estates in the *banlieues* increasingly became home to more economically disadvantaged groups, with an increasing proportion of immigrant residents, who were pushed out of city centres because of prices or housing-market discrimination.

This is also when the first incidents of unrest in the *banlieues* occurred. These were not just mindless rioting; they had to do with material hardships and injuries inflicted by France's colonial past and present. As we will see, there are continuities between the colonial practices of the French state and its treatment of *banlieues* and their residents in the post-colonial period. This is why I prefer using the term 'colonial present' to emphasize how the colonial imaginary still persists and is today played out in French *banlieues*.[2] These continuities are most visible in police practices, urban policy, official discourses and in a series of legislative initiatives. Our exploration of *banlieue* uprisings will provide plenty of examples that suggest a colonial present in France, with 'race', class and spatial stigmatization as the main ingredients of urban rage. This, however, will not be a linear history; we will also see discontinuities and breaks, such as the economic crisis of the 1970s and its effects, or the shift to a more authoritarian approach to *banlieues* and changing priorities of urban policy from the 1980s to the 2000s. Let us start with the 2005 urban uprising, the most significant disruption the country had seen since

May 1968, and work our way backwards to see both changes and continuities.

Fire in Clichy

It was a war atmosphere, which took the generation of my parents back to the Algerian War.
– Mohamed Mechmache describing Clichy during the 2005
uprising

The massive revolt of November 2005 is certainly anti-colonial.
– Sadri Khiari, *La contre-révolution coloniale en France*

The coincidence is almost uncanny: the three teenagers who suffered an electric shock – which killed two of them and seriously injured the third – in an electricity substation while trying to escape from the police had origins that made them more likely to live in a poor *banlieue*, face hardship at school, end up unemployed or underemployed, and suffer discrimination, including in relations with the police as the tragic incident exposed. Such was the finding of two official studies.[3] The descendants of immigrants from North and sub-Saharan Africa – like Zyed and Bouna – and from Turkey – like Muhittin, the only survivor – are economically the most vulnerable in French society even when they are born and raised in France. Indeed, even when factors such as educational level, social status of parents and place of residence are controlled for, these studies found, they still have higher risk of unemployment compared to white French or the children of European immigrants simply because of who they are (something Muhittin would probably not have been able to escape in Turkey either because he is Kurdish).

This was the greatest injustice of all. And they knew it. Zyed, Bouna and Muhittin did not need a government report to tell them about discrimination, so they started running when they saw the police, even though they had done nothing wrong. The others knew it too. This is why, once rage erupted in Clichy in the autumn of 2005, it found resonance in 300 other places across France. They too did not need a government report to tell them that they were not, and would likely never be, on an equal level with their fellow citizens in terms of life opportunities. We, however, will need to come back to this report, because it provides insight into structural inequalities in France. But let us first get a sense of what happened during that autumn of 2005.

On 27 October 2005, three teenagers in Clichy-sous-Bois, a *banlieue* to the north-east of Paris, took refuge in an electricity substation in order to escape identity checks by the police – a form of daily harassment not uncommon for the youth of working-class *banlieues*, especially those with a darker skin. They were escaping not because they had done something wrong, but because they were coming back from a game of football and did not have their identity cards with them. This meant, if caught, a visit to the police station about forty-five minutes away. It also meant that their parents had to come and fetch them from the station, which is an inconvenience, all the more so that day because it was Ramadan, and *iftar* time – the time of the meal to break the fast – was approaching.

Little did they know that there was a police intervention in their neighbourhood because of a suspected theft from a construction site. When they saw officers from the mobile BAC (*brigade anti-criminalité*) police unit, created to catch offenders in the act and known for their aggressive policing in the social housing neighbourhoods of the *banlieues*, the group of teenagers started running.[4] Two of them were caught by the officers, but Zyed Benna (seventeen years old, family from Tunisia), Bouna Traoré (fifteen years old, family from Mauritania) and Muhittin Altun (seventeen years old, family from Turkey) managed to run across a field and reach the electricity station where they hid from the police. They were electrocuted shortly after 6 p.m. Muhittin, despite his burns, managed to get out and go back to the neighbourhood, and firefighters were called – by the youth, not by the police who had chased the teenagers, seen them entering the electricity substation, and blocked the exit.

Firefighters were called shortly before 7 p.m. and, an hour later, groups of young people had already started attacking public buildings and setting cars on fire. It is significant that the early attacks were focused on institutions: the cars set on fire belonged to the municipality and the post office, the buildings attacked included schools, a postal distribution centre and the town hall.[5] Thus started an uprising that was to prove unprecedented in scale and intensity.

As the lawyers for the families of the victims wrote in their book, the revolts could have been prevented had the government not tried to present the victims as thieves, had they acknowledged the seriousness of the situation by immediately opening a judicial investigation (which took one week, despite two deaths, one serious injury and expanding uprisings), and shown that they were willing to listen with compassion rather than react with repression.[6] The day after the incident, in their first public statements, Prime Minister Dominique de Villepin and Minister of the Interior Nicolas Sarkozy both suggested a link between the three teenagers and the suspected theft attempt. Sarkozy also insisted that the teenagers were not being pursued by the police – a claim that was allegedly corroborated by Muhittin, who was interrogated by the police in his hospital bed less than twenty-four hours after receiving an electric shock of 20,000 volts, witnessing the death of his friends and suffering serious burns himself.

Once out of hospital, Muhittin gave an account to the contrary, stating that they had started running because the police were chasing them.[7] They had heard the sirens of the police approaching, panicked and hidden in the electricity substation. 'I wanted to come out,' he said, 'to go home, after all, we hadn't done anything!' But they were intimidated by voices and the barking of dogs outside, and ended up staying inside the substation for about thirty minutes. In the end, it was officially established that the link to the theft attempt was misleading, that the police were indeed chasing them, and that the police knew they had hidden in an electricity substation and were thus in danger. Yet, during the thirty minutes the teenagers stayed in there, no warning was issued by the police.

The initial official statements portraying the teenagers as thieves fuelled the anger, and the uprising continued the next day, Friday, 28 October, with confrontations with the police. On Saturday, a silent march was organized in the neighbourhood with the participation of up to a thousand people, some wearing T-shirts with the slogan 'Dead for nothing'. At night the police cordoned off the neighbourhood. By Sunday the situation seemed calmer until a police tear-gas grenade exploded in the local mosque. This was the turning point that rekindled the fire in Clichy and turned the local uprising into a national one.

According to Mohamed Mechmache, who was present during the uprising and co-created an association following it, the incidents lasted six days in Clichy, but in two phases. During the first phase, there were confrontations between the youth and the police in Clichy and the neighbouring Montfermeil, another *banlieue* with social housing estates. With helicopters flying over the neighbourhood, their projectors directed on the flats, and the riot police cordoning off the neighbourhood for the evening, it looked like a war zone. Several eyewitnesses mentioned police provocation and posturing, challenging the youth to fight and hurling racist insults not just at the youths, but at their parents as well.[8]

The second phase started following the tear-gas incident of Sunday, 30 October. Just like the incident that led to the death of the teenagers, this was first followed by an official denial. No official excuses were presented even after the responsibility of the police had been established. The youth were the actors in the first phase of the uprising, but now their parents had joined in as well in 'a moment of amazing solidarity', in the words of Mechmache. Starting from 31 October, the uprising expanded first to the Paris region, then, from 3 November, to the rest of France.

Calm returned after three weeks of unrest, during which about 10,000 cars were set ablaze and hundreds of public buildings (mainly schools, but also town halls, post offices and police stations) were attacked, with some partially or totally destroyed. By the end of November, according to the numbers provided by the Ministry of the Interior, 4,800 people had been arrested by the police, 4,400 of them taken into police custody, and 763 put behind bars, a figure that had gone up to 800 by mid-December.[9] Although Sarkozy had declared that 80 per cent of the arrestees were already known to the police and the justice system for previous acts of delinquency, data from courts in the Paris region suggested that most of them were not habitual offenders.[10]

Sarkozy also insisted on the 'perfectly organized' nature of the uprising. This claim was inaccurate as well, as a report by the French Intelligence Service showed through its interpretation of the incidents as a 'non-organized insurrection', a 'popular revolt' of social housing neighbourhoods.[11] There was no criminal mastermind behind it. As Mechmache put it, although the deaths of the teenagers were a trigger, the source of the uprising was the accumulation of years of injustice, for which state policies, policing practices and inflammatory language used by state officials were responsible. A prime example here is the incident that started it all – the police chasing non-white youth in a social housing neighbourhood. This was routine, not exceptional, police harassment of *banlieue* youth, which explains why the teenagers started running despite their innocence. Police harassment, as we will see with further examples, is part of everyday experience for the youth in working-class *banlieues* such as Clichy-sous-Bois, and a major source of grievance eventually erupting in violent forms. Small wonder Muhittin was among those placed in police custody a few months later for throwing stones at a police car.[12]

The 2005 uprising was unprecedented in terms of its magnitude and geographical extent. It continued for three weeks, touching about 300 communes. We will be able better to appreciate the scale and significance of this geographical expansion once we have reviewed urban uprisings of the past few decades in France later in this chapter. The state response was unprecedented as well: on 8 November, just when calm was returning to the *banlieues*, the government declared a state of emergency, and the fact that the state of emergency was based on a 1955 law dating from the Algerian War only added insult to injury. That this law had been invoked only twice before – during the Algerian War and in France's overseas territory New Caledonia in 1985 – in France's former colonies, but never on mainland France, suggested that critics of the colonial nature of the French state's treatment of *banlieues* are not, after all, so wide of the mark. On 18 November, parliament approved a three-month extension of the state of emergency, even though the uprising was practically over. The exceptional measure eventually ended on 4 January 2006.

Despite all the unprecedented aspects of the 2005 uprising, no official investigation was conducted to gain an understanding of its causes. Who will then tell us why such a massive uprising happened in this land of equality, in areas that have been objects of various state policies for decades, necessitating such an exceptional measure re-enacted from France's colonial past? Let's ask Hélène Carrère d'Encausse.

The Beauty and the Beast

The tragedy of Africa is that the African has not fully entered into history. The African peasant ... only knew the eternal cycle

of time, marked by the endless repetition of the same gestures and same words. In this imaginary . . . there is room for neither human endeavour nor the idea of progress.
– Nicolas Sarkozy, President of the Republic, Dakar speech, 26 July 2007

You may not know her – neither did I – but it seems that her ideas were shared by politicians, including ministers and future presidents. Hélène Carrère d'Encausse is a historian specializing in Russian history, lifetime secretary-general of the Academie française, and recipient of the Legion of Honour. During an interview with the Russian TV channel NTV on 13 November 2005, this is how she explained the uprisings in the French *banlieues*:

> These people, they come directly from their African villages. But the city of Paris and the other cities of Europe are not African villages. For example, everyone is surprised: why are African children on the street and not at school? Why cannot their parents buy an apartment? It is clear why: a lot of these Africans, I'm telling you, are polygamous. In an apartment, there are three or four women and 25 children. It is so jam-packed that these are no longer apartments but God knows what! One understands why these children are running in the street.[13]

As I said, she was not the only one publicly expressing such ideas. On 15 November, the employment minister Gérard Larcher declared polygamy as one reason for the revolts. On 17 November it was Sarkozy's turn, then minister of the interior: 'They [rioters] are absolutely French from a juridical perspective. But let's put it as it is: polygamy and a-culturalization of so many families makes the integration of French youth of sub-Saharan African origin more difficult than those from other origins.'[14] The beast was out in the open.

'The beast' is Achille Mbembe's metaphor for state racism, which can be 'paternalist and accommodating in its postcolonial version, monstrous when necessary, as during the Algerian War'. Mbembe argues that this beast is lurking behind the mask of civility and reason that is on the façade of the French Republic (and other western cultures). It did not come into being with the 2005 incidents, but 'has always constituted the shameful, and for that reason carefully veiled, side of French democracy'. The 2005 uprising, however, exposed the beast. The mask of civility could no longer hide it.[15]

It seems to me that Hélène Carrère d'Encausse's remarks capture the essence of Mbembe's metaphor. On the one side, we have a perfect representative of French high culture, civility and reason: a historian with a noble name, member of the Academie française (the institution that has been safeguarding the French language for nearly four centuries), and recipient of the Legion of Honour, which, even if you didn't know what it was, or were oblivious to the fact that it awarded personal connections more than merit, sounds very distinguished. On the other, however, her remarks betray the beast, subverting all pretension to civility and reason. It is not clear to what extent such a distinguished member of the French cultural establishment was in touch with the everyday lives of *banlieue* residents, but she seemed to have no doubts.

We have seen that the views of this distinguished historian were shared by members of the government at the time, including the minister of the interior. Polygamy, however, is only one component of the colonial imaginary that informs official discourses and practices. Several events leading up to, during and after the uprising exposed the beast, a deeply rooted colonial legacy in France. These ranged from the use of stigmatizing and inflammatory language by government officials to re-enacting colonial laws – as we saw with the state of emergency – or introducing new ones.

The campaign against the headscarf at school, for example, was launched in 2003 by the right-wing government, and was quickly supported by large portions of the Left, eventually turning into a law in 2004, which prohibited 'wearing conspicuous symbols of religious affiliation' in schools. The law was couched in terms suggesting that it did not target a specific religion but all. Everyone knew, however, that it targeted headscarves and Islam, and was even referred to as the 'anti-headscarf law'. The headscarf is stigmatized as an attack on the principle of secularism, though the fact that schools close on every Christian holiday does not give rise to a similar concern. The headscarf is also stigmatized as a symbol of the oppression of women, although, given the rampant sexism that exists in France, it is not only veiled women who are oppressed, but this does not raise much concern either. This stigmatization of the headscarf also occludes the possibility that it may be worn by choice and religious conviction, rather than as a result of coercion.

As Pierre Tévanian has noted, the anti-headscarf law 'unveiled the postcolonial racism that has taken root in France', or, what he has also called 'republican racism' that has its roots in the colonial period.[16] We must remember that the headscarf was an important symbol of resistance to colonial rule, so this law once again exposed the beast with its colonial legacy. It was partly a product of increasing Islamophobia in France in the aftermath of the September 11 attacks and military interventions. Its sources, however, were as much in contemporary geopolitics as in France's colonial history.

It was in this context that a group of activists launched a call – 'We are the Natives of the Republic!' – in January 2005, pointing to parallels between France's colonial and contemporary policies.[17] They argued that France was still a colonial state, treating its citizens of colonial origin with the same condescension and contempt, particularly in working-class *banlieues*, stigmatized as areas incompatible with the Republic. Calling for a demonstration, they asked for a critical re-examination of the Republic's colonial past and present. Perfect timing. The following month, a new law required high-school curricula to 'recognize the positive role of the French overseas presence, especially in North Africa', and academic research to be oriented in the same direction. Asking educators to teach students France's colonial grandeur was reminiscent of the Vichy period instructions urging them to promote National Revolution, but even Vichy had not dared to put that into a law.[18] The controversial Article 4 of the law on the positive role of France in the colonies was eventually withdrawn, but the beast was once again exposed.

The persistence of this strong colonial legacy in France is divisive despite the image of the Republic as 'one and indivisible'. The Republic is at once the product and producer of racialized social relations through its public policies and official discourses. Thus, the republican racism Tévanian criticizes is not a sign of malfunction of the Republic, but part of its normal workings.[19] This is why, Saïd Bouamama notes, there was no significant anti-colonial movement in France. The idea that there were superior and inferior civilizations, as well as superior and inferior people, was so interiorized that colonialism seemed logical, even progressive, for the majority. The same logic is at work today as debates around the headscarf or *banlieues* show. Bouamama argues that the French children of immigrants from former colonies of France are still seen as immigrants and foreigners, and they are treated like that socially, economically and politically. Turks, he observes, suffer the same fate, even though Turkey had not been colonized.[20] This is the beast confronting children like Zyed, Bouna and Muhittin – and their children as well.

The working class *banlieues* of France bear the weight of this colonial legacy. The colonial imaginary is still dominant and shared in a cross-partisan fashion, to varying degrees. Through policies and discourses, 'the State perpetuates, indeed reproduces, forms of colonial domination' in the *banlieues*.[21] One example of this imaginary is the use of military language such as 'reconquest', which is a recurrent term used in connection with *banlieues*, and more recently in urban redevelopment projects aimed at the demolition of social housing estates.[22] Policies and discourses that frame *banlieues* as the 'badlands of the Republic' that are incompatible with its values only exacerbate the already entrenched prejudices, reinforcing the boundaries that set certain spaces and their residents apart from the normalized mainstream.[23] As Mbembe observed:

> for several years the French population has been led to believe that the *banlieues* constitute a direct threat to their lifestyle and to their most cherished values... But as soon as the *banlieue* is defined as a place inhabited not by full-fledged moral subjects but by an undifferentiated mass that can be summarily discredited (as little savages, scum, hooligans, delinquents, gangstas running the parallel economy) – as soon as it is constructed as the domestic front of a new planetary war (cultural, religious, and military all at once), where the very identity of the Republic is being played out – there is great temptation to want to apply colonial methods drawn from the lessons of the race wars to the most vulnerable categories of French society.[24]

The temptation, it seems, was too strong to resist. Now that we have a sense of the persistence of the colonial imaginary and the place of *banlieues* in it, it is time to go back to uprisings. Above we saw how unprecedented the 2005 uprising was, but when we compare the sources of rage that led to it, we see that 2005 was not so extraordinary after all. Indeed, it followed a well-established pattern and history of uprisings in French *banlieues*, following from grievances caused by similar problems over decades. These problems were not new; they 'have been staring French politicians in the face for the past twenty years', as Hargreaves wrote in the aftermath of the 2005 incidents.[25] Their failure to address these problems aggravated them and created a deep feeling of injustice among *banlieue* residents. This feeling of injustice was only exacerbated by the illusions of the French republican model with its alleged commitment to equality, and the French state's failure, or unwillingness, to come to terms with its colonial past and present. These all fed the resentment that then turned into rage with a triggering incident. The sources of resentment and signs of rage were already present in the *banlieues* in the 1970s. So were the bitter traces of France's colonial history.

Algerian War Redux?

Are we still in France, in the Republic? My husband was a conscript in 1956. Will it be necessary to take up arms again to keep our tranquillity?

      – Madame M., letter to the mayor, Villeurbanne, 1979

Let [our street] become what it was before the arrival of this scum. The Algerian War starts again because of public authorities, but this time we are at home, and it is them who will leave one way or another.

      – Petition to the municipality, Villeurbanne, 1980

Lest we take her for a galloping racist, Madame M. clarifies in her letter that she votes 'socialist'. As Michelle Zancarini-Fournel shows, such complaints were common in the housing estates of the eastern *banlieues* of Lyon, an industrial city to the east of France, as early as the 1970s.[26] Particularly notorious were the '3Vs', also referred to as the 'Lyon Bronx': Villeurbanne, Vénissieux and Vaulx-en-Velin, three working-class *banlieues*. The first recorded incident dates from 1971 in La Grappinière, a neighbourhood of Vaulx-en-Velin that included several housing estates built to accommodate repatriated settlers and *harkis* (Algerians who fought on the side of France) from Algeria after 1962. Official documents include references to 'delinquency and criminality', 'rodeos' (racing and performing stunts with stolen cars) and 'skirmish', but the incidents had not yet taken on the national importance that they would in 1981.

In the 1960s, there were already Algerian workers in the industries of the Lyon region, but arrivals increased after Algerian independence in 1962. From 1968 to 1978, the Algerian population in the region doubled to 80,000. They usually did manual jobs and had low incomes, and their situation was further undermined by the economic crisis and diminishing industrial sector. Most of these families were accommodated in the housing estates of Vaulx-en-Velin and Vénissieux, sites of recurrent uprisings in the decades to follow, as we will see. Recall that we have already met Abdel from Vaulx-en-Velin with his bitter observation in the opening lines of this chapter.

Tensions in the social housing estates of Villeurbanne surfaced in the early 1970s, especially in *cité* Simion, which consisted of 350 housing units intended for repatriates from Algeria (a *cité* is a group of buildings constructed according to a single plan and clearly demarcated from the rest of the urban fabric). Tenants in these houses went on a rent strike in 1972 because of poor maintenance, despite the constantly increasing charges. But this was not the only problem in this area. As we saw in the epigraphs above, there were also tensions that carried the traces and bitter memories of the Algerian War. There were complaints about Arab singing, laundry hanging from the windows, rubbish and noise. With time the incidents only got worse, and by 1976 aggression, against females in particular, theft and burnt cars were reported. Mostly it was a small group of adolescents, with problems at school as well, but the *cité* was sealed off several times by the riot police, in a manner reminiscent of military practices in colonial Algeria.

The *cité* Simion was eventually demolished between 1978 and 1984. In August 1984, the local daily newspaper *Le Progrès* ran the following headline: 'A ghetto scraped from the map'. Even the street name was changed. But the demolition removed only the buildings from the map, not the problems that led to Simion's sad reputation. The residents displaced by the demolition were rehoused in Vaulx-en-Velin and Vénissieux, which were to become among the most notorious *banlieues* in France in the 1980s and early 1990s. Let us see what the situation was like in these areas.

The economic crisis and deindustrialization hit the working-class *banlieues* of Lyon hard. Between 1975 and 1982, seven firms were closed in Vénissieux, where the number of unemployed people more than doubled, going from 1,253 to 3,287. This increase corresponded to a dramatic rise in the unemployment rate, which almost tripled from 3.8 per cent in 1975 to 10.8 per cent in 1982. This *banlieue* also lost 10,000 of its inhabitants during this period (from 74,417 to 64,848), which suggests that those who had the means moved away, leaving behind the economically more vulnerable. It was during the so-called hot summer of 1981 that Vénissieux came under the national spotlight with incidents in its social housing neighbour-hood called Les Minguettes. Rodeos and confrontations with the police, which were not unprecedented, put the issue of unrest in *banlieues* on the national agenda. There was no specific incident that triggered events, but, as Adil Jazouli found, anger had been simmering over a feeling of exclusion, generated by economic difficulties, prob-lems at school and police harassment.[27]

The particular context in which the incidents took place gave them additional urgency. The Left was in power for the first time in the Fifth Republic with a contentious political agenda, and was criti-cized for its soft take on immigration. Furthermore, the Brixton uprising had just occurred on the other side of the Channel, which was seen from France as 'race riots', something inconceivable under the allegedly one and indivisible Republic. As we saw in the previous chapter, however, the Brixton and other British uprisings of 1981 were not race riots, but involved, as did the 2011 English uprising, ethnically heterogeneous participants. The menace of race riots fed by dystopian images of US and UK inner cities, however, was a powerful one that summoned the ghosts haunting the French Republic and nurtured the beast lurking in the shadows.

The events of 1981 were not limited to the *banlieues* of Lyon. By the end of the summer, similar unrest had occurred in the working-class *banlieues* of Marseille, Roubaix, Nancy and Paris. Though perplexed, the new government saw these as expressions of discontent and initiated an urban policy programme, which was unprecedented in many ways. One of the unique aspects of this programme involved spatially designating areas of intervention, which contributed to their stigmatization. Many of the social housing neighbourhoods in the *banlieues* designated as intervention areas in the 1980s are still among those targeted by urban policy today, and they were among the most prominent sites of unrest during the 2005 uprising, a point I will come back to later on.

Although the urban policy programme was conceived with ambitious political ideals – 'democratization of the management of the city', 'appropriation of space by inhabitants', and 'right to the city' – it did not have the means to address structural problems, such as increasing unemployment, which was one of the core problems in the working-class *banlieues*.[28] Police brutality, another major problem, also fell beyond its remit. The tension between the youth and the police only continued to mount, and France's centralized, bureaucratic and technocratic political tradition left little room for the involvement of inhabitants in the production of their spaces. Despite these shortcomings, however, the government was careful not to demonize *banlieue* inhabitants, an attitude which, as we saw earlier and will see again later on, was in sharp contrast with the government response to the 2005 uprisings.

The 1980s closed with five large-scale uprisings in the *banlieues*. The start of the 1990s, however, gave a sign of the shape of things to come. This time it was Vaulx-en-Velin, another eastern Lyon *banlieue*, that erupted in flames in 1990 following the death of a youth in an accident that involved a police car. We have already noted above that incidents were reported as early as 1971 in this *banlieue*. The 1990 uprising, however, was a surprise, not only because Vaulx-en-Velin was seen as one of the exemplary sites of the urban policy programme owing to its recently completed physical renovation projects, but also because the intensity of the incidents was unprecedented. It involved about 300 youths and lasted for five days. The newly built shopping centre was looted and set on fire.

Vaulx-en-Velin was still rural in the early 1960s, when a top-down decision to construct housing estates was announced in 1962. This was to become the *cité* de la Grappinière, with 640 housing units. The architectural plan also included facilities such as parks, play-grounds, schools and a commercial centre, though these were not delivered at the same time as the estates, and some had to wait for about a decade to be completed. La Grappinière's fourteen four-storey estates were delivered in 1966. A study published in 1976 shows that La Grappinière was home to 2,408 inhabitants, 52 per cent of whom were younger than eighteen. A majority of those with jobs – 83 per cent – were workers without qualification, and 63 per cent of families' revenue was below the minimum wage. It was, in short, a poorly equipped neighbourhood with a concentration of the poor. The first recorded incident dates from 1971, when a group of young people attacked a flower shop in the commercial centre. The archival evidence suggests the trigger was an argument over an insult about the origins of the youths, whose families were from North Africa.[29]

Vaulx-en-Velin is characteristic of many of the social housing neighbourhoods constructed in the peripheries of large cities during the post-war growth era: top-down designation of a priority urbani-zation area, construction of social housing mostly in the form of large housing estates, sudden demographic expansion, major job losses following the crisis in the 1970s and economic restructuring in the 1980s, and gradual degradation of the housing stock due to the poor quality of the buildings and poor maintenance. The effects of the crisis and economic restructuring had been severe for Vaulx-en-Velin, much more than for other municipalities in the region. In the departmental rankings, Vaulx-en-Velin was the poorest commune in terms of per capita income in 1992 and 1993. Its unemployment rate went up from 4.5 per cent in 1975 to 16 per cent in 1990, and to 23 per cent in 1999. The unemployment rates in its social housing neighbourhoods, where the revolts erupted, were even higher: 18 per cent in 1990 and 28 per cent in 1999. And the unemployment rates among its youth, who participated more widely in the events, were even higher, with one in four unemployed in 1990, and two in five unemployed in 1999.

Although unemployment increased throughout France from the 1970s, it hit the designated neighbourhoods of urban policy particularly hard. The figures above indicate two issues that concern not only Vaulx-en-Velin, but social housing neighbourhoods in *banlieues* in general. First, despite having been included in urban policy programmes for years, these areas suffer from an aggravating unemployment problem, leading to severe conditions in the worst-affected neighbourhoods where one in four – and almost one in two among young people – is out of a job. Second, the transformations of such neighbourhoods are closely linked to dynamics that exceed by far the perimeters of designated intervention areas of urban policy.

The government's response to the uprisings of the early 1990s was to create a City Ministry, as well as a special section on *banlieues* at the French Intelligence Service and, a few years later, the BAC police units, mentioned earlier, that intervene mainly in 'difficult neighbourhoods'. The 1990s were something of a turning point with a shift from prevention to repression, which only intensified after

September 11.[30] The right-wing government set up by President Jacques Chirac, who had promised 'zero tolerance' and 'zero impunity' during the presidential campaign of 2002, passed a series of repressive measures targeting *banlieue* youth. Led by Minister of the Interior Nicolas Sarkozy, one of these immediate measures was the distribution of flash-ball guns to the proximity police (modelled on community policing) working in 'sensitive neighbourhoods', although this was criticized by many human rights associations as a provocation of the *banlieue* youth and a departure from the main mission of the proximity police, which originally was prevention. Thus started Sarkozy's offensive with his stated conviction that 'repression is the best of preventions'.[31] For Michel Tubiana, president of the League of Human Rights, these developments were '[t]he worst step back for human rights since Algeria'.[32] As the 2004 annual report of the League of Human Rights put it: '2003 was a dark year for liberties. Seldom in the history of the Republic did any government as rapidly after its accession to power set up, to accompany its regressive social policies, a system as efficient to restrict the citizens' guarantees.'[33]

This shift from prevention to repression was accompanied by a discourse on incompatible cultural differences and the alleged formation of 'communities' menacing the 'one and indivisible' Republic. The intervention areas of urban policy were further stigmatized by such discourses evoking images of ghettos. The shift, however, was not merely discursive; from the arrival of the Right to power in 2002, it also included steady cuts in social provision and urban policy. As the daily *Libération* wrote: 'Brutal cuts in youth employment schemes, severe cuts in subsidies, disappearance of neighbourhood associations. . . . In terms of urban policy, the right-wing governments since 2002 have been a disaster.'[34] This was the context that produced the massive 2005 uprising, which dramatically expanded the geographies of revolt in France.

Revolting Geographies

Unlike in the UK, urban uprisings in France continued to multiply during the 1990s. Indeed, a steady geographical expansion of unrest is one of the distinguishing features of the French case. In the 1980s, there were five large-scale uprisings. These were followed by forty-eight large-scale uprisings in the 1990s, and the 2005 uprising, as we saw, touched about 300 communes. This expansion of revolting geographies suggests that the problems in the social housing neighbourhoods of *banlieues* have been getting worse. With a few exceptions, all the large-scale uprisings – up to 200 youth, confrontations with the police, lasting more than three or more consecutive days – of the 1990s shared two features in terms of their geographies.

First, all but two occurred in the neighbourhoods of urban policy. Second, all the large-scale revolts of the 1990s took place in social housing neighbourhoods, nearly all of them in *banlieues*. These neighbourhoods and the communes where they are located followed a similar pattern in terms of constantly increasing levels of unemployment since the 1970s, as described earlier. This suggests that there is an embedded unemployment problem, constantly aggravating and hitting, more severely than any other place, the neighbourhoods of urban policy in the *banlieues*, which were formerly working-class neighbourhoods. Furthermore, the spatial designation of such areas does not facilitate things; spatial stigmatization is part of the daily lives of the inhabitants, the youth in particular, of *banlieues*, which negatively affects relations with employers and police.

The 2005 uprising basically shared the same geographical features, but dramatically expanded the geographies of revolts. One difference was that some of the *banlieues* that were the principal sites of uprisings in the 1980s and 1990s either experienced incidents belatedly (such as those of eastern Lyon) or stayed relatively calm during the incidents (notably the northern neighbourhoods of Marseille).

Otherwise, the 2005 uprising followed a similar geographical pattern, occurring mainly in the social housing neighbourhoods of *banlieues*, most of which were the designated spaces of intervention under urban policy – the so-called ZUS (*Zones urbaines sensibles*; literally, 'sensitive urban areas'). Only 15 per cent of the neighbourhoods where revolts occurred were not classified as urban policy intervention areas. The remaining 85 per cent were neighbourhoods of urban policy, some since the policy's inception in the early 1980s. Several had urban redevelopment projects that included the demolition of their social housing estates. In November 2005, 85 per cent of the communes with such projects were sites of uprisings.[35]

This geographical pattern merits attention. Percentages and acronyms may get confusing, so let me recapitulate: most of the incidents took place in the *banlieues*, in urban policy intervention areas called ZUS, and most areas with programmed demolition projects experienced riots (note that these areas are also ZUS). What this suggests is that areas that have been targeted by government actions and discourses over the years have been the major sites of uprising, as they were in the 1990s, but this time on a larger scale. In a way, this is not very surprising, because the designated areas are usually those that suffer more problems than others, such as mass unemployment, although this does not automatically lead to unrest. There are, however, serious inequalities between these areas and the rest, and we will need to look at some statistics later on to get a sense of this. For the moment, though, let us consider another possibility: that the form of government action in these areas creates tension, increasing the likelihood of unrest.

Demolition of social housing estates has become one of the primary aspects of French urban policy since 2003. As we saw with the *cité* Simion above, social housing estates were demolished during the 1980s and 1990s as well, but this was not carried out in a systematic way. In 2003, the Chirac government launched a demolition/

reconstruction programme and set up an agency to oversee the projects in a nationally coordinated way. This programme made housing redevelopment central to urban policy, with an aim to diversify housing supply by constructing housing for the market, for rent or for sale, on the former social housing sites. Although in principle all demolished units were to be replaced, the net result was a loss of social housing units in a country where there are already about one million people on the waiting list for social housing.

The programme is a source of tension for several reasons. The stakes are high for social housing residents when demolition is involved. Yet there is evidence to suggest that they are not included in the projects.[36] Participation has never been a particularly strong aspect of French urban policy, but this programme has been unique in its exclusion of inhabitants from a process that involved such high stakes for them as eviction and displacement. This problem is exacerbated by the provision of more expensive and smaller replacement units away from the original site, where the residents may have consolidated social and economic networks. There is also evidence to suggest that in the Paris region, the real estate boom of the 2000s led to demolition projects for speculative reasons in order to replace social housing with profitable market housing – what we can call, following David Harvey as we saw in chapter 1, accumulation by dispossession. Demolition projects create tension because they dispossess people of their resources. Even when there is replacement, there is risk of displacement, which is destabilizing for existing communities. Exclusion of inhabitants from decision-making processes adds another layer of tension.

There is, however, more. Couched in terms such as 'valorization', 'securization' and 'social mixing', as well as openly military terms such as 'reconquest of sensitive areas', this programme also has an important class, racial and colonial aspect. We must remember that the demolition programme targets areas where the proportion of immigrants, foreigners, unemployed and low-waged is particularly high, and the seemingly benign term 'social mixing' is a coded way of referring to an attempt to avoid the concentration of non-white people in these areas. This preoccupation with non-white people, even when they are fully French citizens, belongs to the same colonial imaginary that has guided the French state's management of the *banlieues* since the 1970s – adding another layer of difficulty to the lives of people whose life chances are already reduced because of who they are.[37]

Arab, Black, Turk

This young person was black, very black, which didn't go down well with the clients, so I said no. I work with middle-class people, so even if this man did his job well, it doesn't matter, it wasn't working. I am not racist though.
– Employer explaining why he didn't accept a young black man as intern, 2010

No person of colour, neither black nor North African.
– Recruitment instruction in a financial company, 2010

In the section on Clichy above, I mentioned two government studies suggesting that the three electrocuted victims had origins – Arab, black, Turk – that would make them more likely to live in a poor *banlieue*, face hardship at school, end up unemployed or underemployed, and suffer discrimination and police harassment. It is time to take a closer look at these studies to get a sense of the structural reasons behind inequalities that lead to urban rage. As I have been arguing in the previous chapters, urban uprisings are eruptions of rage accumulated over years, caused by structural dynamics that have become routine. We will see that the inequalities at the source of the rage that led to the 2005 uprising have been disproportionately hitting people of the same origins, same social classes and same urban areas for decades. So bear with me while I go through these studies. It might seem that we are getting lost in a sea of statistics, but I guarantee a safe return to the shore.

The first study, Generation 98, was conducted by INSEE, the national statistics bureau. It involved a survey designed to observe the employment status of 56,000 young people who had completed their studies, at any level, in 1998. The researchers looked at how they fared in the job market in 2001, and then in 2003. Young people whose fathers were from North Africa suffered disproportionately: in the five years that followed the end of their studies, half of them still did not have a stable job. The situation was similar for those whose fathers were born in other non-European countries (Turkey, sub-Saharan Africa, the Middle East). Compared to this, only one-third of those whose fathers were born in France or in a European country did not have a stable job. The report explains this difference in part by the lower education levels of the former groups, and in part by discrimination in the job market. We can also add to this the negative effects of living in a stigmatized area, which was not included in the analysis. Living in a stigmatized area and having the somatic features or names that suggest non-European origins are significant factors of exclusion from the job market, as the epigraphs that open this section suggest.[38]

The second study was conducted by a government economic research and strategy unit.[39] Since ethnicity statistics are not kept in France, the authors of this study used census data on national origin as a proxy, just as the INSEE survey. Their report shows the difficulties faced by children of immigrants in education, employment, housing and living standards. These difficulties are more pronounced for males with both parents from North or sub-Saharan Africa. Tough luck, in other words, if you are Arab or black (or Turk, as the other study showed) even if you are born and raised in France. Let us see in more detail what the findings of the second study are.

Youth unemployment for French-born citizens whose parents arrived from North or sub-Saharan Africa is 32 per cent. In other words, one-third of French-born Arab and black youth is unemployed. This is the figure for those under thirty. For those under twenty-five, the unemployment rate goes up to 42 per cent. So, if your parents arrived from France's former colonies, your chances of finding yourself unemployed would be very high – indeed, twice as high as for your fellow citizens, including those whose parents are European immigrants (the youth unemployment rate for the latter and native French are the same). If the population distribution were even, almost half of your friends, like you, would be unemployed. This, however is not the case: being a descendant of Arab or black parents, you are also more likely to live in a deprived *banlieue* neighbourhood – a ZUS – which will further decrease your chances of finding a job. There is, therefore, a good chance that most of your friends will be unemployed as well. And as we will see in the next section on police harassment and violence, you are not yet at the end of your troubles.

Why is this the case? There are three main and related factors. One has to with class. The children of African immigrants usually have modest socio-economic backgrounds, which may be a relative disadvantage. Second, they have lower educational levels: 30 per cent of them leave high school with no diploma or qualification, a rate twice as high as that for white French. Finally, they usually live in the deprived areas of *banlieues*. Such areas with concentrated poverty, unemployment and limited facilities negatively affect all residents in terms of education and employment, and descendants of immigrants do not seem to be suffering disproportionately from this. The report shows, however, that once the class position of parents, educational level and place of residence are controlled for, French-born descendants of African immigrants still face a doubly high risk of unemployment. In other words, all other things being equal, they will still be twice as likely to end up unemployed than white French,

1. Urban uprisings expose patterns, dynamics, and structures of exclusion and oppression that have become routine and normalized, as they did in the 2014 revolt in Ferguson, Missouri. The Ferguson uprising started on 10 August 2014, the day after a white police officer shot unarmed black teenager Michael Brown multiple times, killing him. Brown is commemorated with this street art in Ferguson.

2. The increasing use of militarized police force, rather than democratic procedures, to address dissent and resistance aggravates grievances towards and tensions with the police. The Ferguson uprising was repressed by police officers equipped with military-grade weapons – with the National Guard referring to the protestors as 'enemy forces' – and by the declaration of a state of emergency. Here, armed police officers force an unarmed black civilian away from the city's business district.

3. Police brutality and discrimination is a major source of rage, with the police often viewed as oppressive rather than protective. In this photo, police officers move to enforce curfew in Charlotte, North Carolina, in an attempt to quell the uprising that started after a police officer shot and killed a 43-year-old black man, Keith Lamont Scott, on 20 September 2016.

4. Urban uprisings are products of justified rage, but they are destructive. The spectacular burning of vehicles is common during riots. Here, a double-decker bus is set alight on Tottenham High Road in London during the 2011 uprising, which was triggered by the police killing of a young black man, Mark Duggan, in Tottenham, north London.

5. Most urban uprisings have stigmatized areas as their epicentres, marked by discriminatory police action and a history of brutality and rioting. This photo shows police officers in riot gear at Broadwater Farm estate in Tottenham the morning after a night of clashes on 6 October 1985. The 1985 uprising in Tottenham was triggered by the death of Cynthia Jarrett, a black woman, during a police raid of her home.

6. Material deprivation is common in stigmatized neighbourhoods. The rundown housing estates here are in Clichy-sous-Bois, a *banlieue* to the north-east of Paris that formed the epicentre of the 2005 uprising in French *banlieues*. Unemployment, discrimination and police violence are among the many problems the inhabitants of areas like this have to deal with.

7. Mistrust and hostility towards the police are common in stigmatized areas that erupt into revolt. This 'Fuck the police' graffiti in Clichy-sous-Bois is typical in similar *banlieues* with a history of brutal and discriminatory policing. The 2005 uprising broke out after three teenagers were electrocuted in an electricity substation in this *banlieue*. They had taken refuge there to escape police identity checks.

8. Urban uprisings expand through resonance. The problems that made rage build up in Clichy-sous-Bois resonated with the problems facing youth living in similar *banlieues*. Here is a much too literal interpretation of drive-through in Corbeil-Essonnes, a *banlieue* to the south of Paris with so-called 'sensitive urban areas'.

9. Increasing inequalities and exclusion mark the context of urban uprisings, even in countries with a strong democratic and egalitarian tradition. The Rosengård neighbourhood of Malmö is perhaps the most emblematic of Swedish 'badlands' in terms of concentration of poverty and deterioration, and it was the site of uprisings in 2008 and 2009. These were smaller in scale compared to the *banlieue* riots in France, but they followed similar patterns of ritualized unruliness, including clashes with the police and the burning of bins and cars, as we can see in this photo, taken during the December 2008 uprising in Malmö.

10. Police action is the main trigger of urban uprisings. The 2013 uprising in Husby, a stigmatized suburb of Stockholm, started after the police failed to account for the circumstances surrounding the killing by a SWAT-team member of a 69-year-old pensioner of Portuguese origin at his house. There was no looting, and the extent of material destruction was limited. Cars, however, were set ablaze, and the police remained the main target of the youth during the uprising, which extended to other cities across Sweden. Here, police in riot gear block a road in Husby during the uprisings in May 2013.

11. Looting is not an extensive feature of all urban uprisings. During the 2008 uprising that started in Athens, looting was not widespread. The rioters' main targets, apart from the police, were chain stores and banks, with about 200 bank branches attacked, many of them destroyed. Millennium Bank, since then bought by Piraeus Bank, was among those.

12 and 13. Urban uprisings involve unruly practices. These photos show riot police throwing stones at protestors in Athens, Greece, 2008 and Ankara, Turkey, 2013. The extensive use of tear gas, water cannons and rubber bullets marked these uprisings, but the police did not neglect less sophisticated weaponry either.

14. Disproportionate use of force by the police to suppress dissent has become common. This image instantly went viral and further fuelled the rage that had erupted into a civilian uprising unprecedented in its extent in Turkey's modern history. It was captured at Gezi Park, Istanbul. Activists had managed to block the government's first demolition attempt on 27 May 2013, and the following day police attempted to disperse the peaceful protestors using tear gas. Images like this exposed the police's violence against unarmed civilians, and helped turn a local protest into a wholesale uprising.

15. Urban uprisings are linked to legitimate grievances over different forms of exclusion, but they are increasingly repressed by brutal measures. The use of tear-gas canisters, fired directly at the crowds by the police during the 2013 Turkish uprising, created new opportunities for local businesses to cater for the protestors. This sign in Istanbul from June 2013 offers an entire protective set: double-filter gas mask, goggles and hard hat.

16. One of the factors behind urban rage is the way in which urban land and property development have become important areas of investment and profit to the detriment of the common good, democratic procedures and even the rule of law. This photo, taken in March 2009, shows the Başıbüyük neighbourhood in Istanbul, an 'illegal' settlement developed in the 1950s, which came to the attention of TOKI in the early 2000s because of its favourable hilltop location. Despite opposition from the inhabitants and an ongoing court case, TOKI built these six sixteen-storey towers in less than a year on what was the neighbourhood's central park. The towers were themselves as illegal as the settlement TOKI wanted demolished, since they were built while the project was still being reviewed in court.

which is a sign of discrimination. The report notes that it is again this group that suffers most from discrimination in the job market related to origin and place of residence. In short, if you were Arab or black, living in a notorious *banlieue*, you would see your life chances shrink, more so if you were male, even if you were born and raised in France – not because of your lack of will or laziness, but simply because of who you are.

We have been talking about the ZUS, and I think it is time to look a bit more closely at these areas. Let us refresh our memories first: the ZUS are the 'sensitive urban areas' (*zones urbaines sensibles*), the designated intervention areas of urban policy. They were created in 1996, but designating urban policy areas is a measure that goes back to the early 1980s, so several of these areas have been urban policy intervention areas since the 1980s. This has contributed to their stigmatization, as this policy is sometimes referred to as 'anti-ghetto policy'. The ZUS usually, though not exclusively, involve deprived neighbourhoods with social housing estates in the *banlieues*, and it is safe to say that it is not a flattering designation (indeed, despite the additional financial resources it would bring, some mayors resist it because of the stigma attached). Firms locating in these areas benefit from tax breaks, a failed measure conceived to reduce unemployment in these areas. As we saw earlier, since 2003, there has been emphasis on housing redevelopment, which involves demolition of social housing estates in the ZUS through a top-down approach, creating tension among residents of these areas. In 1999, there were 751 ZUS with about 4.5 million people, which was about 8 per cent of the total population (and 10 per cent of the urban population). As noted, several of these areas had been designated areas under different labels since the 1980s.[40]

The ZUS are of particular importance to us if we want to understand urban rage in France, because it is almost always these areas that are the sites of intense revolts. This was, as we saw above, the case in the 1990s. Of the 300 areas touched by the 2005 uprisings, 85 per cent were ZUS. Indeed, they were the only sites of intense revolts. Incidents that took place in other areas were minor and isolated, such as a few sporadic rubbish bin or car burnings. More serious incidents, and especially confrontations with the police, took place in the remaining 85 per cent, the areas designated as ZUS (even though not all the ZUS saw revolts). In the end, all large cities and practically every middle-sized city with a ZUS were touched by the 2005 uprisings.[41]

ZUS residents have to deal with many material difficulties, and poverty and unemployment are among them. The poverty rate is about three times higher in ZUS compared to their surrounding urban areas. In 2011, 36.5 per cent of ZUS residents were living below the poverty line compared to 12.7 per cent in other urban areas. More than half (51.5 per cent) of ZUS residents under eighteen lived below the poverty line. Unemployment, especially youth unemployment, is high in these areas, and has increased dramatically since the 1980s.

From 1990 to 1999, the unemployment rate in these neighbourhoods increased by almost 50 per cent. In 1999, a quarter of the active population in ZUS was unemployed. Among the youth, the unemployment rate was even higher, with two out of five unemployed. This rise in unemployment was not exclusive to ZUS; it was the case in general in France. But these areas were the hardest hit. In 2005, the year of the uprisings, the unemployment rate for mainland France was 8.7 per cent; for cities containing ZUS, it was 9.6 per cent; for ZUS, it was more than twice as high at 20 per cent. Youth unemployment in the same year was 37.4 per cent in ZUS, almost twice the rate for surrounding urban areas. In the ZUS of Clichy-sous-Bois, for example, the unemployment level went up from 17.6 per cent in 1990 to 27.9 per cent in 1999. During the same period, youth unemployment (those aged fifteen to twenty-four) went up from 27 per cent to 37 per cent. In Vaulx-en-Velin, which was the site of the pivotal uprising of 1990, unemployment went up from about 18 per cent in 1990 to 28.4 per cent in 1999, while youth unemployment went up from 25.5 per cent to 40.5 per cent. I do not have the breakdown for descendants of immigrants in these areas, but other data we have seen above suggest that among them unemployment would be disproportionately high.[42]

Who lives in these areas? Another INSEE study, which focuses only on the eighteen to fifty age group, provides some answers.[43] In 2008, practically one-fifth (19 per cent) of immigrants and 14 per cent of their direct descendants in this age group lived in a ZUS. For native French, the figure was only 4 per cent. The figure was higher for non-European immigrants, approaching 25 per cent. African (North and sub-Saharan) and Turkish immigrants and their descendants are more concentrated in the ZUS than any other group. In 2008, a quarter of African immigrants and one-third of Turkish immigrants lived in ZUS, compared to 4 per cent of native French and 5 per cent of European immigrants. The situation was similar for the descendants of immigrants: a quarter of descendants of African immigrants and almost a quarter (23 per cent) of those of Turkish origin lived in ZUS, compared to 6 per cent for descendants of European immigrants. The study notes that lower income levels do not suffice to explain the concentration of African and Turkish immigrants and their descendants in the ZUS, suggesting the possibility of discrimination in the housing market. We saw above how descendants of African and Turkish immigrants were at a disadvantage in the job market. Living in a ZUS does not help either, which makes them 1.5 times more likely to end up unemployed, all other things being equal.[44] As we have seen, however, nothing is equal for the non-white in France.

It is time to get out of this sea of statistics to face other unpleasant facts, on police discrimination and violence. This time, however, we will not have the relevant statistical data as we had with the US and UK cases, because the French police do not systematically collect statistical data to see whether they discriminate or not. Other evidence suggests they do.

Police Everywhere, Justice Nowhere

I can't count how many times I've been stopped. I talk with people who say they've never been stopped in their lives, and I say to myself but how can that be?
– Dedé, of North African descent, Saint-Priest, *banlieue* of Lyon with ZUS, 2011

What do you want me to say? That it [ethnic profiling] doesn't exist?
– Christophe Cousin, Head of Political and Administrative Affairs, Lille prefecture, 2011

'Police everywhere, justice nowhere' was Victor Hugo's description of the government established after the coup of 1851, which became one of the slogans of a popular immigration and *banlieue* movement (MIB) in the 1990s. There is, then, another layer to the overlapping geographies of unemployment, urban policy, stigmatization and revolts: geographies of repression. This, once again, is not a matter of Right or Left. Even before the arrival of the more authoritarian right-wing government of 2002, *Le Monde* had already reported that police repression was targeted at the social housing neighbourhoods, and that abusive identity checks in these areas aggravated the tensions.[45]

A study found, ten years later, that not much had changed: that Arab and black youth in the social housing neighbourhoods of *banlieues* were frequently stopped by the police for identity checks. The French police have broad powers to stop and search individuals, which gives rise to such frequently reported abuses as repeated stops, lengthy questioning and intrusive pat-downs. Citizens are required by law to submit to an identity check. Carrying an identity card is not obligatory, but if a citizen is unable to prove their identity, they can be detained for up to four hours to establish it, which normally means they will stay in the local police station during this time. Expressions of discontent and failure to cooperate increasingly lead to charges for insulting or assaulting an officer. And it all remains opaque, because police identity checks are not adequately documented. This not only prevents the verification of the lawfulness of a stop, it also makes it impossible to assess whether these stops work or not, and to document discriminatory police practices.[46]

While discriminatory police action feeds the hostility of the youth, police violence triggers most of the uprisings. The triggering incidents are the third common feature shared by the revolts of the 1990s and 2005. The majority of the large-scale revolts of the 1990s (thirty-four out of forty-eight) were provoked by the killing, accidental or not, of a young person (second- or third-generation immigrant) from the neighbourhood in question. In more than half of the triggering incidents of revolts (twenty-nine out of forty-eight), the police were implicated (questioning, wounding or killing).[47]

A year before Clichy-sous-Bois, for example, it was the *banlieues* of Strasbourg that revolted following the allegedly accidental killing with a bullet in the head of a person of North African origin by the police during a routine police road check – a form of casualty not uncommon as the triggering incident of unrest in the *banlieues*. In a book entitled *La police et la peine de mort* (The police and capital punishment) Maurice Rajsfus documented 196 deaths between 1977 and 2001. There is no centralized data on police killings. A more recent attempt established the figure at 320 since the 1960s (excluding the Paris massacre of 1961, where the police killed hundreds of Algerians, and the Charonne metro station massacre of 1962). The typical profile of victims of police killings, both studies found, is of Arabs and blacks living in deprived neighbourhoods in *banlieues*.[48]

There are six aspects of French police killings that make them a persistent source of grievance, especially for Arabs and blacks in working-class neighbourhoods. First, practically all the victims are non-white, and the majority are men with North or sub-Saharan African origins, aged twenty to thirty, Muslim, and resident in social housing neighbourhoods, usually in the *banlieues* of Paris or Lyon. Second, in each case, the Ministry of the Interior and other government authorities systematically protect the police officers involved, while representing the victims as delinquents, as we saw with Clichy-sous-Bois. Thus, the presumption of innocence is respected for police officers, but not for their victims. Third, in the rare cases when a police officer is taken to court, the process takes several years, indeed sometimes more than a decade. Fourth, in the court, the prosecutor and the presiding judge minimize the responsibility of the police officers, and focus on the personality, behaviour and the past of victims, the bad image of the neighbourhood where they lived or were from, as if to show they had deserved what they got. Fifth, witnesses for the victims are not taken seriously. Witnesses for the police officers are other police officers, and their accounts are usually given more credence. The fact that the court and the police routinely work together complicates the situation when the former has to judge the latter. Finally, in the rare cases brought against police officers, the police are often acquitted or given sentences seen as unfairly light.[49]

The final point, in particular, aggravates hostility among the *banlieue* youth towards the police, who are seen to be immune, and encourages dubious practices by the police, who think they can act with impunity. This was documented and openly criticized by several observers. In a report published a few months before the 2005 uprisings, Amnesty International had already expressed concern about what they called 'the effective impunity of law enforcement officers', which they defined as 'a widespread failure of the judicial system to effectively investigate, prosecute and punish human rights violations in matters of law enforcement'.[50] The same year, the Council of Europe commissioner for human rights expressed a similar concern following his visit to France a month before the uprising:

> [I]t would seem that at present the prevailing mood among police officers is one of impunity. As a result, few cases of police violence result in convictions which are proportionate to the offences committed. Procedures are highly complicated for victims and investigations are a delicate matter. The sense of mutual loyalty between the different branches of the security forces accounts partly for the fact that statements very often match one another perfectly. In many cases, police officers anticipate the victims' complaints and file their own complaints for insults to or the obstruction of officers in the course of their duties.[51]

Amnesty International has documented allegations of police violence, including ill treatment, excessive use of force, torture and possible unlawful killings. Its findings, supported by other studies we saw earlier, suggest the following: immigrants or French citizens of non-European, especially North or sub-Saharan African, origin are more likely to suffer discrimination and ill-treatment at the hands of the police, even more so if they are from social housing neighbourhoods of *banlieues* – which would also make them more likely to be incarcerated, as a study on the Paris region found.[52] In other words, police discrimination and violence expose racial, class and spatial stigmatization, as we recently saw again with Adama Traoré's death by asphyxiation in police custody and another young man's rape by a police officer – both young black men from social housing neighbourhoods of Paris's *banlieues*.[53] As the Amnesty International report puts it:

> The lack of public confidence in even-handed policing is seen particularly in the 'sensitive areas' ('*quartiers sensibles*') from which

many of the victims of police ill-treatment and excessive use of force originate. Such tensions between the police and these communities have also been exacerbated when cases brought by alleged victims of police violence, or their families, eventually came to court, and resulted in highly controversial acquittals of, or token sentences for police officers. The courtrooms, on these occasions, have been packed with friends and relatives on one side, and with police officers on the other, and scenes of violence within the court precinct have not been unknown, reinforcing the sense of 'us against them' on both sides.[54]

Although Arab and black youth bear much of the burden, in stigmatized working-class neighbourhoods white youth are also subject to police discrimination, whose whiteness, as Bouamama argued, has been erased by their affiliation with the stigmatized area.[55] They too experience similar police abuse, and one of the heaviest sentences following the 2005 uprisings, four years in prison, was given to a young white man from a working-class family in the north of France.

As I have noted, part of the youth's resentment stems from the apparent impunity of the police, with a perception of the police as being 'above the law', which has undermined their credibility and damaged their relationship with the population, *banlieue* youth in particular.[56] For example, the policeman who killed a youth of North African origin in Mantes-la-Jolie in 1991 was only tried in 2001, which contradicted the government's stated commitment to a 'swift, firm and tough response' in the domain of justice, and consolidated the already established perception of impunity. The case was eventually dismissed. The two police officers implicated in the death of Zyed and Bouna in Clichy-sous-Bois also benefited from a similar decision six years after the event. The case, however, was pursued, and despite resistance by the prosecutors to bring a case against the two police officers for failing to assist persons in danger, the officers were tried ten years after the incidents and acquitted in 2015. The five young people arrested after the 2007 uprising in Villiers-le-Bel (another working-class *banlieue* that revolted after a police car killed two youth), however, were less lucky: they have received a 'swift, firm and tough response'. It was 'the vengeance of the state', as a book put it: three to fifteen years in prison, announced in 2010, despite great concern about the lack of solid proof since the accusations were based on anonymous and paid denunciations, and statements by the captured youth made during their four-day police custody.[57]

Despite such a pattern of structural problems affecting the *banlieue* youth, Minister of the Interior Sarkozy chose to use inflammatory language towards them, which certainly did not help to calm things down in 2005, and denied the political significance of the uprisings by confining them to the pathological framework. Three months before the revolts, on a visit to an emblematic *banlieue*, the *cité* des 4000 in La Courneuve, Sarkozy had talked about 'cleaning the *cité* with Kärcher' – a well-known brand of power hose used for cleaning surfaces with sand- or water-blasting. Both before and during the revolts, he referred to the youth who rose up as '*racaille*' – a pejorative term usually translated as 'scum' or 'rabble' – and proposed the expulsion of foreigners (including those with residency permits) implicated in the incidents. The insults did not end there. On 10 November, while the revolts continued, Sarkozy was invited onto a TV programme: 'They are thugs and scum,' he said. 'I'll stick to my guns.' Once the revolts were over, he said he regretted using the term 'scum', not because it was overly pejorative, but because it was too 'weak' a term to qualify the rioting youth.[58]

The use of this kind of inflammatory language is not new, but Sarkozy definitely raised the bar, further stigmatizing *banlieue* youth. That such pejorative terms can be publicly employed, and that this helps climb up the presidential ladder, as it did for Sarkozy, is telling about the French context and the persistence of the colonial imaginary that I evoked earlier. The data we have seen suggest that *banlieue* residents, the youth in particular, disproportionately face many problems on a daily basis – unemployment, discrimination, stigmatization, police harassment and violence, to cite a few. These difficulties are not new, but as the unprecedented geography and magnitude of the 2005 uprising showed, they have been growing.

Is rioting against such intolerable conditions the right answer, then? It depends who is rioting. Here is Sarkozy again, giving a speech about rioting Breton fishermen in 2007: 'Fishermen don't cheat. When people here demonstrate, when they use violence, it's not to have fun, it's never to harm anybody, it's because they're desperate, because they no longer have any option, and they feel condemned to economic and social death.'[59] The revolts of the Breton fishermen are seen as a legitimate manifestation of discontent by honest people, whereas *banlieue* uprisings are reduced to acts of pointless violence committed by delinquents, 'scum' or 'thugs'. The latter, however, carry a significant political dimension in exposing systematic injustices, and in this sense they are political demands rather than signs of political apathy or deprived personality. This confinement of *banlieue* uprisings to the pathological framework masks forms of everyday violence that disproportionately confront *banlieue* residents. These uprisings are not products of personal disorders or cultural traits, but of a burning sense of injustice that has its sources at school, in the job market and in relations with the police, not to mention derogatory remarks by senior government officials.

Exclusion not just from the mechanisms of distribution of resources, but also from equal treatment with respect and dignity can be a powerful source of resentment, turning into hate over years. Unfortunately, the two terrorist massacres of 2015 in Paris and the one in Nice in 2016 showed what extreme and murderous forms such hate could be channelled into when alienated and resentful youth are given a purportedly divine source and a heavenly objective.

Deep-rooted practices – discrimination, police abuses – lead to such exclusions, which need more than lukewarm responses from the government, and less – much less – of the poisonous mix of xenophobia and Islamophobia that has kept France's colonial imaginary alive to this day. France has since been under a constant state of emergency, with no end in sight for the moment. This exceptional measure has become permanent, dramatically decreasing fundamental liberties. As noted in a 2016 Amnesty International report, rights to liberty, private life, freedom of movement and freedom of assembly have been suspended in France under this regime, which has led to many abuses that seem to fuel resentment.[60]

Let us now move to Sweden, where a similar pattern of urban uprisings has been occurring in the peripheral housing estates. Just as the ghosts of US and UK uprisings haunt the French, the ghost of French *banlieue* uprisings haunts the Swedes. Although the Swedish uprisings have not yet reached the scale of those in France, we will see that Swedes have reason to worry as both the intensity and extent of Swedish uprisings have increased over the years.

5

Even in Sweden

In 1995, after the French extreme-right leader Jean-Marie Le Pen secured unprecedented support in national and local elections, Margareta Grape, head of Stockholm's Integration Commission, saw a parallel. 'Le Pen is a French phenomenon,' she said, 'but the soil which made [his] victories possible exists in all the large cities of Europe – even in Sweden.' She cited high unemployment, concrete suburbs, tensions between immigrants and natives, and the falling apart of welfare systems as elements of this worrying context.[1] Yet international observers were surprised when the Stockholm suburbs went up in flames in 2013 – even in Sweden? After all, wasn't Sweden 'the most successful society the world has ever known', as a British journalist put it in 2005?[2]

In this chapter we will challenge this myth of Sweden. We will see for how long Sweden has been experiencing major economic changes, even going as far as letting private companies run its tax-funded schools. Sweden had the fastest-growing inequality rate among rich countries in the past decades. It heads the list of largest unemployment gaps between natives and foreign-born. It is also in this context that the Swedish housing market has been deregulated and a 'growth first' urban policy become mainstream. The first major signs of trouble came from the Rosengård neighbourhood of Malmö in 2008, a rapidly gentrifying city in the south with a shortage of affordable housing. Others followed the next year, culminating in an uprising of unprecedented scale and intensity in 2013. Not so successful after all.

We will put these uprisings in the context of Sweden's changing economic, urban and welfare policies to see how they make sense in Sweden as well. It is important, however, to note that these uprisings were less intense and widespread than others in this book. It is also important to note that Sweden is still relatively egalitarian compared to most western liberal democracies. That the uprisings occurred and recurred, however, is significant. Although the overall level of inequality may seem less alarming compared to that of the other countries discussed here, the pattern of inequality in Sweden is a cause for concern. Stigmatized suburbs of large cities have been hard hit by increasing inequalities, not just in economic terms but also in terms of the unfair treatment of their residents, who are mainly non-white Swedes or immigrants. Racism and discriminatory police practices are persistent problems. The situation, in many ways, resembles the French case, although the uprisings, for the moment, are less intense, and the mainstream political discourse is more moderate, less openly racist and much less inflammatory compared to France. Furthermore, Swedish uprisings do not bear the heavy colonial legacy that marks French *banlieue* uprisings. It seems to me, however, that Sweden has taken a big step in the same direction, and what we have seen up to now may only be the beginning of recurrent and expanding uprisings to come, as was the case with the French *banlieues* in the early 1980s.

Let us start with an account of the changing Swedish welfare state since the 1980s, which is also when inequalities started their steady ascent. As we will see, many sacrifices had to be made in order to turn one of the most equal countries in the world into a champion of increasing inequalities, to move student success from the top of the OECD list to the bottom, and to create a severe affordable housing shortage in a country where the state had once built one public housing unit for every three households.

Sacred Cows of Stockholm

The streets of Stockholm are awash with the blood of sacred cows.

– *The Economist*, 2 February 2013

The economic reforms moving Sweden away from social democratic ideals have been implemented in the past three decades or so, under both social democratic and centre-right governments. With these reforms, austerity policies started cutting welfare back, the emphasis on full employment and redistribution of income gave way to deregulation, benefit cuts, deficit reduction and even to the introduction of collectively financed but privately organized public services such as education and healthcare. Privatization took employment in state-owned public companies from 500,000 in 1983 to about 120,000 in 2010. A series of tax reforms increased income at the top level, widening inequalities: inheritance tax was eliminated in 2005, wealth tax in 2007 and taxes on residential property in 2008. As a 2013 article in the *Financial Times* put it: 'As for the welfare state, it is almost 20 years since Sweden turned from being the Nordic country that took social democracy the furthest to the one that experimented most radically with market liberalisation.'[3]

These changes have made high earners richer and the poor poorer. The inequalities have deepened in terms of income and access to public services, especially in the quality of schooling since the school reform that opened schools to the private sector, making the residents of the already deprived areas more vulnerable.[4] In a 2012 report documenting the changes to the Swedish welfare state, *The Economist* ran a piece subtitled: 'A bit more unequal, a lot more efficient'.[5] Those on the wrong side of increasing inequalities – not those who can afford to accumulate less wealth, but those who cannot afford the additional hardship induced by the reforms – seemed less enchanted with efficiency. The reforms, combined with discrimination in the labour and housing markets, have made the life of many poor citizens harder, citizens who also happened to be mostly non-white, dramatically reducing their chances of integration into the labour and housing markets as effectively as their better-off and white fellow citizens.

Between 1985 and 2010, income inequality grew faster in Sweden than in any other OECD member country. The trend towards polarization that we saw in chapter 1 was also present in Sweden: its richest 1 per cent earners saw their income nearly double from 1980 to 2012. Credit Suisse observed in its 2016 annual report that the richest 1 per cent of Swedish households controlled 24 per cent of total wealth, which made Sweden slightly less unequal than India.[6] While the rich are getting richer, and also benefiting from tax reforms that favour the wealthy, Sweden's benefit system for the disadvantaged has become less generous. Sweden is still among the highest spenders on public services in the OECD, but the surge of inequality has taken its toll on its less advantaged populations.[7]

Unemployment has increased steadily, reaching 8 per cent in 2013, up from 6.6 per cent a decade earlier. This is a big increase for Sweden, given that its unemployment rate was only 1.5 per cent in 1989. Youth were the hardest hit by changes in Swedish economy and policies. Although youth unemployment is not in itself among the highest, Sweden has the highest ratio of youth unemployment to unemployment in general among OECD countries: while the average unemployment rate is 8 per cent, the unemployment rate for those under twenty-four is three times that, standing slightly above 24 per cent – up from 4 per cent in 1989. This high ratio points to problems with the education system, suggesting that many young people graduate without the necessary skills to secure a job.[8]

So what happened to Sweden's famous schools? That was probably one sacred cow too many. The public school system was partly privatized in the 1990s, which not only resulted in a dramatic decline in overall student performance, but also increased the gap between the rich and the poor. Higher-income families living in the better parts of cities had more educational opportunities and resources for their children, while schools in deprived suburban neighbourhoods suffered. Privately organized but still financed by taxpayers' money, the so-called independent schools have become the choice of the upper classes, widening inequalities in education. As the current minister of education Gustav Fridolin put it: 'This used to be a great success story of the Swedish system. We could offer every child, regardless of their background, a really good education. [Now] the parents' educational background is showing more and more in their grades.'[9] The decline in education quality and increase in inequality have reached such levels that an OECD report urged Sweden to 'urgently reform its school system to improve quality and equity'. The report highlighted problems with the funding of schools, the heavy workload and low salaries of teachers, and the overall declining performance as well as the gap between immigrants and native-born students. Almost one in two immigrant students performed below the baseline level in maths, the study found, compared to about one in five for native-born students.[10]

We are now getting closer to our main topic, the Swedish uprisings. These inequalities have hit the segregated housing estates on the peripheral areas of cities hardest, several of which were sites of uprisings in 2008, 2009 and 2013.[11] Before we move on to the uprisings, however, there is one more metaphorical sacred cow to be put down – indeed, a million of them.

Welcome to Modernity: The Million Programme

Between 1965 and 1974, as a response to the housing shortage, the Social Democratic government in Sweden embarked on an afford-able housing project called the Million Programme.[12] It was an ambitious project, and the adjective is not superfluous: when the government launched this project to build a million new public housing units, the country's population was under eight million. The programme meant, at the time, that the state would build one dwelling for every three households in Sweden. And it did, in the peripheral areas of cities, using a variety of forms that included mainly three-storey buildings, small detached or semi-detached houses, and larger housing estates.

The Million Programme projects housed mostly the Swedish working class, as well as immigrants and young people. It was a successful initiative, which raised the standard of housing for many families, providing them with more modern accommodation. As Per-Markku Ristilammi put it, moving into these houses was a sign of modernity: 'you differed from the rest of the society by being ahead of it... It was a youthful stage, full of hope for the future.'[13] But the image of modernity did not last long. Deterioration came quickly, followed by demographic changes and stigmatization. The peripheral Million Programme suburbs lost their appeal as early as the 1970s, and those who could moved out of these areas. Policies that encouraged single-family housing and the rebuilding of city centres facilitated these departures during the early 1980s. Better-off families left the projects for single-family houses or for renovated city centres, which led to a concentration of the more disadvantaged populations in the peripheral suburbs. In the early 1990s, Million

Programme houses were already among the least desirable dwellings. Non-European immigrants and refugees, guided by municipal housing and welfare authorities, started to replace native Swedes, and by the mid-1990s, constituted 65 to 85 per cent of the population of these suburban estates.[14] This is a disproportionate concentration given that the foreign-born population in Sweden is about 14 per cent of the total.

These poor suburbs, however, are not dominated by any single ethnic group: one of their distinguishing features is their diversity. Indeed, it is 'difficult to find neighbourhoods having more than 10 per cent of the population originating in a specific foreign country'. Yet, there are neighbourhoods with concentrations of immigrants from diverse backgrounds, typically from Muslim countries, which is one reason behind their stigmatization. These are often the peripheral housing estates of the Million Programme, and the poorest neighbourhoods are such immigrant-dense areas.[15] Part of the reason for this concentration of immigrants in these areas is the existence of social networks, which make them destinations of choice for new arrivals. It is, however, the government's previous resettlement programme that placed immigrants in such areas, as well as discrimination in the housing market, which then made them destinations for new arrivals.[16] Irene Molina, for example, found in a study of Gottsunda, a Million Programme neighbourhood in Uppsala, that most of the immigrants in the area felt that they were not given any choice of residential location.[17]

These demographic changes were accompanied by hyperbolic constructions of deviancy associated with these areas, making them Sweden's badlands. Like France's *banlieues*, the term suburb in Sweden – *förort* – has negative connotations: images of high-rise housing estates, minority populations that do not fit in, crime, fundamentalism and terrorism, although, again as in France, Swedish suburbs are not uniform. In the popular imagination, these places started to figure as problem areas as early as the 1970s, and their residents as problem populations. Even though research on Rosengård and Gottsunda, two such neighbourhoods, the former in Malmö, the latter in Uppsala, suggested this badlands image is more imagined than real, the stigma remained. The stigmatization of these areas also led to the stigmatization of their residents, contributing further to their treatment as inferior and suspect in job applications and relations with the police.[18] These, as we will see, are among the major sources of grievance that led to the uprisings. There is, however, more that has to do with changes in Swedish urban and housing policies.

The Million Programme homes were commissioned and maintained by publicly owned housing companies, which rented them out as affordable public dwellings. The public housing sector was one of the pillars of the Swedish welfare state. Starting in the early 1990s, however, it has been nearly dismantled, leaving fewer, and a constantly diminishing number of, affordable homes. When the Conservative government came to power in 1991, it abolished the Ministry of Housing, introduced a series of deregulation measures and reduced housing subsidies and allowances. When the Social Democrats came back to power in 1994, they continued what the Conservatives had started, which turned the Swedish housing market into one of the most liberal and market-oriented in the western world.[19]

State support for housing was removed through the legislative reforms of the 1990s. The financial risks associated with such public ventures were transferred from the central state to the municipalities. Deregulation led to the privatization of part of the public housing stock. Remaining formerly non-profit municipal public housing companies started to operate for profit, especially after new legislation in 2011 obliged them to act according to 'business-like' principles. Thus, municipal housing companies were forced to function like profit-seeking actors in the private market rather than as administrators of affordable public housing. Other measures encouraged home ownership, discouraged investment in rental housing and reduced housing subsidies and allowances; from 1995 to 2009, the number of households entitled to and claiming housing allowances went down from 576,000 to 174,000 – a 70 per cent drop.[20]

The consequences of this shift in policy were a decline in new construction, an increase in over-crowded housing, less affordable housing as municipal companies started to operate for profit and, overall, increasing polarization and segregation. Public housing in attractive locations is being privatized, and even when it is retained by public housing companies, the choice of tenants has become more selective, given that profit is now a priority. Municipalities sold large quantities of their public housing stock to private landlords and, more often, to sitting tenants. In Stockholm, for example, 30,000 municipally owned flats were sold to tenants between 2000 and 2009. One consequence of this conversion was that it left the municipal companies with the least desirable properties since they were able to sell only the more attractive ones.[21] Municipally owned public housing as a percentage of Swedish housing stock went down from 23 per cent in 1990 to 18 per cent in 2010. Much of this reduction took place in Stockholm.[22]

Other consequences of this shift in housing policy were reduced construction of new housing and increased rents. Around 70,000 new housing units were constructed in 1990. This figure went down to about 10,000 in 1997, in a period when population increased by a quarter of a million. Between 1986 and 2005, rents rose by 122 per cent. A study found that 90 per cent of the hike in rents was due to political decisions, including reduced subsidies to and increased taxes on rental properties.[23] The shift in housing policy benefited property owners and owner-occupiers, but hurt tenants, in particular those on lower incomes.

With the reforms, the public housing sector went from being a burden on state finances to an income generator. In the late 1980s,

Swedish public housing policy – including subsidies for construction and housing allowances – cost the state 25 to 35 billion Swedish crowns. A decade later, in 1999, the state received a net income of 31 billion crowns from the housing sector.[24] This may look like a good thing, but going from 30 billion cost to 30 billion income in a decade suggests costs in other areas. The other costs in this case were severe shortages of rental housing and decrease of affordable housing. This not only made the life of poor residents more difficult, but also intensified existing inequalities by expanding the gap between those in the market – a minority in major cities – and those on the outside.

These measures also displaced many poor residents who could not afford rent increases from municipal housing. A process sometimes referred to as 'renoviction' – eviction caused by renovation – led to the displacement of the most disadvantaged from public housing. While the old housing stock is renovated to make it more attractive for the market, tenants are asked to pay for the cost of renovation, and rents increase, sometimes up to 60 per cent, which is a prohibitive amount for poor residents living in these areas. As a study of Million Programme renovation projects found, in some areas up to half of the residents had to move because of renoviction.[25]

Overall, then, these policies again hit the peripheral housing estates hardest, first by disinvestment, then by renoviction. The current housing system in Sweden creates, reproduces and intensifies social and economic inequalities and their reflection in urban space. The political decisions made in the past two decades gave more freedom to the market to shape housing construction and allocation, which increased the cost of housing for renters and buyers alike. As *The Economist* found in a 2011 study, the housing market in Sweden is one of the world's most overvalued, measured in terms of affordability for both rent and income.[26] Housing has become less affordable for low-income groups, especially for non-European immigrants who also have the most difficulty in the job market:

while 84 per cent of native Swedes have a job, only 51 per cent of non-Europeans do. Almost half of the unemployed in the country are non-Europeans, and 40 per cent of non-Europeans in the country are classified as poor. The figure stands at 10 per cent for native Swedes. Having a job, however, does not redress inequalities. The steady growth of inequalities since the 1990s is also reflected in the difference between household incomes of native Swedes and those of non-Europeans. In 1991, median household incomes of non-European immigrants were 21 per cent lower compared to native Swedes. In 2013, they were 36 per cent lower.[27]

Understanding these changes and their implications for disadvantaged groups is important in order to make sense of the Swedish urban uprisings, which might have looked like an aberration had we not taken time to dispel some of the myths about Sweden. These changes and their undesirable consequences were not unknown to researchers. Studies from the early 1990s had already shown how changes in housing policy were creating and intensifying inequalities in urban space.[28] Stigmatization of immigrant-dense, poor suburban estates was already documented extensively in the mid-1990s.[29] In a book published in 2000, American geographer Allan Pred had shown the extent of racism and discrimination, despite Sweden's idyllic image as an egalitarian and tolerant society.[30] Uprisings, as we saw in other chapters, exposed these problems by making them a matter of public concern.

Sweden had its share of violent protest and unrest in the 2000s. In 2001, protests in Malmö and Gothenburg, the former during the ECOFIN meeting in April and the latter at the EU Summit in June, turned violent. Unlike the uprisings in the suburbs, these protests took place in city centres, were motivated by different concerns, and had a transnational participation. But car burnings and clashes with the police in suburbs are not unprecedented. Malmö, Gothenburg and Uppsala all experienced uprisings in their poor suburbs in 2008 and 2009. These suburbs were also the most stigmatized. Uppsala's Gottsunda was labelled 'Ghettosunda', although this play on words is not a reflection of the social conditions of this suburb. It is ethnically diverse, but not a ghetto. But Rosengård is perhaps the most emblematic of Swedish 'badlands' suburbs in terms of concentration of poverty and decay.

Rosengård, site of uprisings in 2008 and 2009, is a Million Programme neighbourhood in the southern city of Malmö. Some of the housing has been renovated, while the rest is practically left to rot, with sewage leaks and rain creating ponds in front of some of the most deteriorated buildings. Malmö was formerly an important industrial city, but lost most of its industrial base with economic changes. The massive shipyard crane that was once the city's symbol was dismantled and shipped to South Korea in 2002, marking the end of the city's industrial legacy. Malmö also has the sad reputation of being the scene of a series of racist shootings during 2009–10 by a Swedish man who targeted people with dark skin. At least fifteen shootings were attributed to him; one victim was killed and several were seriously injured (similar incidents had occurred in Stockholm and Uppsala during 1991–2).[31]

Rosengård is home to 24,000 residents, of whom more than 80 per cent are immigrants or of foreign origin. Only 38 per cent of Rosengård's residents have a job. Media reports typically represent Rosengård as a dangerous place that does not fit in, but, as a detailed study of the area suggests, many people who live and work there do not think about their neighbourhood in this way. Interviews with the residents show, however, that both youth and adults living in Rosengård feel that they are treated differently, especially by the police. The neighbourhood is not far from Malmö's city centre, but the feeling that Rosengård is excluded from it is strong among its residents.[32] As the head of public relations for the city put it, although Rosengård is not geographically a suburb, mentally it is.[33]

After the 2008 and 2009 uprisings, Carl-Ulrik Schierup and Aleksandra Ålund argued that they were the signs of the end of Swedish exceptionalism, with its image of an egalitarian and tolerant society supported by a strong welfare state.[34] A few years later, in 2013, that image took another hit with uprisings of an unprecedented scale, exposing problems of discrimination, segregation, exclusion and racism. It started in the Husby neighbourhood of Stockholm, another poor and stigmatized Million Programme initiative subject to renovation projects. Two days into the uprising, the prime minister Fredrik Reinfeldt further fuelled anger by claiming at a press conference that the culprits were 'angry young men' who, because of the 'cultural barriers' they suffered, did not know any other way of expressing their discontent. This pathological approach, as we have seen many times, is a typical political tool because it puts the blame on individuals and their behaviour whereas the rage leading to such incidents, as we will see again, is produced by policy choices.

But Reinfeldt's reaction to the incidents was also significant in another sense, as it evoked an image of the residents of these areas as alien to the nation. This image was not his invention. As early as the mid-1990s, newspaper reports on suburbs that read like colonial encounters had become common. Stories about them were no longer stories about modernity, but about ethnic otherness – a colonial form of storytelling that presented these suburbs as 'big-city-jungles'.[35]

Welcome to the Jungle

Machete-man ... machete sounds like jungle, it sounds un-Swedish, even better.

– Megafonen, 14 May 2013

On 13 May 2013, the police shot a man dead in Husby. Following a call that a man was wielding a knife on his balcony, a SWAT team arrived, broke into the house, launched a flash-bang grenade and shot the man dead in front of his Finnish wife. The man was a sixty-nine-year-old pensioner of Portuguese origin. The police claimed his wife was in danger, which she denied.

The police also claimed that the man had died of his wounds in the hospital. However, some residents had already taken photographs of the police bringing the corpse of the old man out of the building and putting it into a hearse, not an ambulance. He was killed in his own house, but the police chose to hide this in the first public statement published on their website. He was not taken to the hospital in an ambulance at around 8 p.m., as the police website had it, but was put in a black hearse at around 2 a.m. 'How can the police serve the people when they lie to us?' the local association Megafonen asked the next day, and organized a peaceful protest in front of the police station, located in the neighbouring Kista area.[36] Despite calls for an independent investigation, the incident was handled by the police, who announced in August that the SWAT-team member who had killed the pensioner – already dubbed 'machete-man' by the media – had acted in self-defence.

The Swedish uprising did not start immediately after the killing, but six days later, on 19 May, in Husby. It then extended to other poor Stockholm suburbs and to eight other cities across Sweden, and lasted for about a week. In Husby and similar peripheral estates, cars were set on fire, but the real target of the youth was the police. There was no looting, and the extent of material destruction was limited. Nevertheless, the country had not seen unrest on this scale since the food riots during the First World War.[37]

Let us try to get a sense of what the situation was like in Husby, the epicentre of the 2013 Swedish uprising, before the incidents. Husby was constructed as part of the Million Programme, in an area that used to be a green field to the north-west of Stockholm city. Most of the housing consists of five-storey buildings. The metro station opens onto a market square, surrounded by higher apartment buildings. It is a pleasant area with plenty of open space, though the buildings show signs of deterioration. Its alleys and bridges keep pedestrian and vehicle traffic separate.

According to 2015 figures, 85 per cent of Husby's 12,000 residents are of foreign origin. And 86 per cent of Husby's foreign-origin population come from non-European countries, mostly from Africa and the Middle East.[38] Husby was not a neighbourhood with predominantly non-European immigrants from the start. It was only towards the end of the 1980s that non-European immigrants started to become dominant in the neighbourhood as the demographics changed with the government's urban renewal and immigrant settlement policies, as we saw earlier. Husby suffers from strong stigmatization, like other Million Programme suburbs with a majority of non-white residents. This sense of stigmatization was expressed clearly in the response of the local association Megafonen to the police killing:

> How can a team of SWAT-police break into a flat against a 69-year old man and kill him? . . . If this had happened against Karl-Erik [a typical, though slightly old-fashioned, Swedish name], 69 years, in Kungsholmen [a mainly white and rich neighbourhood of central Stockholm] it would have been a scandal. Now it will become just another story about a mad man in the hood. . . . But listen: this is neither the first nor the last time. The police does not exist to serve the common people, the workers, the community, the kids . . . the police is here to protect the political and economic elite: terrify us, discipline us. . . . The police teach us in practice what the school teaches us in theory: as a poor and non-white worker, you are inferior and worthless, in Sweden and around the world.[39]

The youth organization Megafonen was founded and is based in Husby. Active since 2008, this association regularly organizes homework help for children, as well as lectures on segregation, housing and education with the participation of guest speakers. They have also been at the forefront of resistance to 'renoviction' in Husby. Their activism may lead some readers to think that their comments on the stigmatization of their neighbourhood are politically motivated, but the strong spatial stigmatization of such neighbourhoods is confirmed by researchers as well. Research on the youth in poor suburbs found that spatial stigmatization of these areas affected every domain of life, from school to the social welfare office, from associations to relations with the police and between individuals.

But perhaps the most depressing finding of this research is the feeling of powerlessness. For many young students in these areas, school seems to have no place in their plans for the future; it is not seen as a place to accumulate the necessary cultural capital for advancement. As Ove Sernhede writes, 'most young people realise that their immigrant background means a life as second-class citizens', with or without education.[40] They feel they do not have the same opportunities as native Swedes, and they know they will be discriminated against in the job market, in housing and in their relations with the police, regardless of their educational achievements. 'At an early age these young people develop a perception of themselves as subordinate and as not belonging.'[41] These findings were also confirmed by interviews conducted after the uprisings with Husby residents, as we will see later on.

Stigmatization, then, was one of the grievances behind the 2013 uprising. Another was rising inequalities that set Husby and similar areas apart from the rest of the city. As we saw above, peripheral housing estates were the hardest hit by rising inequalities from the 1990s. In the city of Stockholm, for example, income levels increased 9 per cent between 1990 and 1995, but fell by 14 per cent in Husby.[42] As a 2013 government report found, 20 per cent of young people in Sweden aged twenty to twenty-five were neither working nor studying. In the designated 'urban development areas', including Husby and other poor suburbs, this rate went up to 40 per cent, in some places reaching 55 per cent. In Husby, the proportion of young people who were neither working nor studying was just under 30 per cent.[43]

We saw in earlier chapters that profit-driven urban policies and real-estate dynamics displace and create resentment among less advantaged residents, something we will also see in the last chapter on the 2013 Turkish uprising. Grievances linked to urban development were another important factor that set the context for the Swedish uprisings. This is not unique to Husby; we have already seen that changes in Swedish housing policy have led to increasing inequalities, displacement and added financial burden for the less well off, especially in the poorer suburbs of the Million Programme.[44]

There was an organized resistance to renovation in Husby before the uprising, which increased tensions between the administration and the residents. The residents of Husby felt that the renovation project was not aimed at meeting their needs and, despite its rhetoric of participation and citizen dialogue, it was imposed from the top. As one local activist told me during a visit: 'They do things for you, not with you.' Moreover, renovation costs fell on the residents through rent increases. Renovation, Husby residents knew, was eviction by another name. Husby is in a prime location, and opening its public housing to the market would be very profitable. It is only twenty minutes away from central Stockholm on the metro, and just a stop away from Kista, a technology hub referred to as 'Chipsta', or 'Sweden's Silicon Valley'.

The Husby uprisings exposed increasing inequalities in Swedish cities and, in particular, in Stockholm. As a City of Stockholm report pointed out, Stockholm's disadvantaged neighbourhoods had less access to services, and socio-economic segregation had been increasing in Stockholm in the 2000s, as it had in the previous decade.[45] Moreover, segregation has become increasingly ethnic, leading to the concentration especially of non-European immigrants and their descendants in the poor areas. As a result of the housing policy decisions we saw earlier, the proportion of rental units in Stockholm went down from 62 per cent of the housing stock to 40 per cent between 1998 and 2014. This meant about 70,000 fewer rental units at a time when the population of the city had increased by 175,000 people. This decrease not only led to an affordable housing shortage for renters, but also reduced locational choice. As rental units in the most attractive parts of the city became privatized, the only remaining options for rental housing were concentrated in the already disadvantaged parts of the city.

Overall, then, it does not seem to me an exaggeration to say that current housing policy and dynamics in Stockholm and other big cities in Sweden work to concentrate the most socio-economically disadvantaged groups of the population in the less desirable parts of cities. This is a remarkable change in a country that once built a million public housing units, some of which have now turned into the least desirable and most stigmatized areas of Swedish cities. The disadvantaged populations pushed into these areas, as we have seen, are mainly non-native Swedes or immigrants, so increasing socio-economic segregation in Sweden is also marked by an ethnic dimension with non-Europeans as the most vulnerable in the housing and job markets.[46]

These problems were pointed out by Husby residents themselves. In a study inspired by the *Guardian*/LSE *Reading the Riots*, a group of researchers interviewed Husby residents in the aftermath of the uprising.[47] They found that a major reason for the uprising was the accumulated resentment of the youth, especially in their relations with the police. The shooting of the sixty-nine-year-old man and the attempt by the police to cover up the incident were also cited by the interviewed residents. As with other examples we have seen, the residents of Husby expressed a deep mistrust of the police.

Five main themes emerged from the Swedish version of *Reading the Riots*. First, many residents felt they had little or no influence in the policies affecting their neighbourhood – 'a democratic deficit', as the study put it. Second, there was a strong sense of community shaped by the residents' shared experiences of discrimination, racism and exclusion. Third, there was a feeling of frustration among residents, who felt their expectations were not met. A fourth theme was resentment of the way the media and politicians stigmatized Husby. Finally, there was strong concern about police conduct. Interviewed residents of Husby mentioned abusive and repeated identity checks by the police as an indication of everyday racism and as a source of resentment.

As we have seen, Swedish public housing has been subject to new policies, and the current emphasis on renovation puts excessive financial burdens on the poor, leading to displacement. Husby is also subject to policies of renovation leading to prohibitive rent increases, and residents mentioned this in the interviews, pointing to their lack of participation in the process. As one resident put it: 'We never asked for renovation, we requested the maintenance of the houses by the local tenants' association . . . I don't know who has decided all this.' Increased rents as the result of a renovation policy decided over the heads of Husby residents were a major source of resentment.

This lack of participation, the feeling of powerlessness against the authorities, was also evident, residents felt, in the aftermath of the fatal shooting. As we have seen, the uprising only started six days after this incident; it was not an immediate reaction. The immediate reaction of the residents was to organize a peaceful demonstration to denounce police violence and to ask for an independent investigation, given that the police had already misinformed the public. Yet nothing happened, and so anger simmered, and eventually erupted.

The stigmatization of Husby and its residents is also a major source of resentment, and the frustration caused by this shared feeling of exclusion was expressed by several interviewees. As one put it, they would always remain second-class citizens because of their skin colour, and since they were not about to become white, there was no reason to strive for full and equal citizenship. Their skin colour, they believed, was also the source of their unfair treatment by the police. The feeling of exclusion is strong, but so is the feeling of community. Husby is not a socially disorganized area that has eventually slipped into violence. There is a strong feeling of community built on the shared experiences and frustrations of residents faced with undemocratic policy decisions, the indifference of politicians to their grievances and discriminatory police conduct.

Interviewed residents also expressed frustration over their unmet expectations. They felt they were denied the rights enjoyed by others, such as employment, good public services and treatment with respect in their interactions with the authorities. Again, the feeling of exclusion, of not being equal members of Swedish society, was strong among the residents. This feeling of exclusion was aggravated by negative media representations. We have already seen how research on other Swedish 'badlands' pointed to a gap between the media construction of such areas and the residents' views of their neighbourhoods. Interviewed Husby residents felt the same, failing to recognize themselves in the media images and feeling powerless against such stigmatization. The representation of Husby as a 'ghetto' is a source of frustration for its residents.

Some residents felt the police had used excessive force during the incidents, and several mentioned racist slurs, 'monkey' being the most cited. Police brutality is a matter of concern in Sweden. In 2011, more than 5,600 complaints against police officers were registered, but less than 2 per cent of them led to prosecution or punishment. Between 2005 and 2012, only fifty-three cases against the police were brought to court, and twenty-seven of them resulted in acquittal.[48] Like the other examples we saw in previous chapters, police brutality and abusive identity checks targeting darker residents were a main source of resentment for the youth. The Husby study found that for the youth in the area, everyday police harassment had reached such a point that it was almost normalized, becoming part of their everyday lives. This was not, as we have also seen in other examples, a matter of a few rogue police officers, but a product of policy decisions that routinized and legitimized such conduct. The most striking example of this was the REVA initiative. As a Husby resident put it: 'First it started with the cuts, then came REVA, and then came the fatal shooting. It was these three processes that led to frustration among the people.' Let us see what REVA was all about.

Dear Beatrice . . .

Controls are and should be a natural part of everyday police work.
– Department of Justice's response to the critics of the REVA
project, 1 March 2013

The suburbs are always flooded with this feeling. You know. Feeling. That no one listens, that no one wants to hear the stories about racist police, harassment, brutality. That maybe it has to be on fire for someone to hear certain voices. Now it's burning.
– Panthers Writing Group, 'To a nation in flames', 24 May 2013

Those on the receiving end of discrimination and who choose to speak up know how the suggestion that perhaps *they* are being too sensitive hurts more than the discriminatory practices themselves. Jonas Hassen Khemiri, a Swedish novelist, must have felt like that when he heard Beatrice Ask, then minister of justice, brushing off racial profiling as a matter of 'personal experience'. In an open letter to the minister, he wrote:

We're both full citizens of this country, born within its borders, joined by language, flag, history, infrastructure. We are both equal before the law.

So I was surprised [when you were] asked whether, as the Minister of Justice, you are concerned that people (citizens, taxpayers, voters) claim they have been stopped by the police and asked for ID solely because of their (dark, non-blond, black-haired) appearances. And you answered:

'One's experience of "why someone has questioned me" can of course be very personal. There are some who have been previously convicted and feel that they are always being questioned, even though you can't tell by looking at a person that they have committed a crime . . . In order to judge whether the police are acting in accordance with laws and rules, one has to look at the big picture.'

Interesting choice of words: 'previously convicted'. Because that's exactly what we are. All of us who are guilty until we prove otherwise. When does a personal experience become a structure of racism? When does it become discrimination, oppression, violence? And how can looking at 'the big picture' rule out so many personal experiences of citizens?

Khemiri then made an unusual request: that they borrow each other's bodies for twenty-four hours, so that he could see what it is like to be a woman in the patriarchal world of politics. And she would see, in Khemiri's body that was darker than hers, how it feels 'when you go out into the street, down into the subway, into the shopping centre, and see the policeman standing there, with the Law on his side, with the right to approach you and ask you to prove your innocence'. The letter definitely touched a nerve: by the end of the day of its publication in the newspaper, it became the most shared article, and went on to become 'the most linked text in Swedish history', in the words of its English translator.[49]

What prompted this incident was the REVA project. REVA is the acronym for an internal migration control programme presented as a 'legal and effective' execution of the return policy aimed at deporting immigrants without legal residency permits. It was conceived within the framework of an EU-funded collaboration to facilitate the expulsion of undocumented immigrants. Run during 2009–14, REVA gave the Swedish police the authority to stop people to this end. The project was implemented in Stockholm in the spring of 2013, a few months before the uprising, where the police started identity checks in metro stations, targeting non-white people.

We have seen in previous chapters how policy decisions put pressure on the police and force them to engage in legally dubious practices to meet quotas set by their superiors. The REVA project had the same effect. As a border patrol agent in Stockholm's Arlanda airport explained, the concern to meet performance goals put pressure on agents, who started taking shortcuts and stopping passengers based on their appearance. Overall, the REVA project did not significantly improve the efficiency of internal border controls, but dramatically increased their numbers, creating tension and conflict.[50] Being detained and questioned in public is a humiliating experience for those stopped by the police. Even the deputy chair of the Police Board in Stockholm, Katarina Berggren, called the practice 'deeply offensive' for those stopped.[51]

But not everyone was stopped – only those who looked foreign. It turned out that nine out of ten people the police stopped were Swedish citizens or legal residents, a disproportionality that betrayed the nature of stops, guided by somatic features rather than a justifiable suspicion, which effectively made these stops illegal within the framework of a programme that was promoted as being legal and effective.[52] REVA was heavily criticized, and generated public protests. In a radio interview, Minister of Justice Beatrice Ask was asked whether she was concerned by the racial profiling brought about by the implementation of the project, but she brushed the question off by saying it was a matter of 'personal experience', prompting Khemiri's open letter.

Try to imagine the implications of the REVA project for the youth of Husby. As we saw, almost nine out of ten of Husby's 12,000 residents are of foreign origin, of which again about nine out of ten have non-European origins, mostly from Africa and the Middle East – something that would make them stand out in overwhelmingly white central Stockholm. What the REVA project means for them is that every time they take the metro to go to Stockholm city centre, only twenty minutes away, they are subject to police stops just because of the way they look. They might choose not to go there for fun, but imagine they have a job there and have to commute. They would then risk police stops twice a day, five or six times a week, on the way to and from work. Such measures further exclude the non-white populations of the suburbs from the city centre, deepening their sense of exclusion and resentment. They also aggravate tensions with the police, which is a major grievance that set the context for all the uprisings that we have examined in this book.

Following the 2013 Swedish uprising, one journalist argued that the killing of the sixty-nine-year-old man and police conduct during the incidents had exposed the violence and racism in the police as an X-ray would reveal the skeleton.[53] This was also the finding of an earlier government study, although the tone was less acerbic. In a 2008 report, the Swedish National Council for Crime Prevention pointed out that people with foreign backgrounds were subject to police checks because of their origins, and were treated unfairly compared to native Swedes. They were also subject to disrespectful and degrading treatment by the police. The council's study also found that people with foreign backgrounds were considered less trustworthy than native Swedes at a crime scene, during a criminal investigation or in court hearings. The report stated that the discrimination against people of foreign origin by the police and in the judicial system was driven by stereotyping, with Muslim and black men, Roma people and Eastern Europeans suffering the most from this bias.[54]

A more recent survey in the Million Programme neighbourhoods confirmed these findings, and found that distrust of the police was strong among immigrants and children of immigrants living in these areas, deriving from what was perceived as unfair treatment.[55] These two reports formed the basis for a motion to the parliament in 2014. Maria Ferm, a Green Party member, brought a motion asking for changes in the organization of police work. Requesting better oversight of police activity, the motion raised several points relevant to our case, in particular the mistrust of the residents of poor Million Programme suburbs like Husby and Rosengård towards the police because of discriminatory practices.[56]

This was not the first time discrimination was highlighted in official reports. In 2005, Masoud Kamali, in a report prepared for SOU (Swedish Government Official Reports) had documented the extent of discrimination that had had devastating effects on the lives of many Million Programme residents.[57] Through hearings and focus-group interviews with residents of the stigmatized suburbs of Malmö, Gothenburg and Stockholm, Kamali found evidence of structural and institutional discrimination based on origin, skin colour, name and presumed religion. From labour and housing markets to education, from police and the judicial system to welfare services, the residents of these areas suffered routine discrimination. People of foreign origin were directed to areas with similar populations, and usually got stuck there because of discrimination in the housing market, even if they had the means to leave. They were discriminated against in job applications and their children were regularly directed to vocational courses at school. As for relations with the police, the study not only found widespread distrust among residents, but even fear of the police.

Resentment was already simmering in the early 2000s: 'The voices vibrate with anger and despair,' Kamali wrote about his conversations with the residents, 'but also with resistance.'

Resentment turned into rage, and eventually erupted in 2008, 2009 and, to a much more extensive degree, in 2013. In terms of scale and intensity, the Swedish uprisings were not as severe as the others we have encountered in previous chapters. There were no deaths during the incidents, no looting, and the extent of material destruction was limited. They are, however, a sign of things to come: urban rage and unrest are geographically expanding in Sweden. The 2013 uprising exposed the injustices of the current pattern of racialized urbanization in Sweden, which aggravate inequalities between the poor suburbs and the rest of the city.[58] Having suffered years of disinvestment, these suburbs are now at the forefront of renovation projects that make them prohibitively expensive for their existing residents, who already have to contend with other hardships caused by widespread discrimination.

The use of renovation projects that force poor and stigmatized populations out in the city's search for more profit from urban land is not unique to Sweden. The same process, though more widespread and aggressive, was also at work and was a major source of resentment in Turkish cities, where urban rage erupted a couple of weeks after that in Sweden. Before moving on to Turkey, however, let us first make a short stop on the way, in Greece, where an uprising of an unprecedented scale in the country's recent history took place in 2008.

6

Days of Rage in Greece

Even the hard-nosed Sarkozy had to postpone his controversial education reforms, fearing a 'European May 68' during Christmas. Such was the scale of the Greek uprising in December 2008. It was, some observed, 'the most intense social crisis in the thirty-four years since the democratic transition of Greece' in 1974. Others thought it was 'one of the most acute challenges to the Greek political establishment since the end of the Greek Civil War' in 1949. Some went further and argued that in terms of its scale and intensity, the Greek uprising was 'unique in modern Greek history and there are very few examples of such unrest in recent European history'. It was, indeed, 'the worst civil unrest in Europe since 1968'.[1] Overall, there was broad agreement that what had happened in December 2008 in Greece was unprecedented in many ways.

Unprecedented in scale and intensity perhaps, but not novel – Greece, as we will see, has a long history of direct political action and struggle. Yet, unlike others we have studied, the 2008 Greek uprising was not marked predominantly by racial discrimination, although this was not altogether absent either. The main source of grievances, as with other uprisings we have seen, was the widespread feeling of exclusion and powerlessness within an established political system whose legitimacy was deeply undermined. Protestors gathered in central Athens in December 2008 after a police officer killed a fifteen-year-old boy. The city was brought to a standstill for days. The uprising spread to most of the national territory, something we will also see in the next chapter on Turkey.

The Greek uprising brought people from different backgrounds together, without necessarily unifying them under the banner of a shared ideology or demand. It was a revolt by citizens who felt politically excluded in a context marked by rising unemployment, eroding social rights, corruption, investments in urban space that exacerbated inequalities, and tensions with the police. Decades of capitalist urban development had created a real estate boom and gentrification, accompanied by a steep rise in precarious employment and unemployment. A steady increase in inequality and polarization marked, as it did in our other examples, the context that led to the uprising. The urban development fever followed the priorities of the market and reached its peak with the 2004 Olympic Games in Athens, leaving many citizens embittered as they felt increasingly excluded from the production of their urban spaces. It is in this context that we must understand the Greek December – the 'days of rage', as one slogan put it – as citizens standing up for their right to the city and right to participate in the political process.

Let us first try to understand what made this period of capitalist urban development particularly unpalatable for Greek citizens. After all, Greece is not the only country to have had such a period of capitalist expansion and, at the time of the revolts, it was certainly not the weakest economy in the Eurozone, or at least not the only weak one, although it was on its way down. We will see that the legacies of Greece's historical development marked by authoritarian regimes made the transition to capitalism peculiar, and sowed the seeds of many problems that later surfaced once growth was over.

Public to Precarious

Twentieth-century Greek history is marked by cycles of authoritarian rule and strife, from the Metaxas regime of the late 1930s to the Civil War in the second half of the 1940s, and, more recently, to the military junta of 1967–1974, known as the 'Rule of the Colonels'. The fall of the junta marked not just the end of the colonels' dictatorship, but also the end of this long twentieth-century history of repressive regimes. What followed after 1974 was an era of vibrancy and political radicalization referred to as *metapolitefsi*, which means politics after, or political transition. This is the era that saw the conviction of the high-ranking members of the military junta, expulsion of the king, and foundation of the Third Hellenic Republic. The fact that revolts on such a scale erupted in this context is important, and we will come back to this.

Greece's transformation after the end of the Civil War in 1949 provides insight into the economic situation that set the context for the 2008 uprising – and the depression a year later. Between the early 1950s and the mid-1980s, the Greek economy expanded, turning a largely rural society into an increasingly urban and more affluent one. The key factors that made economic growth in this period possible were tourism, shipping, banking and foreign remittances. The change was as rapid and significant as it was peculiar: practically all the growth in employment took place within the state sector, in self-employment and the informal economy. So, you either worked for the state, which was the safest option, emigrated or were self-employed. In the 1970s and the 1980s, up to two-thirds of all university graduates were employed by the state. This pattern of economic growth enabled Greeks to avoid some of the less desirable elements of capitalism, in particular 'the disciplining effects and insecurities of the private labour market'.[2]

Post-war Greece did not have a welfare state, wages were low, and workplace politics remained repressive. Social provisions were improved slightly in the post-dictator era, first by the conservative New Democracy government in the late 1970s, then by the socialist PASOK government that came to power in 1981. Therefore, in the 1980s, when many western countries were moving away from social democracy towards neoliberalism, Greece was moving in the other direction. However, the resources for this social-democratic expansion did not come from taxes – the wealthy were left unburdened by taxes as in previous periods – but paid for partly by European adjustment funds. This meant that despite the political transition, earlier social and economic structures of privilege remained. The result was an accumulation of public debt.

Moreover, public sector employment could not expand for ever, and it eventually stopped doing so in the 1990s. Decline followed stagnation. Under EU pressure, a series of privatizations started shrinking public-sector employment in the late 1990s. Thus, neoliberalism ended up arriving in Greece later than in any other European country. Financial deregulation and privatization were among the immediate neoliberal policies applied, which produced a frenzy of speculation, especially in the run-up to the 2004 Olympic Games in Athens. The speculative financial activity was also facilitated by joining the euro in 2001, although Greece was not really qualified: Eurostat revealed in 2004 that the Greek government had paid $300 million to Goldman Sachs to shift debt off its public accounts to give the illusion that it had cut the deficit, a necessary condition for qualification.[3]

Although the Greek economy steadily grew from the mid-1990s to the mid-2000s, this growth was not based on a firm foundation. The prominence of international shipping and banking resulted in the neglect of investment at home. Greek economic growth during this period was due largely to EU subsidies, a shipping boom that followed China's export boom, banking and financial speculation, and construction for the 2004 Olympic Games. The frenzy in banking and financial speculation also produced a lending boom to

Greek consumers, which would prove dramatic when the economic crash hit. None of these helped to consolidate a stable job market with decent wages.

What emerged instead was a precarious job market and the so-called '€700 Generation' – the generation of young Greeks who, despite their qualifications, are trapped in low-paid and temporary jobs where they earn 700 euros maximum a month. Of all new jobs created in 2006, 70 per cent were part-time. In terms of income inequality, measured as the ratio of the richest 20 per cent to the poorest 20 per cent, Greece was fourth among the European Union members in the same year. More than one-fifth of the population lived below the poverty line.[4] Although a latecomer to neoliberalization compared to its European counterparts, Greece has also had its share of generalized precariousness and widening inequalities, which, as we saw in the first chapter, have been a feature of OECD countries since labour markets started to change in the 1980s.

Therefore, the insurrection of 2008 was not necessarily a sign of Greece's failure to become a fully modern country, as western media tended to depict it during the early days of the uprising, but a result of neoliberal reforms that it pursued like its European counterparts, only later. Stathis Kouvelakis highlights this tendency and how it soon changed by looking at the representation of the Greek uprising in mainstream French media.[5] Four days after the start of the incidents, *Le Monde* presented Greece as a somewhat backward society that is not quite European. A couple of days later, however, when French politicians expressed concern over the risk of a similar eruption in the *banlieues*, the same newspaper ran an editorial that concluded: 'France is not Greece. But.' In less than a week, Kouvelakis observes, the archaic and oriental country had turned into a mirror reflecting France's own problems to itself. The transformations that set the context for the Greek uprising did not result from archaism or backwardness, but were the consequences of policy choices.

The Olympic Legacy

Capitalist modernization of Greece was particularly intense. The countryside was emptied out (which also had to do with the Civil War), millions emigrated overseas, and millions moved to cities, to Athens in particular, which is still home to about one-third of the whole population. What this meant for Athens was a phenomenal concentration of population and unregulated urban growth. The post-war period in general was characterized by unregulated urban expansion with small-scale and illicit constructions on the peripheries of large cities – the period of urbanization and economic expansion. This pattern changed in the 1990s when the government, following EU urban policy agendas, opened urban land to markets and encouraged entrepreneurial strategies for urban development. Both the government and the private sector thus invested in urban space through mega-events such as the Olympic Games and city-branding projects. Urban space became a site of investment and a source of profit for private entrepreneurs. However, the necessary regulatory and institutional mechanisms to curb the negative effects of such a shift were not in place.

The early 2000s, in particular, was a period of intense construction activity, which was particularly visible in Athens. The Olympic Games were used to direct huge amounts of public money to large urban projects carried out through public-private partnerships. Indeed, Eleni Portaliou has argued, the Olympic Games served as a tool for a broader restructuring of Greek capitalism and urban policy.[6] Using the Olympics as an excuse, politicians abandoned earlier ideas about regional development, decentralization, social cohesion and environmental care. Athens turned into a huge construction site where public funds flowed.

The projects benefited from the use of public land and cheap labour, but working conditions and wages remained below standard levels. Workplace accidents soared, and any attempt to protest or go on strike was seen as betraying the nation. Yet, projects focused less on the needs of local residents and more on attracting tourists and global investors, and resulted in the privatization of public land and services. The development of new commercial districts and office buildings was prioritized, which exacerbated the already high levels of inequalities in the city. An airport expansion project quickly followed. However, gentrification of city centres and environmental destruction in this period, especially with the Olympics preparation, created tensions. Mounting grievances gave rise to mobilizations during the 2000s that focused on two issues in particular: the environment and urban space. So, when rage erupted in 2008, there was already an important legacy of urban activism and a contingent of activists who had cultivated their skills, know-how and solidarity networks over the previous years of activism around local struggles.[7]

There was also the legacy of corruption, which, as we will see, continued to undermine the legitimacy of the government in the years leading up to the incidents. In the absence of effective regulatory mechanisms, and in a political environment marked by corruption, this focus on urban space as a tool for city-marketing and a source of profit displaced residents, exacerbated inequalities and degraded the environment. Privatizations, the awarding of public contracts, and public-private partnerships all gave rise to high-profile corruption scandals that undermined the legitimacy of the state.

Another legacy of the Olympic Games was the introduction of new forms of policing and surveillance in Athens. This intensification of policing was also the product of the post-September 11 context. In the years leading up to the Olympic Games, Greece passed new laws and created special units in line with the militarization of the police that we saw in our other examples. Police activity focused on certain areas, such as the Exarcheia neighbourhood in central Athens, the epicentre of the uprising. In a country with a police force that has a long history of abuse directed at young people, political activists and immigrants, and where there is already widespread anti-police sentiment owing to its history of authoritarianism, such intensification of policing only exacerbated the tensions.[8]

It was in this context of building frenzy, political corruption and police repression that the Greek youth, in particular, started to see a bleak future. Youth unemployment and underemployment were a problem in Greece even in the high economic growth period in the mid-1990s, reaching 22 per cent in 2008. In the year the revolts erupted, more than one-fifth of youth aged between fifteen and twenty-four were unemployed, and the following year more than one-quarter. The steady increase in youth unemployment, which was an important source of resentment that led to the eruption of 2008, continued, reaching a whopping 58 per cent in 2013.[9] Youth who managed to find employment had to put up with low wages, part-time and precarious jobs, as we saw above. The shrinking labour market affected youth across the board, regardless of educational level and social status – one of the factors that brought different segments of Greek youth together during the uprising.

It was also in this context that the government announced, in early 2006, that it would legalize private universities, although the constitution explicitly banned private higher education. This was part of a larger reform package that the government was trying to push through, which also included more managerial strategies for public universities, reduced funding and an end to university asylum.[10] Many students and teachers saw the proposed reform, and the way the government handled it, as an authoritarian and disciplinary attack on public education. This was the start of a prolonged wave of protests in March 2006. By the end of May, almost all Greek universities were occupied. The protests continued during the following academic year, with primary school teachers joining as well to oppose austerity measures. The police response was typically heavy-handed.

Huge demonstrations in June 2006 and later in March 2007 were attacked by the police, leading to mass arrests, as well as to several allegations of excessive use of force, torture or other ill treatment.[11]

Police violence during demonstrations only fuelled anger, and further radicalized the students participating in the demonstrations. Thus, already before the December 2008 uprising, students, high-school students in particular, were mobilized and politicized through the 2006–7 protests, and now had a taste of police baton and tear gas. However, the 2006–7 mobilizations not only politicized the youth and made them more wary of, indeed hostile to, the police; they also undermined the legitimacy of the state, not just through the violent repression of the protests, but by the very nature of the proposed reform as well. As we saw above, although its share had been declining, the prominence of the state in the employment structure of Greece made the question of education a fundamental one. A good job within the state required a good university degree, which made the provision of universal and free higher education key to the legitimacy of the Greek state.[12] The government's reform attempt, which included a proposal to legalize private universities, and its heavy-handed police response to dissent, undermined the legitimacy of the state in the eyes of many young people.

Legitimacy crises of the state, however, had other sources as well, including high-profile corruption scandals. One such scandal broke in August 2008, a few months before the uprising, in which several senior ministers and the Vatopedi monastery were implicated in an illegal exchange of land. Although ministers and construction firms with close links to the governing New Democracy party made huge amounts of illegal gains from the scheme, the prime minister did not resign and the government tried to block a full investigation of the case. Some of the slogans during the 2008 uprising referred to this scandal, such as 'the looting is not the job of the *koukouloforoi* [hood-wearers], it is the job of bankers, clergymen and monks'.[13] A couple of months after this scandal, in October 2008, the government announced a 28 billion euro package to bail out the banks, which, again, was a source of anger among citizens as several slogans and writings during the December uprising showed.

The concentration of incidents suggesting government corruption and incompetence during the year leading up to the 2008 uprisings was spectacular: an abruptly proposed and highly contentious education reform, heavy-handed police repression of the reform's opponents, inability to deal with the forest fires of August 2007 that left dozens dead and thousands homeless, a real-estate scandal that involved monks and ministers and, to top it all, a 28 billion euro bail-out for unscrupulous bankers in a country with steadily increasing levels of unemployment, underemployment, inequality and polarization. Yet, it was a single bullet that caused the bitter cup to overflow.

Now the Streets do the Talking

Now the streets do the talking. . . . These days are for the hundreds [of] migrants and refugees murdered at the Greek border, in police stations, at workplaces. . . . For the people that died at the Olympic Games construction sites. For the undocumented labour. . . . These days are for all those marginalised, excluded. . . . 18 years of mute anger are enough.

– Albanian Migrants' Haunt, 2008

But it was clearly much more than street protest. Imagine Westminster and Whitehall or the White House and Congress under siege every day for two weeks.

– Costas Douzinas, *Philosophy and Resistance in the Crisis*

At about 9 p.m. on 6 December 2008, the police shot and killed an unarmed teenager in the Exarcheia neighbourhood of central Athens. Alexis Grigoropoulos, a high-school student from a middle-class family living in the suburbs of Athens, was only fifteen. He was out on a Saturday night with friends, when two police officers from the 'special guards' unit approached them after what seems to have been an exchange of verbal insults. Although there was no threat of physical violence, one of the officers pulled out his gun. Eyewitness accounts and the police ballistics report established that the officer had pointed his gun at the youth, and not in the air as the police officers claimed. Alexis Grigoropoulos died from a bullet through the heart. Given the circumstances, recourse to a firearm was both disproportionate and unlawful. The officers were suspended, charged with unlawful use of firearms, manslaughter with intent, and with complicity. Later, one was given a life sentence, the other ten years.

Within an hour of the murder, a crowd had already gathered in Exarcheia, throwing stones and petrol bombs at the police. Three universities were occupied that night (Athens Polytechnic, the Law School and Athens University of Economics and Business), and the protestors marched in the streets of central Athens, damaging and burning banks and commercial chain stores along the way, which were the main targets during the uprising. By midnight, Athens was in flames.

The unrest intensified during the week, quickly spreading out of the Exarcheia neighbourhood and beyond Athens to cover most of Greece. But let us first get a sense of what Exarcheia is like. With its vibrancy, political culture and history, it is an object either of love, or, for those who like their law and order, contempt. As *Guardian* reporters put it, 'it resembles the Lower East Side of Manhattan: a vortex of alternative culture, lifestyle and politics, but with more political edge'.[14] Or, as a hotel manager said when I told him I was on my way to Exarcheia with my three young children: 'Why do you want to go there? It is for anarchists.'

Exarcheia is a dense neighbourhood in the centre of Athens, highly politicized, but also highly policed. It is a neighbourhood of students, artists and intellectuals, with small bookshops and other shops, bars and bistros, offices of political parties and NGOs, as well as political organizations of the Left. Several anarchist groups and social movements also have spaces there. It was connected to every youth mobilization in the twentieth century, and its political and symbolic importance is no secret to Athenians. Exarcheia is adjacent to prominent universities: the Law School, Athens University of Economics and Business and, not least, the Athens Polytechnic, which was the epicentre of the student uprisings against dictatorship in 1973, and since then has become an important site for manifesting political dissent.

It would not be far-fetched to characterize Exarcheia as an anti-establishment youth stronghold, which is why it is stigmatized by the establishment. This is also why the area has been subject to heavy police presence and surveillance, which had intensified in the few years leading up to the incidents. In addition to the more colourful features listed above, the streets of Exarcheia are also marked by the presence of riot police patrol cars as well as by special unit members wearing bullet-proof vests and carrying machine guns. This looks like overkill, given that Exarcheia has an almost non-existent crime rate, and the unjustified police presence serves rather to provoke and antagonize than to protect and to serve.[15]

The immediate mobilization after the murder was mainly by anarchists and radical Left militants, who were in their element in Exarcheia and already had an uneasy relationship with the police. But they were soon joined by youth from all segments, including, on Monday, high-school students who joined the protests in huge numbers. The police's response was typically heavy handed, with enormous amounts of tear gas and several episodes of brutality. The protests were most intense in the first two weeks, but continued for over a month. Several university campuses and schools were occupied. About 200 bank branches were attacked, and many of them destroyed. Looting was not widespread, but many expensive stores were smashed up. In addition to physical violence that also involved clashes with the police, and destruction of ATMs and traffic lights, the protests involved diverse actions, including performances, occupation of theatres and of the studios of the National Television Company. The government toyed with the idea of declaring a state of emergency, but this was later abandoned. However, the police response grew more violent, and they were joined by extreme-right vigilantes who attacked protestors, targeting immigrants in particular. By mid-January, the Greek uprising was over.

Immigrants, then, were also on the streets protesting, one of several features that made the Greek uprising of 2008 unprecedented in many ways in the country's modern history. The uprising lasted much longer than any other since the country's transition to liberal democracy in 1974. It went beyond Athens, expanding into most of the national territory, including not only all the large cities and urban areas, but also some of the agricultural heartlands and rural borderlands. This diffusion of the uprising has led Loukia Kotronaki and Seraphim Seferiades to argue that the 'Greek December' was not simply a riot, but a particular form of claim-making they call 'insurrectionary collective action', characterized by its geographical and social expansion, as well as its mix of violent and non-violent disruptive acts.[16] Or, in the words of Stavros Stavrides, it was an expression of 'a common rage' and a way of 'collectively reclaiming the city'.[17] The duration and the geographical expansion of the uprising showed that although the immediate cause was the murder of an unarmed teenager by the police, the resentment had been brewing for a long time and had many sources.

The young people were in the majority and played a leading role in the uprising, which was another distinguishing feature. Indeed, as Panagiotis Sotiris noted, for the first time it was a whole youth movement, and not just a student movement. The struggle of the previous two years against educational reforms, as we saw above, had already favoured the development of a culture of struggle among students. But the Greek December united students with young workers, lower-class youth with their middle-class peers and, perhaps most remarkably, native Greek youth with second-generation immigrant youth, which was a unique aspect of the uprising. Different segments of the population were thus united in revolt during the Greek December. Their diversity and the shared sources of their resentment were evident in the public announcement issued during the first week of the incidents, on 12 December 2008, by the Athens Coordination of Student Unions' General Assemblies and Occupations:

> The revolt of the youth is an expression of social anger against the politics that murder life, education and work, against the government that attacks the youth and at the same time is handing 28 billion euros to the banks. It is a political answer to state murder and repression ... Workers ... are the natural allies of our movement that is expressing the anger of high-school students, university students, precarious young workers of the '700 euros generation', the unemployed, and immigrants.[18]

Job insecurity was a shared concern across the board, including workers and Greek youth of different education levels, social status and origin. Before the uprising, the main trade unions had already called for a general strike on 10 December, which is yet another indicator of the widespread feeling of discontent. The future looked particularly bleak to the youth, which was an important factor that brought them together.

Another issue that brought the youth together, and especially the native Greek and second-generation immigrant youth, was police brutality, which, as Andreas Kalyvas has pointed out, was something that 'both the foreign and the native can associate with'.[19] As noted above, the Greek police have a well-established history of abuse and brutality, which had already been documented in several reports published since the early 2000s. These expressed concern over human-rights violations committed by the police during demonstrations, arrest and detention, including excessive use of force, arbitrary detention, torture or other ill treatment, and denial of access to legal assistance. Indeed, on several occasions in the 2000s the European Court of Human Rights found Greece to be in violation of the right to life and the prohibition of torture or degrading treatment. The 2009 report by Amnesty International was quite clear about the relationship between the history of police violence and the December uprising: 'The demon-strations are the culmination of a pattern of serious human rights violations by law enforcement officials.'[20]

A Second French November 2005

For us, organised migrants, this is our November 2005 French uprising.

– Albanian Migrants' Haunt

When so called liberal states resort to massive police violence, they testify to their own social and political weakness.

– Stathis Gourgouris

Many mainstream Greek intellectuals were not kind to the December protestors. They interpreted the uprising as a form of deviance, exposing a culture of violence and lack of civility. Mainstream media did not refrain from referring to the protestors as 'rabble'.[21] Such unflattering comments were probably conditioned by the level of violence against property and general destruction. Even observers sympathetic to the uprising admitted that the 2008 incidents were 'far more intense, violent, and destructive' than anything Greece had witnessed since the end of the Civil war. Hundreds of banks, stores and public buildings were destroyed, hundreds of cars were torched, transport was paralysed. The extent of physical destruction had taken everyone by surprise.[22]

Yet the uprising, violent as it was, was an eruption of rage in response to other forms of violence, which it exposed. It was violence that destroyed the established order, because the established order was seen to be a source of violence. This point was forcefully made by the public announcement of a popular assembly that occupied the town hall of Agios Dimitrios, a municipality in the southern part of Athens metropolitan area, during the December revolt:

> There has been a lot of talk about violence. For the people in authority and the media violence is only what destroys order.
>
> But, for us:
>
> Violence is to work for forty years for extremely low wages and to wonder whether you will ever be able to retire.
>
> Violence is the bank bonds, the robbery of pension funds, the stock exchange fraud.
>
> Violence is to be forced to take a housing loan that you are going to have to repay with massive interest.
>
> Violence is the right of the employer to sack you whenever he pleases.
>
> Violence is to be unemployed, precarious, to be paid 700 euros per month, sometimes without insurance.
>
> Violence is workplace 'accidents', because the bosses are reducing costs to the detriment of workplace safety.
>
> Violence is to be an immigrant woman, to live in constant fear of being thrown out of the country, and to have a permanent feeling of insecurity.[23]

Although marked by violence against property, with banks and chain stores as core targets, the Greek December exposed and spoke to other forms of violence that ruined many lives, ranging from unemployment to corruption, precariousness to police brutality. A deep distrust of the political establishment was apparent throughout the uprising in the form of slogans and writings. In this sense, the Greek uprising showed that the established political order was unable to address the grievances and meet the political ideals especially of the younger generation of Greeks and immigrants who were born and lived in Greece. The majority of the participants, Costas Douzinas has noted, 'were people whose interests are never heard, accounted or represented'.[24] The uprising grew, in the words of Eirini Gaitanou, 'out of an awareness that, for the first time, a generation was facing a future that was worse than that of previous generations', and out of frustration that their 'accumulated rage' could not be expressed through traditional channels of political communication and representation.[25] This is why the streets did the talking for over a month.

And when the streets did the talking, there was also room for voices otherwise suppressed. As noted above, the participation of second-generation immigrants – now rebellious and in the public eye – was an important aspect of the Greek insurrection. In their public announcement posted on the Internet on 19 December 2008, the Albanian Migrants' Haunt stated their demand for equality:

> Immigrants' children are massively and dynamically involved in the movement. . . . They do not want to be and they are not like their parents, who came in Greece with their head's [sic] down, and were treated like beggars. They are part of the Greek society, since they know of no other society. They do not beg but demand to be equal with their Greek peers: equal in struggle in the streets, equal in the dreaming of future.[26]

On 22 December, Konstantina Kouneva, a Bulgarian immigrant working as a cleaner, was attacked with sulphuric acid, which attracted

more immigrants into the uprising and fuelled the rage. The participation of immigrants was an important political aspect of the Greek
December, because it implied the emergence of new political subjects,
and thus a redefinition of the political community.[27] The reference to
the 2005 uprisings in the French *banlieues* and the demand for
equality showed how second-generation immigrants in Greece, like
the stigmatized groups in France, felt excluded and oppressed in
their country of birth and residence. However, as the extent of the
uprising suggested, the feeling of exclusion was not limited to
second-generation immigrants.

Another politically significant aspect of the Greek uprising was
that unlike the previous revolts of twentieth-century Greece, it took
place in a liberal democracy. This led some to disregard its political
meaning. As one member of the 1973 university occupation against
the military junta, now leading a left-wing parliamentary group wary
of the December uprising, said: 'we were rebelling against a dictatorship, they are rebelling against a democracy.... Who are they
fighting, exactly?'[28] But this, perhaps, is precisely the point. As we
have seen with the urban uprisings in the US, the UK, France and
Sweden, you do not need a military dictatorship to produce injustices
that enrage ordinary citizens. Our democracies are perfectly capable
of doing this, though under conditions very different from a military
regime. The fact that these are democratic regimes is not, in other
words, a guarantee against devastating inequalities, oppressive practices and injustices left unaddressed. Indeed, the fact that these are
democratic regimes is not even a guarantee of democracy, if by this
we understand the equal worth of every citizen and resident.

We saw with the Greek and other episodes of urban rage that
revolt remains the ultimate form of dissent by citizens who are not
recognized as legitimate or equal political interlocutors – not just
voters – in the processes that affect their everyday lives. Urban uprisings, in this sense, are not episodes of mindless destruction, but

reminders of the presence of a body of citizens who feel wronged by the workings of the established order. As one participant observed about the Greek uprising: 'smashing things up is not what matters. Above all, this revolt was an assertion of dignity and a statement of presence. Of all the slogans, our most important was, "We are here."'[29] Urban uprisings involve the bodily presence of citizens asserting themselves as equals in urban space in order to question and challenge the order of things. As graffiti in Athens put it following the December 2008 uprisings: 'December was not an answer. It was a question.'[30]

Since 1974, Greece has been a democratic state, its constitution in place, parliament working, multiple political parties trying to woo voters, and free elections regularly organized. Yet, the workings of this order left many feeling excluded and resentful, as the unprecedented unrest showed. Liberal democratic processes failed to combat – and failed to give voice to those who wanted to combat – police brutality, speculation, top-down planning, economic exclusion, discrimination and widespread corruption, all of which accumulated rage over the years. And when rage eventually erupted, as it does, this liberal democratic order had recourse to more police violence, testifying to its own social and political weakness.

Let us now move to Greece's eastern neighbour, Turkey, the last of our case studies. As noted, the 2013 Turkish uprising was similar to the Greek one in its geographical expansion to practically all national territory. As we will see, similar processes were at the source of urban rage in Turkey as well, though with the added layer of forced Islamization under an increasingly authoritarian, yet popular, government.

7

Young Turks Find Peace in Revolt

On Monday, 17 June 2013, at about 6 p.m., a man in his thirties arrived in Istanbul's Taksim Square. This had been the site of massive protests since the end of May that year, set off by an urban redevelopment project to replace Gezi Park, one of the last remaining public green spaces in central Istanbul. He walked towards the cultural centre building, where a portrait of Atatürk, the founder of the modern and secular Turkish Republic, was hanging. Then he stopped – and did not move for the next eight hours. We have to remember that the square where he was standing looked like a battlefield after tens of thousands had shown their capacity to step into action over the previous days, despite a violent police response. What the 'standing man', as he came to be known, so wonderfully showed was that a people capable of stepping into action is equally capable of stepping back from it in order to stop and think – capacities political thinker Hannah Arendt associated with politics and believed were shared equally by all.

Recep Tayyip Erdoğan, then prime minister, now president of the Turkish Republic, was not happy. He called the protestors 'marauders', 'vandals', 'marginals' and 'terrorists', denying them all political capacity and legitimacy. They were following, so went his reasoning, orders from 'foreign powers'. He even responded to the standing man, who later received a human rights award in Germany and the Human Rights Foundation's Creative Dissent award. What bothered Erdoğan about the standing man was not his expression of dissent, but his lack of movement – the fact that he was standing still, not moving forward, thus showing no sign of progress or development. That did bother Erdoğan, and he made it known: 'We say: no standing still, onwards we continue. What do they say: Standing man!'

I will come back to this later, but wanted to bring it up here because, in order to understand the 2013 Turkish uprising, and indeed to get a sense of much of what has been going on in Turkey, we need to understand this mentality of moving forwards as a sign of progress and development. This mentality has guided all Turkish governments since the foundation of the republic in 1923, but the current one has taken it to new levels, creating grievances with a frenzy of reckless projects over the years, of which the Gezi Park redevelopment project that triggered the 2013 uprising was but one.

Like the Greek uprising we examined in the previous chapter, and unlike those we saw earlier, racism was not the main catalyst for the Turkish uprising, although discrimination based on ethnic and religious identities had caused rage to build up over the years. As we will see, one of the injustices that the Turkish uprising threw into sharp relief was the stigmatization of certain ethnic and religious groups, who suffered disproportionately from police violence, something the almost exclusive media focus on Gezi Park overshadowed.

Unlike the Greek government, however, the Turkish government did not suffer from a lack of legitimacy. As we saw in the previous chapter, the New Democracy government at the time of the 2008 Greek uprising was in a deep crisis of legitimacy, which resulted in defeat in the elections held the following year. In Turkey, however, the AKP government that prepared the context for and brutally repressed the 2013 uprising won clear electoral victories in local elections a year later and general elections in 2015, and survived a military coup attempt in 2016. Unprecedented revolts at a time of such seeming political stability raise interesting questions about democracy, but I am getting ahead of myself. Before looking at what happened during that memorable summer of 2013, let us first take a look at the context that led to it.

The Sultan's Palace

Do you build on every hill a mansion to amuse yourselves?
— *Quran*, Surat Ash-Shu'ara, 26: 128

We cannot say that an executive presidential system is incompatible with the unitary structure of the state. There are already examples in the world. You can see it when you look at Hitler's Germany.
— Recep Tayyip Erdoğan, President of the Turkish Republic, 2016

The Presidential Palace, built on top of a hill in Ankara, the Turkish capital, was inaugurated in October 2014. Not that one was needed. But Erdoğan wanted a new, bigger palace, ideally in the middle of a first-degree protected natural and historic site where construction is not allowed. It was not originally meant to be a presidential palace, but a palace for Erdoğan himself. When the idea dawned on him in 2012, he was prime minister, so he wanted a new palace for the prime minister. After he became president in 2014, he decided it should be for the president. The imposing palace has more than a thousand rooms and a state-of-the-art bunker. Plans include a 250-room residence for the president's family, and a giant mosque to accommodate 4,000 people. You may think it must have cost a fortune, and it has:

nearly half a billion euros – for the moment – plus prodigious maintenance costs.

I start with this example, because if we understand the construction process of this palace, we will also get a sense of the nature, extent and impact of this government's authoritarian interventions in cities and other sites during the past decade, which were one of the major sources of resentment that led to the 2013 uprising. The only elements missing from the picture would be the eviction of residents, police violence and enforced Islamization, but I will make sure those are not forgotten. It is not going to be a pretty picture. Indeed, some episodes of police violence are downright ghastly, government officials' remarks repulsive and the government's urban and infrastructure projects crazy – but that is something the government is actually proud of.

I am not being sarcastic. Since the 2005 release of a best-selling semi-documentary novel on the Turkish War of Independence entitled *Şu Çılgın Türkler* (Those Crazy Turks), the term 'crazy' (*çılgın*) has become part of nationalist rhetoric, and been appropriated by the government to legitimize projects facing public opposition. The 2012 publication of the book *Osmanlı'nın Çılgın Projeleri* (Crazy Projects of the Ottomans) by a conservative publisher reinforced this trend, and resonated equally well with the government's nationalist rhetoric with an Ottoman and Islamist twist.[1] The environmentally disastrous canal project (Kanal Istanbul) to join the Black Sea and the Sea of Marmara, constructing artificial islands in the latter are just some of this government's 'crazy projects', as Erdoğan himself refers to them. Turkey now is a country where government officials justify projects by their craziness rather than, say, their value for the public good, well-being of citizens or the environment. God willing, of course. 'I pray to God that this crazy project will be blessed for our Istanbul,' said Erdoğan in 2011, then prime minister, when announcing his Kanal Istanbul project. Folly has replaced reason.

Little wonder citizens went crazy over the Gezi Park project. It was, after all, another of Erdoğan's 'crazy projects' announced in June 2011.[2]

But let's go back to the palace. As I said, the history of this palace – the decision to build it, the choice of location, construction process, architectural style – is in many ways the history of this government's urban interventions and infrastructure projects. The decision came from the leader, and the palace was built to satisfy Erdoğan's ego rather than to respond to a real need. There was already a nice one in Ankara. The new palace was built with utter disregard for the environment, on top of a hill, on a site that was created by and carried the name of Atatürk, nemesis of Islamist Erdoğan. The site has been a first-degree natural reserve since 1992, where construction was prohibited. Putting a presidential compound large enough to cover twenty football fields on top of this natural reserve not only created great environmental concern, but was also against the law. Indeed, a court order was issued to stop construction that had, typically, already started. Erdoğan responded: 'Let them demolish it if they can. They cannot stop this construction. I will inaugurate this building and settle in there' – which he did.[3]

This kind of action and reaction has been the norm rather than the exception since Erdoğan's Justice and Development Party (AKP) came to power in 2002. It is not limited to Erdoğan's whims, but manifest all over the country in the form of extravagant urban and infrastructure projects. Utter disregard for the environment, law, planning and citizens characterizes most of these projects. As the palace example shows, size is of great importance. So is history, or a certain interpretation of it. These projects of excess are wrapped in and justified by glorified images from Turkish history. The Gezi Park project was defended as a resurrection of Ottoman legacy by reconstructing the Ottoman-era artillery barracks that once stood on the site where the park is now. 'Read the history of Gezi Park,' Erdoğan challenged the protestors. 'We will bring that history back to life.'[4] Though, he might have added, the new 'barracks' would have shopping malls and rich home owners rather than soldiers. As we saw with the new palace, this pragmatic use of history takes such ludicrous forms that it makes you cringe – look at the photographs and see for yourself.[5]

So how extravagant do these projects get? Erdoğan has built this monster of a palace, which claims to be one of the biggest in the world. A third bridge is currently being constructed over the Bosporus, a giant suspension bridge with ten lanes and two railway lines. When completed, it will have the highest pylons of any suspension bridge in the world. The contract for the third international airport was awarded in 2013 after the greatest bid in Turkish history. Yes, you guessed it: it will be the largest airport in the world, covering such a vast area that it will be visible even from the moon.[6]

Then there is Venice in Istanbul: Viaport Venezia, another massive structure, an upper-end real estate project with office buildings, residential blocks with more than 2,000 units, a hotel, and, of course, a shopping mall. 'You no longer have to travel to Venice to experience Venice,' the publicity says, 'Viaport Venezia has more, not less, to offer than Venice. . . . The perfect life you could not even find in Venice awaits you.'[7] I cannot quite comprehend why one should go to Istanbul to experience Venice, but this is a country where they even built a replica of Istanbul's Bosporus in Istanbul – the 'Bosporus City', with flats selling for millions. It is an exclusive residential compound with a canal imitating the Bosporus, a bridge imitating the Bosporus bridge, houses imitating Ottoman-era houses along the Bosporus, and towers imitating, as far as I can tell, nothing in particular.

Such projects have produced criticism and opposition, but, as usual, that did not register with the government. With projects so futile, corrupt, ridiculous even, how, you may wonder, did Erdoğan manage to win three consecutive electoral victories as prime minister and the

AKP remain in power since 2002? Part of the answer is that the AKP adopted an economic growth model that prioritized construction, and managed to present construction and real estate as signs of development and progress – which is why Erdoğan was unhappy with the standing man. Let us now take a look at this model, which will help us understand the context that led to the 2013 uprising.

Development Everywhere, Justice Nowhere

In issues such as family we are conservative. In economy and relations with the world we are liberal. And in social justice and poverty we are socialist.
– Finance Minister Mehmet Şimşek describing the Justice and
Development Party, 2011

They couldn't sell their shadows so they sold the forests
They knocked down, closed down movie theatres and squares
Covered everywhere with shopping malls
What happened to our city?
It is packed with buildings on steroids
– From the song *Tencere Tava Havası* by Kardeş Türküler, 2013

The Justice and Development Party (AKP) was founded in 2001 in the wake of a major economic crisis in Turkey. Voter discontent made itself felt in the elections a year later: the AKP secured a landslide victory in 2002, and has since governed the country. This was not, however, the first electoral victory of an Islamist party. In the municipal elections of 1994, the Islamist Welfare Party (predecessor of the AKP) won six out of fifteen metropolitan municipalities, including those of Ankara and Istanbul, where Erdoğan served as mayor between 1994 and 1998. This unprecedented entrance of political Islam into metropolitan governance was a turning point, and helped consolidate the networks that would later bring about the electoral victory of the AKP.

Both the Welfare Party and, later, its offshoot AKP focused on the urban poor in the municipalities they controlled. The AKP had a strategy of what they called a 'social' approach to local government, which involved charity for the urban poor in return for votes. Giving food, clothes and coal to the poor not only secured votes, but also reinforced the AKP's self-styled image as providing service to citizens and as free from corruption. Even the party's acronym played on the Turkish word *ak* – clean – presenting the party as a 'clean party', tainted neither by corruption nor practices inappropriate for devout Muslims. Ironically, the bulk of the funding for this form of 'municipal aid' came as donations from firms and contractors that had close business ties with the municipalities in question, all belonging to similar Islamist business networks. There is also evidence that municipal aid was discontinued in neighbourhoods that did not support the AKP, including predominantly Alevi areas.[8] The latter suffer from strong spatial stigmatization because of their religious and political affiliations. We will come back to this, because it is key to understanding police violence and the 2013 uprising (all six people killed in relation to the uprising were Alevi, which was no coincidence). For the moment, however, let us note that Alevis make up 15–25 per cent of Turkey's population. They practise a more liberal form of Islam, and are broadly associated with left-wing politics, both of which lead to their discrimination by those committed to Sunni Islam, who consider Alevis nonbelievers, and by nationalists. The AKP is firmly committed to Sunni Islamic principles and nationalism has been on the rise.

In addition to buying votes and establishing networks through charity, Islamist mayors also made Islamic practices and customs more visible, for example by rendering public spaces and municipality-owned facilities 'family friendly' through the creation of separate

sections for single men and families, and banning alcohol. Such practices consolidated a strong support base for the AKP. So while the
AKP presented itself internationally as fresh, moderately Islamist yet
democratic, and, above all, open for business, at home it consolidated
informal networks through donations and favours, controlled and
manipulated the media for its own political purposes, and emphasized its attachment to tradition and Islam – much more than many
foreign observers realized, until the 2013 uprising exposed things
more clearly (even *The Economist*, which loved the AKP for its
economic policies and referred to it as 'moderately Islamic' eventually
dropped the first adjective).

Since the AKP came to power in 2002, economic growth has been
impressive. In 2011, Turkey had the fastest growing economy in
Europe, with an 8.5 per cent growth rate. This growth, however, was
not equally shared. In the same year, the richest 20 per cent had
almost half of national income, whereas the poorest had only 6 per
cent. Despite its economic growth, Turkey has the third-highest level
of income inequality among the thirty-four OECD countries, with
16 per cent of the population living below the poverty line.[9] The
economic growth of Turkey in this period was based on land speculation, financial services and overseas trade. It created fortunes for a
select minority of investors aligned with the government, and benefited only a portion of the upper middle classes. In the meantime, real
wages have declined. The informal sector has grown dramatically, not
least with the arrival of rural migrants, especially more than two
million Kurds displaced by violence in the east. By 2011, 55 per cent
of the labour force were working in the informal sector. The urban
manifestation of this pattern of urban growth was neighbourhoods
of poverty, and increasing polarization between urban poor and
upper middle classes.[10] Such neighbourhoods have been targeted
by so-called 'urban transformation' projects, as we will see in more
detail below.

The AKP's economic growth model relies on foreign capital inflows, which seek high and fast returns on investment. Thus, although foreign capital inflows increased, they fed speculation-driven developments for higher and faster returns, which made construction and real estate major domains of investment. Bank loans for construction increased more than eighteen times in a decade, rising from 4.6 billion in 2004 to 85 billion in 2013.[11] Thus, in the 2000s urban space has become a major site of investment and profit with a frenzy of projects, ranging from infrastructure to housing, from shopping malls to mosques, both of which mushroomed under AKP rule. The number of new construction permits went up from about 43,000 in 2002 to over 75,000 in 2004, reaching 116,500 in 2013.[12]

These projects, however, do not follow a masterplan, and are generally not conceived to respond to pressing needs, but follow an urge to build more, bigger, higher and, as we saw, crazier. When there is no longer enough vacant space to build, the government starts to re-build cities by demolishing poor inner-city and other neighbourhoods, including historic sites. This has been a consistent pattern since the mid-2000s, which only accelerated in the years leading up to the Gezi uprising. The AKP has turned all available space into a source of profit by making state-owned land, forests, settlements built informally on public land but tolerated until then, and historic inner-city areas available for private investment, and even moving inner-city schools and hospitals to peripheral campuses to make space available for property development. A particular target of this strategy has been poor, inner-city neighbourhoods sitting on valuable land. The government passed laws that gave it practically unlimited authority to expropriate these properties, which it has been doing steadily in the name of urban transformation. The affected residents were not always informed about these projects, as we will see. When the eviction of six million households was on the agenda in 2012, Erdoğan even asked the residents not to make their job difficult. This was among the sources of urban rage that erupted a year later.

This emphasis on construction is as politically driven as it is economically. The AKP has been very successful in presenting construction and real estate as signs of development and modernity. Indeed, the AKP consolidated its power by investing in urban space and large infrastructure projects. This strategy resonated well with the development mentality that has always had good purchase in Turkey. Although the AKP is clearly an Islamist party, which distinguishes it from other governments of the modern Turkish Republic, it shares the same approach to development, guided by an image of forward movement and progress through projects initiated by leaders.[13] The historical legacy and dominance of this approach make it difficult to oppose proposed projects: opposition is seen as hindering the development of the nation, if not as outright treason. If one opposed a project, one opposed the development of Turkey, nothing less.

Here Prime Minister Erdoğan's response to the 2013 uprising is typical. In a rally called 'Respect for national will rally', organized the day after the massive police raid in Istanbul that cleared Gezi of protestors, Erdoğan claimed that the protestors were not motivated by environmental concerns, but by a desire to hinder Turkey's growth. The protestors, he said, did not want Turkey to 'grow, become powerful and earn prestige'.[14] We see once again the association of construction and real estate development with the growth, power and prestige of the country – a vision the AKP made central to its economic policies from the early 2000s. Now we can understand better why Erdoğan was so annoyed by the standing man: 'We say: no standing still, onwards we continue. What do they say: Standing man!' It is noteworthy that 'No standing still, onwards we continue' (*Durmak yok, yola devam*) was the AKP's slogan for the 2009 local elections, and for its twelfth anniversary in 2013.[15] The standing man contradicted the very idea of progress that the AKP made central to its economic and political strategy.

The vision the AKP consolidated was one where investments were seen as good, modern, a service to the public – even if they led to eviction of the poor, commodified urban spaces and were ecological disasters. The AKP's economic growth policies based on construction and real estate transformed cities and damaged the environment. Like the new palace on the hill, the number and extent of these projects were not justified by any pressing need. Rather, they were motivated by speculation, image building (through, for example, spectacular urban projects), and a desire to keep the construction sector going, which developed into a sector without alternative in the 2000s. As noted, this economic development model based on construction, real estate and infrastructure extended to vast spaces – not just urban, but also rural. The Gezi Park project was a perfect example of this model. Why, otherwise, transform one of the last remaining green spaces in central Istanbul and build in its place yet another shopping mall – of which there are already about a hundred, making Istanbul the fifth city in the world in terms of the number of shopping malls?[16] And why build, in addition to the shopping mall, more luxury residential housing, which also exists in vast quantities and is not even fully occupied, whereas there is a chronic shortage of affordable housing?

The answer is this: to make profit through speculation. If you are thinking this is the biased interpretation of a lefty academic who is unsympathetic to this government, here is how the minister of environment and urban planning himself put it in 2013, a couple of months after the uprising and before having to resign because of corruption allegations: 'Citizens will of course buy land for investment, rent will be created. If rent is not created, if the private sector cannot make money, the country cannot develop. Look at CNN or BBC news broadcasts: in the background, they show grandeur, rent and power. We too shall become powerful.'[17] We must note that the Turkish term for rent (*rant*) implies money made through speculation, not through the production of goods or provision of services. Let us also note that the minister who made this comment, Erdoğan Bayraktar, was the head of TOKİ, the government institution at the heart of the AKP's economic model based on construction and real estate. Bayraktar directed TOKİ for a decade, between 2002 and 2011, with exactly the same approach, as TOKİ's record shows. It is time we meet this institutional monster.

Creating an Institutional Monster

Irregular urbanization breeds terrorism.
                                    – Erdoğan Bayraktar, head of TOKİ, 2007

Now we'll go ahead and demolish houses if necessary. . . . Don't make our job difficult.
                    – Prime Minister Erdoğan on urban transformation, 2012

Turkey received Marshall funds after the Second World War, which helped the country expand its existing industries, develop new ones and mechanize agricultural production. One consequence of these developments was the move of agricultural workers, made redundant by mechanization, from rural areas to cities. Since there was no official housing policy to accommodate this new urban population, the newcomers built their own houses – the *gecekondu* (literally, landed overnight) – mostly on publicly owned land. Though not particularly elegant, this was an effective solution to the emerging housing problem, one that satisfied both the industrialists, who needed this labour force, and the rural migrants, who needed cheap shelter. It was a solution that also benefited short-sighted politicians, who promised *gecekondu* residents protection from demolition and basic infrastructure, provided they voted for them. And they did. Not only water, electricity and roads arrived, but also new concessions that allowed the building of *gecekondus* of several storeys. By the 1980s, *gecekondu* areas had become dense neighbourhoods.

A tepid response was the creation of the Mass Housing Administration (TOKI) in 1984, which produced very little housing and not really for the masses. In the 2000s, following the AKP's institutional reforms, TOKI started to build a lot of housing, though still not really for the masses. TOKI has been the main actor in the government's urban transformation projects. It has an impressive range of powers – at once planner, constructor and developer – and an unimpressive system of checks. Indeed, TOKI is effectively unaccountable, and reports only to the prime minister, not even to the Ministry for Environment and Urban Planning. The transformation of TOKI from an insignificant government institution in the 1980s and 1990s (I know well because I was an intern there during the summer of 1993) to a central player in the 2000s with more than a 10 per cent share of the Turkish housing market has been spectacular.[18] How did this happen?

In order to understand this, we must first take a look at what the AKP did with this institution, and how the latter works.[19] The AKP turned TOKI into a central player by putting public land under its control, legally empowering it to expropriate private property, and, to top it all, to make plans itself. In other words, this single institution was endowed with powers to plan something, take the land for it and construct it, which it usually does through public-private partnerships, with investment bids going to allies and friends, including a company whose CEO is Recep Tayyip Erdoğan's son-in-law. These are the so-called 'TOKI princes' – a select group of big construction firms that have religious, political and personal ties with the government.[20] What makes TOKI even more dominant is that its urban transformation projects are exempt from taxes and duties, which puts it at a considerable advantage over other constructors. Thus, TOKI, with public land at its disposal, exempt from tax, unrestrained by any mechanism of financial oversight or building quality control, and blissfully free from cumbersome processes of public participation, has unchecked control on shaping cities. All the more so because TOKI's competences go beyond housing, and include shopping malls, office spaces, football stadiums, mosques, schools, hospitals, prisons and police stations.

This is how TOKI works: it opens state-owned land to private developers for high-end housing. The developer who offers the highest share of revenue to TOKI gets the contract. Thus, both the private developer and TOKI profit from developing state-owned land for the upper classes. But there is more. TOKI values the land at a price lower than its actual market rate, which works as a hidden subsidy for the developer, who can then afford to sell the units at a lower price than competitors. This creates unfair competition, which TOKI itself admits, but justifies as an inevitable side effect of its affordable housing policy.

Now we must deal head-on with two common misconceptions about TOKI. First, there has never been an official social housing policy in Turkey, and TOKI does not provide social (or public) housing. It builds market-rate housing and promotes home ownership. Second, even though TOKI claims to be building affordable housing for lower income groups, these are not affordable to people evicted as a result of its projects. It is true that TOKI uses revenues generated through the model described above to build housing for lower income groups, but these are sold to the urban poor. Those who want to buy these houses, unless they are built for the 'poor' category, must first make a down payment (ranging from 10 per cent to 25 per cent) and then pay monthly instalments – indexed to public sector wage increases – for between eight and twenty-five years. Failure to do so transfers ownership of the house back to TOKI.

Most of the residents evicted through TOKI urban transformation projects simply do not have the means to afford these housing units, and those who do usually find it impossible to live in TOKI's dense, high-rise apartment blocks, sometimes referred to as 'coffins'. Karaman calls TOKI's so-called 'affordable' housing scheme a 'market-disciplinary tool', incorporating the urban poor into the mortgage market by coaxing or coercion. Residents to be evicted are not offered affordable housing units, but mortgage loans for market-rate housing. The cost for the evicted urban poor goes beyond the price of the new housing unit. Making monthly mortgage payments is close to impossible for many, because they do not have stable or well-paid jobs. Moreover, moving to TOKI units also brings the additional costs of property tax and service charges, contracted to private companies, which they cannot afford.

Thus, TOKI is a profit-making state institution, and the source of its profit is selling public land, including protected forest land, for real estate development, and reconstructing entire urban neighbourhoods for speculation. TOKI projects transform space with little or no regard for affected citizens, the environment, urban planning or history, unless the latter serves to justify new and more construction. For years leading up to the 2013 uprising, TOKI engaged in a systematic destruction of living spaces and natural environments, causing evictions and displacement, producing irreversible natural damage, all with the aim of generating more profit by constructing more, higher and denser. This was part of the context that led to the uprising – one of the sources of pent-up rage – and the Gezi Park project was the last straw.

Istanbul, groomed to be Turkey's 'global city', has been at the centre of the AKP government's urban transformation projects. These efforts to transform Istanbul to integrate it into global real estate markets had two main pillars: redevelopment of squatter settlements in the peripheral areas and the enforced gentrification of deprived inner-city neighbourhoods. The attempt to develop Istanbul into a global city is not new. What is new is the way the AKP government is trying to achieve it by the wholesale redevelopment of Istanbul's informal and deprived neighbourhoods rather than just building a few prestige projects – 'bulldozer neoliberalism', as John Lovering and Hade Türkmen have called it: a massive demolition programme to erase much of the city's pre-AKP physical and social heritage. This is a programme that extends to other cities as well, since construction is the main pillar of the AKP's economic growth model.[21]

One particular target of the AKP's urban transformation policy has been the *gecekondus*, especially those sitting on profitable land. As we saw at the start of this section, the *gecekondu* was once tolerated because it helped with the provision of cheap labour and shelter, which turned such settlements into dense neighbourhoods over time. In the 2000s, however, toleration came to an end. Both official discourses on and mainstream media representation (increasingly controlled by the government) of *gecekondu* changed once the AKP had consolidated its power. In the new discourse, residents of such areas were portrayed as shamelessly profiting from illegally occupied land, and engaging in other illegal activities themselves. This was a shift from the image of the *gecekondu* resident as poor yet hard-working; they have now become the new dangerous class, associated with gang activity, muggings, drug-dealing and terrorism – similar to the case of French *banlieues*. Unlike in the *banlieues*, however, many of these residents were sitting on profitable urban land, since what was peripheral when they first arrived was no longer so.

So a discursive offensive started with the stigmatization of these areas and their residents. This is exemplified by the former TOKI director's comments from 2007:

Today *gecekondu* is among the two or three important problems Turkey is facing. But Turkey cannot speak of development without having solved the *gecekondu* problem. It is well known that *gece-kondu* areas are at the foundation of terrorism, drugs, oppositional views about the state, psychological hardship, ignorance and health problems.[22]

Such language is more readily deployed when the residents are Kurds, who are portrayed as primitive, anti-social, criminal and disloyal to the nation. Such strong stigmatization not only serves to justify demolition projects, but also to undermine any resistance to them. As a resident of a now demolished *gecekondu* area put it:

> Our fear, as the media films us and broadcast the situation, is that if the municipality comes tomorrow, or the day after tomorrow with machine guns, they will say 'They were terrorists, they were PKK'. How many times have they already come in, raided us, thrown us out, and the media only report that 'They are Kurdish'. We are living with this fear.[23]

It is important to note that migration is driven not only by adverse economic conditions in the least developed parts of the country in the east, but also by what increasingly looks like a civil war. Most of the Kurdish population thus pushed out of their living spaces simply have nowhere to go back to.[24]

Stigmatization is even stronger if the residents are Alevi. Gülsuyu in Istanbul, for example, was a predominantly Alevi neighbourhood targeted for urban transformation. The neighbourhood was under constant surveillance with police cameras and a permanently stationed police vehicle. As one local woman put it: 'If I say "I am from Gülsuyu," the boss would say that they don't have a job for me.'[25] Such neighbourhoods were also sites of clashes over urban transformation projects, suffering disproportionately from police violence because of their residents' ethnic identities, religious affiliations and political orientations. In the 2013 uprising, although most of the media attention was focused on the more peaceful and festive protests around Gezi Park, such peripheral and poor neighbourhoods in Istanbul and other cities were sites of violent clashes with the police. I will come back to this later, in the section on police violence.[26] Let us note for the moment that all the protestors who were killed by the police during the 2013 uprising were Alevis, and most of them were killed in Alevi neighbourhoods.

The discursive offensive was accompanied by a legal one, with a penal code passed in 2004 that made *gecekondu* construction punishable by up to five years in prison. Thus, during the 2000s, the *gecekondu* has been represented as a space of criminality and problems, subject to the harshest comments and practices. Authoritarian interventions in these areas were enabled by new laws and powers granted to TOKI – and as we saw with the president's palace, not even first-degree protected natural and historic sites are immune from construction. Between 2002 and 2008 alone, fourteen new laws or amendments to existing laws dramatically expanded the field of action and resources of TOKI.[27] A notorious 2012 law on the transformation of disaster-risk areas further expanded TOKI's reach, giving the government a free hand to transform (that is, demolish and build more instead) any area designated at 'risk' – targeting not just Istanbul, but every single city, not only cities, but every settlement all the way down to villages. As the head of TOKI put it in 2011 when announcing the government's reinforced urban transformation agenda: 'From now on, starting with cities, we will go down to counties, towns, and villages.'[28]

With its eviction and displacement of people on a massive scale, destruction of the environment and commercialization of urban space, the government's urban policy has created a great deal of tension over the years. The Gezi Park project showed how reckless the government's urban agenda had become. But Gezi Park showed something else, something even more powerful at the source of the pent-up rage that erupted over this particular project, which, unlike many others, did not even lead to the eviction of people: the way projects were imposed by the government. The government executed its projects in a top-down manner, at times not even informing the residents in advance. This was the extent of this government's democratic will or capabilities; some residents were not even informed about urban transformation projects that would lead to their eviction or displacement, and citizen consultation and participation seemed too wild to even think about, given the government's increasingly authoritarian interventions. When resistance took place, as it did in Gezi, it was violently repressed by the police, which in Gezi turned a peaceful sit-in into a nationwide uprising. Gezi Park, therefore, not only exposed the dubious economic model of the government based on using urban space for profit, but also the increasingly authoritarian nature of its interventions in people's living spaces.

Here Prime Minister Erdoğan's response to the Gezi resistance exemplifies the government's approach. Speaking at the groundbreaking ceremony of the third bridge over the Bosporus, another contested yet imposed government project, Erdoğan defied the protestors, who had already been attacked by the police the previous day and were now growing in numbers: 'Do whatever you want at Gezi Park,' he said. 'We made our decision, and we are going to execute it.'[29] Imposed projects destroying life spaces of people and ruining the environment were not the only source of grievance. The government had also become increasingly authoritarian, severely limiting civil liberties and trying to impose its Islamist agenda as it imposed its crazy urban projects. Encouraged by its successive electoral victories, the AKP government, and Erdoğan in particular, were corrupted by the power to rule them all. No, we have not slipped into Middle Earth by accident or for rhetorical effect. Who does what in that fictional world is of great importance for some people in Turkey. Their freedom depends on it.

Gollum's Wrath

Among several other important duties of Turkish courts, one of them is to decide, with help from experts, whether Gollum of *The Lord of the Rings* is evil or not. You may wonder why this would require the commitment of the Turkish judicial system. Gollum, after all, is a figment of Tolkien's imagination, and the matter has already been the subject of many literary studies. You would be right to wonder, but it is very important that the court establish the disposition of this fictional character because the freedom of a real person hangs on it. Bilgin Çiftçi, a doctor employed in the public sector, shared images of Gollum and Erdoğan in similar poses and expressions in his private Facebook account in 2015. As a result, he lost his job because his status as civil servant has been rescinded, and the court is now waiting for the expert report. The Turkish courts can afford to take the time to deal with such a peculiar case, because President Erdoğan felt insulted by the comparison. And insulting Erdoğan is a crime, punishable by up to four years in prison. Incidentally, the newspaper that reported the court case was also taken to court.

I am not interested in Erdoğan's physical resemblance to Gollum, although it is my scientific opinion that the juxtaposed images are hilarious. What I am interested in, and what worries me most as it does so many other Turkish citizens, is the parallel between Gollum's blind obsession with the ring of power and Erdoğan's with political power. Erdoğan, unlike Gollum, is not a loner but a ruler with popular support, as the election results show. Where Gollum's wrath derives from his obsession with the one ring, Erdoğan's derives from anyone and everyone who criticizes him, or simply does not agree with him. In the first eighteen months of his presidency, 1,845 cases have been opened against people, including schoolchildren, accused of insulting him – more than three court cases a day. But Erdoğan's attempts to censor criticism go beyond national borders. Between July and

December 2014, Turkey filed more than two requests per day to Twitter for removal of content, approaching 500 requests in a six-month period. In March 2016, the German ambassador to Ankara was summoned twice, first over a music video on the Internet, then for attending the opening of a court case for two journalists accused of espionage. The video exposes and mocks the authoritarian tendencies of Erdoğan, whom it calls the 'Big Boss from Bosporus'. It is telling that the Turkish government deemed it appropriate to ask the German government to censor German media. As one German journalist put it, 'Erdoğan now reacts hysterically to any criticism.'[30]

It would be a mistake to focus merely on Erdoğan's personality or on the government's crazy projects, even though these are major sources of grievance. Granted Erdoğan gets on people's nerves by telling them how many children they should have (three, in case you missed it; and remember birth control is 'treason'), that they should not smoke or eat white bread, and that they should drink *ayran* (a traditional Turkish drink made with yogurt, water and salt) rather than getting drunk with *rakı* or any other alcoholic beverage. His political rhetoric is divisive and inflammatory. But the resentment that led to the 2013 uprising had been simmering for years over the government's conservative and Islamist agenda, marked by the erosion of civil rights and liberties, suppression of dissent, and authoritarian governance.

Since coming to power in 2002, the AKP has implemented a revanchist politics against the military, journalists and intellectuals, and against what Erdoğan named the 'White Turks' (the urban secular elite he distinguished from the 'Black Turks', the poor and less educated classes and his voter base). Through reforms and practices that established networks facilitated by religious connections and a clientelistic political culture, or, when those did not suffice, through the mobilization of the state's coercive powers, the AKP has tightened its grip on the media as well as on business. As the AKP's power consolidated over the years, dissent was suppressed and civil rights and freedoms started to erode. Thousands of activists, mainly Kurdish, are jailed through the use of loosely formulated anti-terror laws that make the flimsiest charges possible. The judiciary is filled with AKP nominees, army generals are jailed (not that anyone wants another military coup, as we saw with the citizen resistance to the 2016 attempt), and the opposition has been so incompetent over the years that referring to them as 'opposition' seems generous.

In this context, the AKP has started to implement its conservative agenda more openly, limiting civil liberties, especially for women. 'A woman is above else a mother,' declared Erdoğan in a speech on none other than International Women's Day. Legislation limiting women's rights was introduced, such as tightening of the law on abortion and informing the families of pregnant women of their condition, as well as attempts to limit the morning-after pill and Caesarean sections. Violence against women and transgender people surged under AKP rule. Honour killings of women increased by a factor of fourteen between 2002 and 2009.[31] Stricter regulation of alcohol sales and consumption was also introduced. You can, for example, no longer have alcohol on Turkish Airlines' domestic flights, as I learned the hard way. This is not a serious, life-threating issue like the others evoked above, but it is telling of this government's façade to the world and crackdown at home. Turkish Airlines has been running a huge publicity campaign to show how global, open to the world it is, endorsed by such celebrities as Lionel Messi, Kobe Bryant, Kevin Costner and, more recently Ben Affleck – all male, but that should hardly come as a surprise. Islam goes out of the window when global business is in question but, at home, you are expected to live by its rules – or, better yet, by this government's interpretation of them.

The AKP government's Islamization agenda was once perhaps less obvious, to international observers at least, but in 2012 Erdoğan openly admitted in an address to parliament that his government wanted to 'raise a religious youth'. 'Do you expect the conservative democrat AK Party to raise an atheist generation?' he asked. 'We will raise a conservative and democratic generation embracing the nation's values and principles.'[32] Of course the Republic is supposed to be secular and not engaged in raising youth according to any religious doctrines, but that ideal went down the drain a long time ago. Like the French state, the Turkish Republic has never been really secular, with religion courses in school and citizens' religions inscribed on their identity cards. But such openly religious declarations of intent by those in power are certainly a big step towards increasing Islamization of the society on the political agenda. Another indicator of the AKP's Islamization agenda are the resources channelled to the Directorate of Religious Affairs (*Diyanet*), another AKP-revitalized government institution like TOKI. The AKP increased Diyanet's annual budget from half a billion liras in 2002 to 1.3 billion in 2006, and to 4.6 billion in 2013, which was more than the budget of many ministries.[33]

In one domain, the AKP government's authoritarian policies took Turkey to top ranking on a world scale: incarceration. The country did very well indeed in terms of the number of journalists in prison, the number of political prisoners and the number of people convicted on terrorism charges – no mean feat when competing with 1.5 billion-strong China and post-September 11 United States (Turkey's population is about eighty million). When the AKP came to power in 2002, there were nearly 60,000 prisoners in Turkey. This figure exceeded 100,000 in six years, and reached 132,000 by 2012 – a more than 100 per cent increase in prison population in a decade.

Turkey under AKP also enjoys the unique position of having the largest number of political prisoners in the world, as well as the largest number of people convicted on terrorism charges. According to an Associated Press survey, at least 35,000 people were convicted of terrorism worldwide in the decade following the 11 September 2001 attacks. Turkey and China, two countries that regularly use far-reaching anti-terror laws to crack down on dissent, accounted for more than half of the convictions. Turkey alone accounted for more than a third of all convictions, with about 13,000 people convicted of terrorism (this figure must be even higher because the latest year included in the survey was 2009, thus leaving out two years from the count). This increase was facilitated by the AKP's new, stricter anti-terror laws passed in 2006 as part of its war against opposition, which produced an impressive number of terrorism convictions. In 2005, the number of people convicted of terrorism was 273. This figure went up to 6,345 in 2009, more than a twenty-three-fold increase, facilitated by the new laws.[34] The threat of terrorism charges was also levelled at protestors during the 2013 uprising. After the massive police raid on 15 June to 'clean up' Taksim Square, where the protestors had rallied, Egemen Bağış, Minister for EU Negotiations, warned people not to go to Taksim: 'I am asking all our citizens who support these protests to please return back to their homes. From this moment on, unfortunately, the state will have to consider each individual there as a member of terrorist organisations.'[35]

As I mentioned above, Kurdish activists suffered disproportionately from the AKP's authoritarian policies. Another group that suffered excessively were journalists. The AKP government turned Turkey into 'the world's biggest prison for journalists', as Reporters Without Borders called it in 2013. For two consecutive years, in 2012 and 2013, Turkey was world leader in terms of the number of imprisoned journalists, ahead even of China – a position it reclaimed in 2016 following the crackdown after the failed coup. According to Reporters Without Borders's Press Freedom Index, it ranks 149th among 180 countries, which is poor for a 'democracy'.[36]

Under AKP rule, critical newspapers are closed or issued with crippling tax fines to allow their takeover by business groups sympathetic to the government. When these do not suffice, they are seized by the government on terrorism or conspiracy charges, as we saw recently with the country's biggest selling newspaper, *Zaman*, which was critical of the government, but is now publishing pro-government propaganda with new staff. Journalists critical of the government are jailed, or fired at best, and those who are not are intimidated to the point of self-censorship. The silence of the Turkish media during the first days of the 2013 uprising was typical in this sense: while CNN-International was airing live coverage of the revolts, the local channel CNN-Turk was treating its viewers to a documentary on penguins – which turned these lovely creatures into a symbol of resistance.[37]

AKP's Islamization agenda, authoritarian interventions in people's living spaces and ways of life, erosion of civil liberties, dismissal of democratic procedures and repression of opposition led to the radicalization of secular groups in particular, and brought them together during the summer of 2013 in what was to become an unprecedented insurrection against the government. There was, however, another major source of grievance that revolted people: police violence.

The Legendary Deeds of Turkish Police Officers and Shopkeepers

After the legend of the Battle of Çanakkale [Gallipoli], you are writing a second legend.
– Prime Minister Erdoğan praising Turkish police during the 2013 uprising

When necessary, shopkeepers are also soldiers, heroes, police officers, judges.

– President Erdoğan, 2014

What did the Turkish police do to merit such flattering remarks from the country's political leader? They killed five unarmed people, including a fifteen-year-old boy, during the 2013 uprising. The violence of the Turkish police in repressing the uprising was indeed legendary, though I am not sure this is something to be really bragging about. Six weeks into the uprising, 8,000 people had been injured, sixty-one of them seriously, eleven lost an eye and 104 suffered serious head injuries.[38]

What about Erdoğan's multi-purpose shopkeepers then? On 1 June 2013, as the numbers swelled and the uprising started to expand, Erdoğan menaced the protestors with the threat that he could mobilize a million supporters to confront them. Some of his followers listened. There is plenty of evidence showing government sympathizers with clubs in their hands, 'helping' the police in their legendary beatings of protestors. In one tragic incident in the city of Eskişehir, the day after Erdoğan's threat, nineteen-year-old Ali İsmail Korkmaz was beaten with clubs by a group of men, two of whom turned out to be bakers. The governor of the city denied that the police were involved, but this proved to be wrong; the two bakers were giving a hand to four police officers in plain clothes. Korkmaz died after thirty-eight days in a coma.[39]

Eventually the two bakers were sentenced to eight years in prison, but only two of the four police officers involved – all from the antiterrorism unit – were sentenced, one to twelve, the other to ten years in prison. This incident shows to what extremes inflammatory language by government officials can lead. One of the police officers defended himself by claiming that Erdoğan had qualified Gezi as a coup d'état, and that he was trying to prevent that. The bakers were probably emboldened by Erdoğan's call. In any case, they received his full support. Erdoğan's speech praising Turkish shopkeepers as soldiers, heroes, police officers and judges was delivered on the very day they were being judged, by real judges, for murdering Ali İsmail Korkmaz.

This is a depressing topic to write about, but let us look at the other victims of police violence, as this will illustrate the discriminatory nature of it. Abdullah Cömert was hit on the head by a tear-gas canister fired at close range in the city of Hatay on 3 June. He died the following day. Ahmet Atakan died in the same neighbourhood, under the same circumstances, a couple of months later during a protest. Berkin Elvan, the fifteen-year-old teenager, was also hit on the head by a tear-gas canister fired at close range when he went out to buy bread at around 7 a.m. on 16 June. He died after about nine months in a coma, and the investigation still continues.

Ethem Sarısülük was shot in the head by a police officer during a protest in Ankara on 1 June 2013. The incident was captured on video, and shows the police officer separating himself from his colleagues, kicking a protestor lying on the ground, then firing three shots towards a group throwing stones, two in the air, and one towards the protestors, hitting Ethem Sarısülük, who died on 14 June as a result of his injuries. Dilan Dursun, a twenty-year-old student, was among those who attended his funeral in Ankara on 16 June. Shortly before 6 p.m., while she and a group of people were fleeing from police, the police fired a gas canister at them from a vehicle. Dilan was hit on the head. She underwent brain surgery, remained in a coma for four days, and was released from hospital two weeks after the incident. Evidence shows that the police were aware of what had happened – a manually operated surveillance camera panning away from Dilan after she was shot, a police officer reporting on the radio that someone was injured – but no aid arrived, and Dilan was transported to hospital in a private car. A crime scene investigation took place, but only four days after the incident. The investigation continues. The authorities managed to identify the police vehicle in question, whose licence plates were removed, three years after the incident. They now have to identify the officers in the vehicle, but the way the investigation is going, there seems little hope.

Amnesty International reported that police violence was due partly to the fact that the officers were poorly trained and poorly supervised, yet instructed to use force. They were publicly praised by the prime minister on several occasions, and assumed – correctly, as it turned out in many cases – that they would not be identified or prosecuted for their abuses. But there are patterns in the police violence that suggest it cannot be chalked up to poor training or working under pressure, but that it was the result of punitive and targeted police action. The use of the tear-gas canister as a weapon fired to hit protestors was common, as was the use of tear gas in confined areas. Several documented incidents show that the police unnecessarily and deliberately punished people, for example by firing tear gas canisters directly at individuals, like Dilan Dursun, already fleeing the protest scene, or by cornering small groups in the vicinity of protests and beating them, alone or with help from heroic shop-keepers moonlighting as judges and police.

Another example of this punitive police action was the targeting of doctors helping injured protestors. In Ankara, for example, the police made three raids on the evening of 2 June, targeting doctors. As one doctor put it: 'Anyone wearing a white jacket became a target that weekend. We made a decision not to wear them.'[40] During the raids on makeshift clinics, the police beat people receiving medical treatment, as well as some of the doctors, detained medical equipment and fired tear gas inside the buildings. They then beat people escaping from the building outside. There are even reports and video footage of police firing tear gas inside a makeshift health clinic and removing masks from the faces of people inside. Such actions were not condemned by the authorities. Indeed, the authorities encouraged them. The prime minister, as we saw, called the actions of the police 'legendary'. The government participated in the repression of medical aid as well. On 13 June, the minister of health declared makeshift health clinics illegal, and threatened medical staff treating injured protestors with criminal investigation. He was duly reminded by the Turkish Medical Association that it was a crime not to help injured people.[41]

A particularly gruesome incident took place in the Sarıgazi neighbourhood of Istanbul on 3 June. Hakan Yaman, a thirty-seven-year-old father of two, was returning home after his work as a minibus driver. He was first hit by water cannon, then by a tear-gas canister in the stomach. Five police officers attacked and beat him. One of them gouged his eye out with a hard object. Then they dragged him to a nearby fire, threw him on it and left him to die. He survived, but suffered life-changing injuries, as the medical report showed. He lost one eye and 80 per cent of his sight in the other. His skull was fractured from the top of his head to his jaw. His nose, cheekbone, chin and the bones of his forehead were broken. He also suffered second-degree burns to his back. The investigation still has not produced anything, despite the fact that part of the incident was filmed by an eyewitness, showing Hakan Yaman being dragged by four officers to the fire. As Amnesty International noted, 'Police officers in Turkey have long enjoyed de facto immunity from prosecution, especially in the context of demonstrations,' and the 2013 uprising was a sad reminder of this.[42]

Who were these victims and where were they killed? All the victims killed by the police were Alevis, and they were all killed in areas peripheral to the centre of protest and media attention. Ali İsmail Korkmaz, who was beaten to death, was Alevi. Abdullah Cömert, Ahmet Atakan and Berkin Elvan, who died after being hit in the head by tear-gas canisters, were Alevis and were killed in neighbourhoods marked out for their Alevi and leftist identities – two in the Armutlu neighbourhood in Hatay, and one in Okmeydanı in Istanbul. The neighbourhood where Ethem Sarısülük lived, Tuzluçayır in Ankara, was also marked out for its Alevi-leftist identity (he was not killed there but his status in the protest during which he was killed must have made his political orientation visible to the police). The Sarıgazi neighbourhood in Istanbul where Hakan Yaman was tortured and left to die is another area marked for its Alevi-leftist identity.

Police repression of the 2013 uprising was brutal in general, but the worst of it was reserved for groups and neighbourhoods stigmatized for their religious and political orientations. This pattern of police violence also suggests a link to the government's urban policy. These neighbourhoods have been objects of urban transformation projects and the leading sites in organized resistance against them. The sectarian policies of the government and its targeted urban interventions were sources of grievances, and Alevis intensely participated in the 2013 uprising. They did not necessarily participate with a particular Alevi agenda, but as citizens protesting against the government's policies and authoritarianism. They were, however, targeted during the uprising as they were before it. Istanbul police reported that 78 per cent of those taken into custody were Alevis. The overwhelming majority of Alevi deaths, injuries and imprisonments suggests targeted violence against them and neighbourhoods associated with them.[43]

The 2013 uprising was the product of this context, marked by urban and environmental destruction driven by profit, enforced Islamization of secular lifestyles, and police repression and violence. State officials' divisive rhetoric, led by Erdoğan, only added insult to injury. It was only a matter of time before the pent-up rage erupted.

The Sultan of Pots and Pans

Huzur isyanda.

– Graffiti in Istanbul

Legally this is a crime, I have the constitution here, a crime! Is someone banging pots and pans in your building? Take them to court right away.

– Prime Minister Erdoğan, 21 July 2013

The triggering event for the 2013 uprising was police violence against protestors in a dispute over the redevelopment of Gezi Park in Istanbul's Taksim Square into a commercial and high-end residential complex. Taksim Square is a symbolic place for the secular Republic as well as for Left politics. At the centre of the European section of the city, it is the place for official ceremonies celebrating the Republic (with a monument to its founders), as well as for May Day celebrations (though these are only occasionally allowed). When the first Islamist prime minister of Turkey, Necmettin Erbakan, came to power in 1996, he had promised to construct a mosque in Taksim Square. He was ousted the following year.

The Gezi Park project was part of a broader plan to turn Taksim Square into a pedestrian zone, which was approved by the Istanbul Metropolitan Council in 2011, typically without deliberation, following neither planning processes nor democratic procedures. According to this plan, the main roads leading to the square would be moved underground. Gezi Park would be replaced by a building imitating the old military barracks that once stood there. The project also involved the demolition of the cultural centre that overlooked the square, which carried the name of the founder of the modern and secular Turkish republic, Atatürk. And yes, a mosque was planned as well.

The central district where Taksim Square is located is called Beyoğlu. The cultural life in Beyoğlu is at odds with the Islamist vision of the AKP and its supporters, who see the area as decadent. This plan was part of a broader objective to sterilize and commercialize the central districts of Istanbul, and make the most out of urban space by transforming it into tourist and retail zones and high-end housing. This strategy has already replaced small shops and independent bookstores with shopping malls, chain stores and boutique hotels, and drawn in foreign investment in real estate. Gezi Park is a unique refuge from all the concrete and commercial spaces in this area. It is also a meeting ground for LGBTQ individuals.[44]

Thus, the Gezi Park and the broader Taksim Square project reflect the government's use of real estate for profit with no consideration for people or the environment, and its agenda of Islamization of life-styles deemed incompatible with its own vision. But opposition to the project did not turn into a wholesale uprising until protestors staging a peaceful sit-in in the park were brutalized by the police. Activists learned about the arrival of vehicles for demolition of the park towards midnight on 27 May 2013, and that night a few activists managed to stop the cutting-down of the trees. Another attempt to demolish the park was made the next day, this time backed by the police, but the resistance started to grow. This was the day when the image of the 'lady in red' tear-gassed in the face was captured. The following day, Prime Minister Erdoğan defied the protestors in his speech at the groundbreaking ceremony of the third bridge, which was to be named after Yavuz Sultan Selim, the Ottoman sultan who had ordered the massacre of 40,000 Alevis in the sixteenth century. 'Do whatever you want at Gezi Park,' he said, as we saw above. 'We made our decision, and we are going to execute it.'

Thus, having the public support of Erdoğan, the police became bolder. At dawn on 31 May, the police attacked the park and set fire to the tents of the protestors. Increased police violence and Erdoğan's defiant and inflammatory language attracted more people, and by noon on 1 June, the sit-in had turned into an uprising with the participation of hundreds of thousands. A night of clashes with the police followed, after which Taksim was established as a free zone for two weeks, while the uprising expanded geographically in Istanbul and to other cities. Erdoğan still remained defiant, and announced on 2 June that they would continue with the project, the Atatürk Cultural Centre would 'be demolished, God willing', and yes, they would 'also build a mosque'.[45]

According to figures provided by the Ministry of the Interior, 5,000 demonstrations across seventy-nine cities (out of a total of eighty-one) took place during the first twenty days of the uprising, with over 3.5 million people participating, according to police estimates. Those who were not on the streets took to banging pots and pans in their windows as a sign of solidarity with the protestors, which led the vigilant Erdoğan to declare that such banging of pots and pans constituted a crime and would be punished. As soon as August 2013, one criminal case was opened.

Three points, it seems, need to be emphasized about the uprising: its diversity, its relation to previous resistance movements and its structural sources. The uprising brought together people from various walks of life: there were women in headscarves, 'anti-capitalist Muslims',[46] gays, lesbians, transsexuals, union members, football club fans, Alevis, Sunnis, Jews, Christians, atheists, Armenians and Kurds as well as Turks. It was not organized or structured around particular social, cultural, gender, ethnic, religious or political identities or affiliations. What brought the protestors together was their political capacity as equals and their political desire to resist repression and authoritarian governance.

Some commentators unwittingly gave support to Erdoğan by characterizing the incidents as an elite middle-class affair, a characterization Erdoğan himself used to undermine the legitimacy of the uprising. As it turned out, this was not an accurate portrayal of the participants. The uprising was much more than just the Gezi Park, covering practically all the cities of Turkey with the active involvement of millions. The profile of the participants was much more diverse than an elite middle-class characterization could capture, and as especially the profile of those who died or were seriously injured shows, there was a strong working-class cohort, who suffered police violence much more than those who were at the park, where international media attention was focused. Although professionals and students were overrepresented in Gezi Park, overall most of those taking part in the uprising were workers or wage earners. Rather than an elite middle-class affair, the 2013 Turkish uprising was a popular revolt deriving from grievances expressed in terms of rights, freedom and democracy, and against oppression and dictatorship.

These grievances were not the products merely of the Gezi Park project, but of years of government policies and authoritarianism. The number of political protests was already on the rise all over the country before the Gezi uprising. Yörük and Yüksel documented some sixty political protests in July 2012, more than a hundred each month between September and December 2012, 150 in January 2013, over 200 in March, 250 in May and over 400 in the 'hot June' of 2013. These protests included thousands of Kurdish prisoners on hunger strike, Alevis discriminated against by the sectarian policies of the government, feminist groups opposing the new abortion law, strikes by workers, LGBTQ activists protesting against hate crimes, environmental activists opposing proposed nuclear and hydroelectric plants, secularists, students, football fans – all these groups were already mobilized for months on different agendas, opposing the government's projects and divisive rhetoric, engaging in street fights with the police. What Gezi did was to bring them all together in an uprising against the government.

Therefore, although the 2013 uprising was not planned or organized by any urban group or social movement, it did not happen independently of them either. There were already a growing number of protests against the government's projects, authoritarian interventions and conservative agenda in the years leading to the uprising. The skills and know-how acquired by activists during these struggles came in handy. So the unprecedented extent and diversity of the 2013 uprising were already in the making in the previous months. Political protests were on the rise with movements of resistance against the government's projects, authoritarian interventions and conservative agenda. However, the fact that rage erupted over an urban redevelopment project is significant, and shows how the unrestrained use of urban space for profit had become a source of grievance.[47]

The Turkish uprising was, like the others we saw, spontaneous in the sense that it was not planned or organized in advance. It was an eruption of pent-up rage against interventions in urban space, environment and lifestyles by an increasingly authoritarian government trying to impose its Islamist morals and practices on the one hand, and selling public land for profit on the other. This is not to suggest that activists and previous movements against such projects were not present; they were, and they took on important leadership and organizing roles once rage had erupted in the streets. But they were not the ones who planned for this to happen. Indeed, resistance to the Gezi Park project had started months before the uprisings, in the autumn of 2011, with such slogans as 'Occupy Istanbul' and 'Rebel Istanbul'. Organized through social media, this movement produced some meetings, but these remained modest, and did not turn into an occupation, let alone rebellion. It was police violence and the inflammatory language of officials that triggered the eruption of rage that had been simmering over the years.

There were signs of grievances produced by the AKP government's socially conservative and authoritarian policies and practices, as well as by what was generally perceived as the plundering of the urban environment with no regard for citizen rights, due process or environmental issues, abuses driven merely by profit and the desire for extravagant image-making. The AKP has been quite successful in consolidating a regime of governance characterized by market-oriented property development and mediated by Islamic codes of conduct. Gezi Park was the last drop in the up of growing resentment and urban resistance. 'Capital out! Gezi Park is ours,' chanted the protestors. Some clever graffiti in Istanbul suggested that the recent ban on alcohol had resulted in the sobering up of the people (the Turkish word for sobering up also means 'waking up to something').

While Erdoğan and his followers hoped the people of Turkey would find peace in Islam, millions found it in *isyan* – revolt – as the graffiti that opens this section suggests. '*Huzur isyanda*' is a play on the popular Islamist slogan '*Huzur Islamda*', which means 'one finds peace in Islam', suggesting that one finds peace in revolt.

The response of the authorities, however, was far from peaceful, despite the fact that most of the participants were pacific. The uprising was countered with police violence, with extensive use of tear gas, water cannons, plastic bullets and beatings to disperse the protestors. This police violence has a long history and was not unique to the 2013 revolt – and this is the third point I want to emphasize. As Amnesty International observed, the state's response to the 2013 uprising was 'a continuation of long standing patterns of human rights abuses in Turkey; the denial of the right to peaceful assembly, excessive use of force by police officers and the prosecution of legitimate dissenting opinions while allowing police abuses to go unchecked'.[48] Police officers, both in uniform and plain clothed, and civilians giving them a hand, beat many protestors – one, as we saw, to death. Doctors helping the injured protestors, journalists reporting on the incidents and lawyers providing legal advice also received their share of police beatings. Several women detained by the police reported sexual harassment, and some assault, by police officers.

According to figures provided by the government, 130,000 tear-gas canisters were used during the first twenty days of the uprising alone. This was equivalent to a year's supply, and in August, the government ordered 400,000 more canisters, almost tripling the amount compared to its previous annual orders. The police crackdown during Ethem Sarısülük's funeral on 16 June was equally out of proportion. On that single day, the police fired about 5,000 gas canisters on 20,000 protestors in the centre of Ankara – one tear-gas canister for every four protestors.[49] Water cannons were also used extensively by the police. High-pressure water itself caused injuries, but the nature of some of the injuries caused further concern. The governor of Istanbul eventually admitted that 'medication' had been added to the water, but claimed that it did not contain any chemicals. There is a strong tradition of herbal medicine in Turkey, of course, but it is hard to conjure up images of Turkish police adding herbs to water cannons. Moreover, some protestors suffered skin irritation and first-degree burns after being exposed to said medicinal water. Unless it was too much of a good thing, it was clear that chemical irritants had been added in generous quantities to the water in the cannons.[50]

The 2013 Turkish uprising exposed the sources of urban rage that went beyond Gezi Park. Particularly chilling was the degree and targeted nature of police violence, as the deaths showed, suggesting a link between patterns of authoritarian urban intervention and patterns of police brutality. Let me conclude with an anecdote from an urban transformation project in the Başıbüyük neighbourhood in Istanbul, which was developed as *gecekondu* in the 1950s but came to the attention of TOKI in the early 2000s because of its favourable hilltop location. TOKI's attempt to impose an urban transformation project was met with resistance, and led to violent clashes between the residents and the police. TOKI ended up building six sixteen-storey towers in less than a year on what was the central park of the neighbourhood. Some of the housing units in these blocks were allocated to police officers as subsidized housing, and residents alleged that some of the officers who moved there were on active duty during the clashes. This allegation was supported by none other than TOKI's director, illustrating the government's approach to opposition: 'We prepared a project.... But construction couldn't start as local people were against us. So we sold flats to policemen in the area, and told them "protect us". This meant that construction could at last begin.'[51]

Ironically, the towers built by TOKI were themselves as illegal as the buildings it wanted demolished; they were built while the project was still being reviewed in the administrative court, which ruled that it violated public interest and principles of urban planning, and had to be stopped. But this way of proceeding is the norm rather than the exception in Turkey. Even its president's palace was built in this way, on top of a hill.

8

Ghosts of Stories

During the 1985 Handsworth uprising in Birmingham, a journalist approached a middle-aged black woman to get some local insight for the story he was writing about it. 'There are no stories in the riots,' she said to him, 'only the ghosts of other stories.'[1] Urban uprisings, however, are not enigmatic occurrences.

We have seen what those other stories are about: exclusion, deprivation, discrimination, stigmatization and police violence. We have also seen how these stories have been reduced to what I called a pathological framework in the official responses to the uprisings that insists on the flaws of human nature.[2] This was the case after the 1985 Handsworth riots and others that followed as well. The UK government was once again at pains to dissociate uprisings from the deprivation and material difficulties its policies had done much to aggravate. In the House of Commons, the home secretary claimed that defective human nature and criminality were behind these incidents.[3]

Recourse to the pathological framework to condemn urban uprisings is a typical reaction by the authorities, as we have seen in case after case. But the ghosts of stories behind them suggest that the participants in uprisings are not natural-born criminals, and that each revolt is bound up with grievances over different forms of exclusion. Once we have understood that, we will be better equipped to realize that bullets, batons, dogs, water cannon and tear gas might not be the best of responses.

Urban uprisings are manifestations of urban rage produced by policies and practices that shape and regulate urban space (planning laws, housing policies, private investors, public institutions, job and housing markets, police practices and so on). The participants in the uprisings are almost always, though not exclusively, as we saw with the Greek and Turkish cases, those who are most hurt by these, by the way urban space is organized, transformed and policed. They are the ones who bear the burden of urban change and development without benefiting from its advantages.

All the urban uprisings we have explored had stigmatized areas of cities marked by discriminatory police action as their epicentre. One exception to this was the Turkish case, where the uprising was triggered over the redevelopment project of a park in central Istanbul, although the tipping point came, again, with police action. But closer examination of the Turkish uprising showed that stigmatized neighbourhoods peripheral to this park and in other cities were areas simmering with anger over police brutality and top-down redevelopment projects. They were the sites where confrontations were most intense, police violence most targeted. The Turkish example is also peculiar in another way: the largest anti-government uprising the country has known in its modern history occurred in a context of immense popular support for the government. The government has since continued with its divisive policies, and the crackdown since 2013, intensified following the failed military coup in 2016, has steered the country towards authoritarianism. If a free press, an independent judiciary and political opposition are the hallmarks of liberal democracies that serve as checks and balances against abuses of power, then Turkey no longer looks like one.

Despite differences between and within the countries we have surveyed, we find at the source of urban rage different forms of exclusion in a context of putative equality. To go back to the birdcage metaphor we saw in chapter 1, there are many related factors that systematically produce such exclusions, although the wires of the birdcage are not the same for each city and for each historical context. Inner-city displacement in Cincinnati is not the same as suburbanization of poverty in US metropolitan areas, though related. These are very different from stigmatized suburban estates in France and Sweden, which are also different from each other in many ways, not least including the former's colonial legacy. The polarization of wealth and poverty in London is unmatched in any other city we have seen, but economic deprivation and increasing inequalities are common to the uprisings (even in the Turkish one, which was inaccurately characterized as an elite middle-class affair by commentators who focused exclusively on Gezi Park in Istanbul). 'Race' is a catalyst in most uprisings, but not in all, although it is never altogether absent either. Discrimination and stigmatization are major sources of grievance behind all the examples of urban rage we have looked at, though their sources are not always the same, ranging from racism to religious identities or political orientation. Brutal and discriminatory policing is a source of rage across the board; so is the exclusion of urban dwellers from the decisions and processes that transform their living spaces, such as top-down projects or gentrification.

Although urban uprisings are products of justified rage, I am not trying to suggest that rage is an emancipatory sentiment; it is destructive, including for those involved. But rather than demonizing those involved, we need to be attentive to what enrages them. Their rage is justified as it follows from systematic injustices, not from one-off incidents that can be chalked up to a few bad apples. This is most obvious in relation to police violence. As we have seen with our examples, the problem goes beyond a matter of a few rogue officers, and has its sources in policy choices that pit citizens and the police against each other, such as zero-tolerance approaches, heavy surveillance of stigmatized areas, use of policing to generate income and the increasing use of militarized police forces, rather than democratic procedures, to address dissent and resistance. There is a difference between violence during uprisings – the violence of desperation – and violence that leads to uprisings – the violence of oppression. The former is episodic, the latter systematic, routinely produced through the everyday workings of cities, the police, institutions, housing and job markets, and social interactions in contexts marked by discrimination and racism.

While urban uprisings do contain elements of violence, this violence can be put into perspective rather than dismissed as criminal or pathological once we get a sense of other forms of violence that are at their origins. This is why I propose a shift from a pathological to a political framework for understanding them. Urban uprisings are marked by violence but, as we have seen, they are products of violence as well. They are political because they expose the sources and geographies of legitimate grievances, including injuries of the past, difficulties of the present and anxieties about the future. And the traces of injuries, the ghosts of stories remain. On 14 June 2016, another protest in central Paris against the labour law reform turned violent. Shop windows were smashed, walls were covered with graffiti. One of them read: 'Zyed and Bouna. Rest in peace'.

As we have seen, people do not revolt at the slightest frustration. Urban rage accumulates over time, and erupts when other means for addressing grievances prove futile. As a community activist in Baltimore put it after the 2015 uprising:

We've been down in Annapolis [state capital of Maryland], we've been at the city council, trying to get reforms. We've pursued every one of the avenues we're told to pursue in order to see changes come about. And we've gotten nothing significant. It's unfortunate that only after buildings were burned and cars were smashed, only then did people start listening.[4]

Revolt is a spectacular mode of public appeal to justice, equality and accountability when other forms of appeal prove useless. Urban uprisings, in this sense, are the ultimate form of dissent by the disenfranchised in a context of putative equality.

This brings me to my final point about liberal democracies. That such incidents have occurred and recurred at such unprecedented scale and intensity speaks to the failure of these regimes to address the exclusion of their most vulnerable populations from the processes that affect their lives. These are mature democracies, some of them the most mature the world has known. They operate under conditions of formal equality, with their elections regularly and properly held, parliaments in session and government institutions working according to rules (apart from the occasional corruption scandal). Yet there is a tension between the image – or illusion – of equality that these democracies formally uphold and the empirical inequalities that lead to urban rage and erupt in uprisings. Something, somewhere will erupt when the established institutions fail, as they do, to address exclusion and denials of equality. And when that happens, we would do well to view it with the dignity of politics rather than as a pathological aberration to be dealt with through use of harsh crackdown measures. For it is significant that none of these democratic regimes was able to address urban rage in non-coercive ways. As Tef Poe, a Ferguson rapper, put it during the 2014 uprising: 'I voted for Barack Obama twice, and still got tear-gassed'.

Notes

1 Rage in the Urban Age

1. UN-Habitat, *State of the World's Cities 2012/2013*, v.
2. Although I focus on urban uprisings as expressions of urban rage, we should note that this is not the only way rage is expressed. The feeling of disenfranchisement that has erupted as urban uprisings has also led to Brexit, English Defence League and the growth of other extreme-right groups, the election of Trump, popular support for despots, and, alas, terrorist massacres, which are other expressions of rage. See, for example, Pankaj Mishra, 'Welcome to the age of anger', *The Guardian*, 8 December 2016; Roger Cohen, 'The rage of 2016', *New York Times*, 5 December 2016.
3. Some of the urban uprisings explored here occurred in places that are technically suburbs – Ferguson in the US, Clichy-sous-Bois in France, Husby in Sweden. They, however, are all products of urbanization policies and patterns, and thus inseparable parts of cities (we will see, for example, in the next chapter how the transformation of Ferguson was inextricably linked to urban policies of the city of St Louis).
4. Readers will notice that although I mainly use the term uprising to refer to eruptions of urban rage, I also employ other terms such as revolt and riot depending on the context. One reason for this is to avoid repetition. More importantly, however, these eruptions carry elements of what all these terms suggest: they are acts of rising up against authority (the police, the government) – which is what the terms uprising and revolt connote. They, however, also involve violent disorder or ritualized violence, property destruction or looting – stuff that is more closely associated with the term riot. As we will see, the incidents I focus on in this book bring together features associated with all of these terms. They all start as acts of rebellion, of rising up against authority, and they all involve violent disorder. But, as we will see, it is hard to dissociate the rebellious aspect from the disorderly one. I want to keep in focus that these are acts of defiance, and such acts involve unruly practices; they are violent, but they are also responses to violence.
5. Nancy Fraser, *Justice Interruptus: Critical Reflections on the 'Postsocialist' Condition* (New York: Routledge, 1997); Iris Marion Young, *Inclusion and Democracy* (Oxford: Oxford

219

University Press, 2000). The epigraph is from Stuart Hall, 'Urban unrest in Britain', in John Benyon and John Solomos, eds, *The Roots of Urban Unrest* (Oxford: Pergamon Press, 1987), 48.

6. Young, *Inclusion and Democracy*; Fraser, *Justice Interruptus*; Jean-Philippe Deranty and Emmanuel Renault, 'Democratic agon: striving for distinction or struggle against domination and injustice?', in Andrew Schaap, ed., *Law and Agonistic Politics* (Farnham: Ashgate, 2009), 43–56; Martin Wolf, *The Shifts and the Shocks* (London: Allen Lane, 2014).

7. OECD, *Divided We Stand: Why Inequality Keeps Rising* (Paris: OECD, 2011); Thomas Piketty, *Capital in the Twenty-first Century* (Cambridge, MA: Harvard University Press, 2014).

8. Kate Driscoll Derickson, 'The racial state and resistance in Ferguson and beyond', *Urban Studies*, 53, no. 11 (2016): 2223–37; Don Mitchell, Kafui Attoh, Lynn Staeheli, '"Broken windows is not the panacea": common sense, good sense, and police accountability in American cities', in Jordan T. Camp and Christina Heatherton, eds, *Policing the Planet: Why the Policing Crisis Led to Black Lives Matter* (London: Verso, 2016), 237–57; Paul Routledge, 'Introduction: cities, justice and conflict', *Urban Studies*, 47, no. 6 (2010): 1165–77.

9. Ernesto Laclau, *On Populist Reason* (London: Verso, 2005). Historical research into riots, and research on the US urban uprisings of the 1960s showed this pathological interpretation to be empirically inaccurate. See George Rudé, *The Crowd in History* (London: Serif, 2005 [1964]); Gary Marx, 'Issueless riots', *Annals of the American Academy of Political and Social Science*, 391, no. 1 (1970): 21–33; Michael Haas, 'Metaphysics of paradigms in political science: theories of urban unrest', *Review of Politics*, 48, no. 4 (1986): 520–48; Steven I. Wilkinson, 'Riots', *Annual Review of Political Science*, 12 (2009): 329–43.

10. Alain Locke, *The Works of Alain Locke*, ed. Charles Molesworth (Oxford: Oxford University Press, 2012), 307; Don Mitchell, 'Introduction: the lightning flash of revolt', in Neil Smith and Don Mitchell, eds, *Revolting New York* (Athens, GA: University of Georgia Press, forthcoming). I owe the Locke description to this chapter. See also Andy Merrifield, *The Politics of the Encounter: Urban Theory and Protest under Planetary Urbanisation* (Athens, GA: University of Georgia Press, 2013); Byron Miller and Walter Nicholls, 'Social movements in urban society: the city as a space of politicisation', *Urban Geography*, 34, no. 4 (2013): 452–73; Margit Mayer, Catharina Thörn and Håkan Thörn, eds, *Urban Uprisings: Challenging Neoliberal Urbanism in Europe* (London: Palgrave, 2016).

11. James Baldwin, 'A report from occupied territory', *The Nation*, 11 July 1966.

12. Ferdinand Sutterlüty, 'The hidden morale of the 2005 French and 2011 English riots', *Thesis Eleven*, 121, no. 1 (2014): 38–56; Michael Keith, *Race, Riots and Policing: Lore and Disorder in a Multi-racist Society* (London: UCL Press, 1993).

13. Carole Cadwalladr, 'The man accused of starting the 2011 riots – and what he did next', *The Guardian*, 26 June 2016.

14. Mark Townsend, 'Five years after the riots, tension in Tottenham has not gone away', *The Guardian*, 31 July 2016.

15. The birdcage metaphor is from Marilyn Frye's writings on the systematic nature of oppression: Marilyn Frye, *The Politics of Reality: Essays in Feminist Theory* (Berkeley: Crossing Press, 1983).

16. Anmol Chaddha and William Julius Wilson, '"Way down in the hole": systemic urban inequality and The Wire', *Critical Inquiry*, 38, no. 1 (2011): 164–88; William Julius Wilson, *The Truly Disadvantaged: The Inner City, the Underclass, and Public Policy*, 2nd edn (Chicago: University of Chicago Press, 2012).

17. John Eligon, 'Milwaukee's unrest was no shock to some residents', *International New York Times*, 16 August 2016, 5.
18. David Harvey, *The New Imperialism* (Oxford: Oxford University Press, 2003).
19. Stephen Graham, *Cities under Siege: The New Military Urbanism* (London: Verso, 2010).
20. Judith Shklar, *The Faces of Injustice* (New Haven, CT: Yale University Press, 1990), 49.
21. Martin Fletcher, 'The sad truth behind London riot', NBC News, 7 August 2011, http://worldblog.nbcnews.com/_news/2011/08/07/7292281-the-sad-truth-behind-london-riot (last accessed 2 May 2017).

2 Fatal Encounters in US Cities

1. Joanna Walters, 'Troops referred to Ferguson protestors as "enemy forces", emails show', *The Guardian*, 17 April 2015.
2. We will see that most of the publicized incidents involve black males. This should not make us neglect, however, the grievances of black girls and women. In Cincinnati, for example, activists talked about police officers routinely raping black women. A *New York Times* article recently reported on this problem when a former Oklahoma City police officer was found guilty of raping black women, targeting those with criminal backgrounds so that their stories would not be believed. See Dave Philipps, 'Former Oklahoma City Police Officer Found Guilty of Rapes', *New York Times*, 10 December 2015. As Treva B. Lindsey observes, 'Black women and girls occupied a marginal space in most discussion about Black violability, despite being on the frontlines of protests against anti-Black state violence occurring across the nation.' See Treva B. Lindsey, 'Post-Ferguson: A "herstorical" approach to black violability', *Feminist Studies*, 41, no. 1 (2015): 235.
3. Molly W. Metzger, *Section 8 in the St. Louis Region: Local Opportunities to Expand Housing Choice* (Washington University in St. Louis: Center for Social Development, 2014).
4. Colin Gordon, *Mapping Decline: St. Louis and the Fate of the American City* (Philadelphia: University of Pennsylvania Press, 2008); Richard Rothstein, *The Making of Ferguson: Public Policies at the Root of Its Troubles* (Washington DC: Economic Policy Institute, 2014).
5. Elizabeth Kneebone, 'Ferguson, Mo. Emblematic of growing suburban poverty', Brookings Institute blog, 15 August, available at http://www.brookings.edu/blogs/the-avenue/posts/2014/08/15–ferguson-suburban-poverty.
6. Sasha Abramsky, *The American Way of Poverty: How the Other Half Still Lives* (New York: Nation Books, 2013).
7. Peter Edelman, *So Rich, So Poor: Why It's So Hard to End Poverty in America* (New York: The New Press, 2012).
8. Sean F. Reardon and Kendra Bischoff, 'Growth in the residential segregation of families by income, 1970–2009', report prepared for Project US2010 (2011); John R. Logan and Brian Stults, 'The persistence of segregation in the metropolis: new findings from the 2010 census', census brief prepared for Project US2010 (2011).
9. Elizabeth Kneebone and Emily Garr, *The Suburbanization of Poverty: Trends in Metropolitan America, 2000 to 2008* (Brookings Metropolitan Policy Program, 2010).
10. Rothstein, *The Making of Ferguson*.
11. http://www.stltoday.com/news/local/metro/why-did-the-michael-brown-shooting-happen-here/article_678334ce-500a-5689-8658-f548207cf253.html (last accessed 26 April 2017).
12. Unless otherwise stated, this section is based on this report: Department of Justice (DoJ), *Investigation of the Ferguson Police Department*, United States Department of

Justice, Civil Rights Division, 4 March 2015. The epigraphs are from this report, pages 13 and 12 respectively.

13. *City of Ferguson, Missouri, Comprehensive Annual Financial Report for the Year Ended June 30, 2014.*

14. *City of Ferguson, Missouri, Annual Operating Budget, Fiscal Year 2015–2016.*

15. DoJ, *Investigation of the Ferguson Police Department*, pages 10 and 2.

16. Ferguson Municipal Code defined 'Manner of walking along roadway' as the following: '(a) Where sidewalks are provided, it shall be unlawful for any pedestrian to walk along and upon an adjacent roadway; (b) Where sidewalks are not provided, any pedestrian walking along and upon a highway shall, when practicable, walk only on the left side of the roadway or its shoulder facing traffic which may approach from the opposite direction' (Secs. 44–344). This was eventually repealed in April 2016.

17. ArchCity Defenders, *Municipal Courts White Paper* (St Louis, 2014).

18. Jon Swaine, 'Ferguson judge behind aggressive fines policy owes $170,000 in unpaid taxes', *The Guardian*, 6 March 2015.

19. http://fox2now.com/2014/08/11/video-protester-justifies-the-looting-in-ferguson/ (last accessed 30 November 2016).

20. '$3-million settlement accepted in police raid', *Los Angeles Times*, 6 February 1990; 'The raid that still haunts L.A.', *Los Angeles Times*, 14 March 2001; Mike Davis, *City of Quartz: Excavating the Future in Los Angeles* (New York: Vintage, 1992).

21. Janet Abu-Lughod, *Race, Space, and Riots in Chicago, New York, and Los Angeles* (Oxford: Oxford University Press, 2007); Mike Davis, 'Uprising and repression in L.A.', in Robert Gooding-Williams, ed., *Reading Rodney King/Reading Urban Uprising* (New York: Routledge, 1993), 142–54; Paul Ong and Evelyn Blumenberg, 'Income and racial inequality in Los Angeles', in Allen Scott, ed., *The City: Los Angeles and Urban Theory at the End of the Twentieth Century* (Berkeley: University of California Press, 1998), 311–35.

22. Melvin L. Oliver et al., 'Anatomy of a rebellion: a political-economic analysis', in Gooding-Williams, ed., *Reading Rodney King/Reading Urban Uprising*, 117–41; Jeremy Travis, Bruce Western and Steve Redburn, eds, *The Growth of Incarceration in the United States* (Washington DC: National Research Council, 2014), 2; Elizabeth Hinton, *From the War on Poverty to the War on Crime: The Making of Mass Incarceration in America* (Cambridge, MA: Harvard University Press, 2016). Hinton shows that the support for this punitive approach was bipartisan and had a longer history. Although Reagan made law enforcement much more punitive in the 1980s with an extraordinary expansion of urban police forces, court cases and prison populations, this was the culmination of earlier policies since the civil rights era, rather than a novel approach that marked the beginning of our contemporary militarized and intrusive policing practices.

23. Cited in Robert M. Fogelson, 'Violence and grievances: reflections on the 1960s', *Journal of Social Forces*, 26, no. 1 (1970): 157.

24. Michael Omi and Howard Winant, 'The Los Angeles "race riot" and contemporary U.S. politics', in Gooding-Williams, ed., *Reading Rodney King/Reading Urban Uprising*, 97–114.

25. Oliver et al., 'Anatomy of a rebellion'.

26. Abu-Lughod, *Race, Space, and Riots*.

27. David B. Oppenheimer, 'California's anti-discrimination legislation, Proposition 14, and the constitutional protection of minority rights', *Golden Gate University Law Review*, 40 (2010): 117–27.

28. Abu-Lughod, *Race, Space, and Riots*. For a detailed account, see Robert Conot, *Rivers of Blood, Years of Darkness* (New York: Bantam Books, 1967).

29. Robert M. Fogelson, 'White on black: a critique of the McCone Commission report on the Los Angeles riots', *Political Science Quarterly*, 82, no. 3 (1967): 337–67; *Violence in the City – An End or A Beginning? A Report by the Governor's Commission on the Los Angeles Riots*, 2 December 1965 (the 'McCone Report').

30. Davis, *City of Quartz*.

31. *Report of the Independent Commission on the Los Angeles Police Department*, 1991 (the 'Christopher Commission report').

32. Amnesty International, *Torture, Ill-Treatment and Excessive Force by Police in Los Angeles, California* (New York: Amnesty International, 1992).

33. Michelle Cottle, 'Did integration cause the Cincinnati riots?', *New Republic*, 7 May 2001: 26–9.

34. Expert report of Cecil L. Thomas, United States District Court, Southern District of Ohio, Western Division, Case No. C-1-99–317; Cottle, 'Did integration cause the Cincinnati riots?'.

35. Dan P. Moore, *Mark Twain was Right: The 2001 Cincinnati Riots* (Lansing: Microcosm Publishing, 2012); '2001: A timeline', *Cincinnati Enquirer*, 30 December 2001.

36. Alice Skirtz, *Econocide: Elimination of the Urban Poor* (Washington DC: NASW Press, 2012).

37. Thomas A. Dutton, '"Violence": in Cincinnati', *The Nation*, 18 June 2001; 'Appeals for peace in Ohio after two days of protests', *New York Times*, 12 April 2001.

38. Preliminary technical assistance recommendations to improve the Cincinnati Division of Police, Letter from Steven H. Rosenbaum, Chief, Special Litigation Section, Department of Justice, 23 October 2001.

39. 'Curfew restores calm', *Cincinnati Enquirer*, 13 April 2001.

40. The prosecutors, however, failed to obtain a conviction after four trials, and the remaining charges were eventually dropped. See Baynard Woods, 'Remaining charges dropped against police officers in Freddie Gray case', *The Guardian*, 27 July 2016.

41. Anjali Kamat, 'The Baltimore uprising', in Jordan T. Camp and Christina Heatherton, eds, *Policing the Planet: Why the Policing Crisis Led to Black Lives Matter* (London: Verso, 2016), 73–82.

42. 'Undue force', *Baltimore Sun*, 28 September 2014; 'Freddie Gray not the first to come out of Baltimore police van with serious injuries', *Baltimore Sun*, 23 April 2015.

43. https://www.washingtonpost.com/news/wonk/wp/2015/04/28/these-two-maps-show-the-shocking-inequality-in-baltimore/ (last accessed 30 November 2016); 'Baltimore leaders agree: city has a race problem', *Baltimore Sun*, 14 March 2015.

44. 'As Baltimore mayor, critics say, O'Malley's police tactics sowed distrust', *Washington Post*, 25 April 2015; 'Arrests for minor crimes spur resentment in some Baltimore neighborhoods', *Baltimore Sun*, 23 August 2015.

45. 'Appeals for peace in Ohio after two days of protests', *New York Times*, 12 April 2001; 'Why Freddie Gray ran', *Baltimore Sun*, 25 April 2015. Brandon Ross quote is from Kamat, 'The Baltimore uprising', 77.

46. Charles M. Blow, 'America's problem with policing', *International New York Times*, 27 September 2016, 7. See also Deborah Cowen and Nemoy Lewis, 'Anti-blackness and urban geopolitical economy: reflections on Ferguson and the suburbanisation of the "internal colony"' (2016), available at http://societyandspace.org/2016/08/02/anti-blackness-and-urban-geopolitical-economy-deborah-cowen-and-nemoy-lewis/

3 Of Seditions and Troubles in the UK

1. S. Reicher, 'The St. Pauls' riot: an explanation of the limits of crowd action in terms of a social identity model', *European Journal of Social Psychology*, 14 (1984): 1–21.

2. Home Office, *An Overview of Recorded Crimes and Arrests Resulting from Disorder Events in August 2011* (London: Home Office, 2011), Table A9; Home Office Statistical Bulletin, *The Outcome of Arrests During the Serious Incidents of Public Disorder in July and August 1981*, 13 October 1982 (available at the National Archives, reference HO 496/16). The remark on the St Pauls uprising is cited in Reicher, 'The St. Pauls' riot', 15.

3. *The Guardian*/LSE, *Reading the Riots: Investigating England's Summer of Disorder* (London, 2011), 24–5.

4. Ibid., 24.

5. *The Guardian*/LSE, *Reading the Riots*; Juta Kawalerowicz and Michael Biggs, 'Anarchy in the UK: economic deprivation, social disorganization, and political grievances in the London riot of 2011', *Social Forces*, 94, no. 2 (2015): 673–98.

6. Home Office, *An Overview of Recorded Crimes and Arrests*; Matthew Taylor et al., 'England rioters: young, poor and unemployed', *The Guardian*, 18 August 2011.

7. Katie Allen, 'UK unemployment hits 17-year high', *The Guardian*, 14 December 2011; Office for National Statistics, Statistical Bulletin, 'Public sector employment, Q3 2011'; NGO contributors and Runnymede, *Joint Submission by UK NGOs Against Racism to the UN Committee on the Elimination of Racial Discrimination* (London: The Runnymede Trust, 2011).

8. Office for National Statistics, *Persistent Poverty in the UK and EU, 2008–2013* (London, 2015); Emma Downing and Steven Kennedy, *Food Banks and Food Poverty* (House of Commons Library, 2014); Niall Cooper, Sarah Purcell and Ruth Jackson, *Below the Breadline: The Relentless Rise of Food Poverty in Britain* (London: Church Action on Poverty, Oxfam, The Trussell Trust, 2014).

9. PSE, *The Impoverishment of the UK: PSE UK First Results* (2013; see PSE website: www.poverty.ac.uk); Juliette Garside, 'Recession rich: Britain's wealthiest double net worth since crisis', *The Guardian*, 26 April 2015.

10. Benjamin Hennig and Danny Dorling, 'The hollowing out of London: how poverty patterns are changing', *New Statesman*, 13 March 2015.

11. The quotes in this paragraph are from Mark Townsend, 'Five years after the riots, tension in Tottenham has not gone away', *The Guardian*, 31 July 2016.

12. Alexandra Topping, 'Trouble isn't over yet, says teenager who predicted riots', *The Guardian*, 12 August 2011. The video is available at https://www.theguardian.com/society/video/2011/jul/31/haringey-youth-club-closures-video.

13. Tom Slater, 'From "criminality" to marginality: rioting against a broken state', *Human Geography*, 4, no. 3 (2011): 106–15.

14. Her Majesty's Inspectorate of Constabulary (HMIC), *Adapting to Protest: Nurturing the British Model of Policing* (London: The Stationery Office, 2009).

15. *Hansard*, House of Commons, 23 October 1985, column 359.

16. IPCC Press Notice, 'Release of information in early stages of Mark Dugan inquiry', 12 August 2011. See also Home Affairs Committee, *Policing Large Scale Disorder: Lessons From the Disturbances of August 2011* (London: The Stationery Office, 2011) and Ojeaku Nwabuzo, *The Riot Roundtables: Race and the Riots of August 2011* (London: Runnymede Trust, 2012), 7.

17. For Godwin's statement, see Home Affairs Committee, *Policing Large Scale Disorder*, paragraph 14. For codes of practice, see National Policing Improvement Agency, *Family Liaison Officer Guidance* (2008), 67.

18. Home Affairs Committee, *Policing Large Scale Disorder*, paragraph 12.

19. Home Affairs Committee, *Independent Police Complaints Commission* (London: The Stationery Office, 2013), paragraphs 15 and 13.

20. His Honour Judge Keith Cutler, *Report to Prevent Future Deaths. Inquest into the Death of Mark Duggan*, 29 May 2014, Her Majesty's Coroner. The quotes are from paragraphs 75, 66 and 64.

21. 'The investigation of Mark Duggan's death is tainted. I want no part in it', *The Guardian*, 20 November 2011.

22. Symeon Brown, 'Were the Tottenham riots sparked by the beating of a 16-year-old girl?', *The Guardian*, 7 December 2011.

23. In a letter sent to the families of Sean Rigg and Olaseni Lewis, two black males who died in police custody in 2008 and 2010. The IPCC initially cleared officers implicated in these deaths. An inquest exposed the flaws in the IPCC's Rigg investigation and the High Court quashed the IPCC's first investigation of the Lewis case and made them start a fresh inquiry. See Vikram Dodd, 'Theresa May admits justice system fails families over deaths in police custody', *The Guardian*, 19 April 2015.

24. Her Majesty's Inspectorate of Constabulary, *Without Fear or Favour: A Review of Police Relationships* (London: The Stationery Office, 2011).

25. INQUEST is a charity that monitors deaths in police custody. Their data are derived through monitoring and casework, and can be accessed on their website at http://inquest.org.uk/site/home (accessed 31 July 2015). See also the evidence provided by Deborah Coles, Co-Director of INQUEST, to the Home Affairs Committee report, *Independent Police Complaints Commission* (2013), Ev 15. The quote from the report is in paragraph 34.

26. Home Affairs Committee, *Policing Large Scale Disorder*, paragraph 11.

27. Ben Bowling and Coretta Phillips, 'Disproportionate and discriminatory: reviewing the evidence on police stop and search', *Modern Law Review*, 70, no. 6 (2007): 936–61. The opening epigraph is from Alpa Parmar, 'Stop and search in London: counter-terrorist or counter-productive?', *Policing & Society*, 21, no. 4 (2011): 377.

28. Her Majesty's Inspectorate of Constabulary, *Stop and Search Powers: Are the Police Using Them Effectively and Fairly?* (London: The Stationery Office, 2013), 3.

29. George Greaves, 'The Brixton disorders', in John Benyon, ed., *Scarman and After: Essays Reflecting on Lord Scarman's Report, the Riots and Their Aftermath* (Oxford: Pergamon Press, 1984), 63–72.

30. Philip Stevens and Carole Willis, *Race, Crime and Arrests* (London: Her Majesty's Stationery Office, 1979).

31. Cited in Lord Scarman, *The Scarman Report: The Brixton Disorders 10–12 April 1981* (Harmondsworth: Penguin, 1982), paragraph 4.39.

32. Greaves, 'The Brixton disorders'.

33. Chris Hamnett, 'The conditions in England's inner cities on the eve of the 1981 riots', *Area*, 15, no. 1 (1983): 7–13.

34. Colin Brown, *Black and White Britain: The Third PSI Survey* (Aldershot: Gower, 1984).

35. Paul Gilroy, *There Ain't No Black in the Union Jack: The Cultural Politics of Race and Nation* (London: Routledge, 1987).

36. Cited in David Smith and Jeremy Gray, *Police and People in London IV: The Police in Action* (London: Policy Studies Institute, 1983), 116. As Smith and Gray show, this joke circulated not only among police officers on the street, but among senior officers as well. A year after the Brixton uprisings, Sir Kenneth Newman, Commissioner of the Metropolitan Police and one of the founders of Scotland Yard's Community Relations Branch, was interviewed by the American *Police Magazine*. He said: 'In the Jamaicans, you have a people who are constitutionally disorderly. It's simply in their make-up. They are constitutionally disposed to be anti-authority.' Kenneth later denied the remarks, arguing that the journalist who conducted the interview had distorted his words. But

the journalist himself stated that he was 'quite certain' that was what Sir Kenneth had said. Cited in John Clare, 'Eyewitness in Brixton', in John Benyon, ed., *Scarman and After*, 52.

37. Section 8, *Criminal Attempts Act 1981* (London: Her Majesty's Stationery Office, 1981).
38. Parmar, 'Stop and search in London'. In addition to its disproportionate use against certain groups, Section 44 was also controversial for its (mis)use in harassing photographers in public spaces, in London especially. See the Statewatch analysis at http://www.statewatch.org/analyses/no-105-uk-section-44.pdf (accessed 27 April 2017).
39. Vikram Dodd and Alan Travis, 'Muslims face increased stop and search', *The Guardian*, 2 March 2005; Alan Travis, 'Anti-terror stop and search powers to be scrapped', *The Guardian*, 8 July 2010. Blears resigned in 2009 after her involvement in the MP expenses scandal.
40. This 'nine times out of ten' seems to be the standard statistical myth to justify discrimination. In their 1983 study of the police, Smith and Gray found that some police officers justified stopping black people in cars by arguing that they would find drugs nine times out of ten, even though the actual figures showed that only 3 per cent of stops led to an arrest and charge. The senior policeman's comments in the epigraph are from this study. See Smith and Gray, *Police and People in London IV*, 129.
41. William Macpherson, *The Stephen Lawrence Inquiry* (London: Home Office, 1999), paragraph 6.50. This report on the investigation of the murder of a young black male was the first official document to conclude that the police force was marked by 'institutional racism'.
42. Anna Clancy et al., *Crime, Policing and Justice: The Experience of Ethnic Minorities Findings from the 2000 British Crime Survey* (London: Home Office, 2001).
43. MVA and Joel Miller, *Profiling Populations Available for Stops and Searches* (London: Home Office, 2000), quotes from pages 84 and 87.
44. Metropolitan Police Authority (MPA), *Report of the MPA Scrutiny on MPS Stop and Search Practice* (London: MPA, 2004), paragraphs 248 and 250; Home Office, *Stop and Search Manual* (London: Home Office, 2005), 5; Home Affairs Committee, *Young Black People and the Criminal Justice System* (London: The Stationery Office, 2007), 303.
45. Bowling and Phillips, 'Disproportionate and discriminatory', 961.
46. The figures presented in this section are from Home Office stop and search statistics for corresponding financial years.
47. Ministry of Justice, *Statistics on Race and the Criminal Justice System 2012* (London, 2013).
48. Karen Hurrell, *Race Disproportionality in Stops and Searches, 2011–12* (Manchester: Equality and Human Rights Commission, 2013); Alan Travis, 'Theresa May announces reform of police stop-and-search powers', *The Guardian*, 30 April 2014.
49. *Hansard*, House of Commons, 11 August 2011: column 1060 for Tapsell's question and Cameron's response.
50. https://www.gov.uk/government/speeches/pms-speech-on-the-fightback-after-the-riots, delivered on 15 August 2011 (accessed 3 July 2016).
51. *Hansard*, House of Commons, 6 July 1981, 'Disturbances' (Southall and Liverpool); *Hansard*, House of Commons, 09 July 1981, vol. 8, column 575; *Hansard*, House of Commons, 13 April 1981, column 25.
52. Cited in John Benyon and John Solomos, eds, *The Roots of Urban Unrest* (Oxford: Pergamon Press, 1987), 11 and 165–6.
53. Home Affairs Committee, *Policing Large Scale Disorder*, paragraph 24. Cameron quote is from his speech to Parliament, *Hansard*, House of Commons, 11 August 2011, column 1054.
54. Home Affairs Committee, *Policing Large Scale Disorder*, paragraph 24; *The Guardian/ LSE*, *Reading the Riots*, 21. The official numbers on estimated gang affiliation are from

Home Office, *An Overview of Recorded Crimes and Arrests Resulting from Disorder Events in August 2011* (London: Home Office, 2011).
55. Response of Tim Godwin, then Acting Commissioner of the Metropolitan Police, to the Home Affairs Committee, *Policing Large Scale Disorder*, paragraph 20.
56. Claudia Rankine, *Citizen: An American Lyric* (London: Penguin Books, 2015), 116.
57. Ferdinand Sutterlüty, 'The hidden morale of the 2005 French and 2011 English riots', *Thesis Eleven*, 121, no. 1 (2014): 38–56.
58. *Hansard*, House of Commons, 11 August 2011, column 1075.
59. *Hansard*, House of Commons, 13 April 1981, vol. 3, column 28.
60. Prime Minister, 'Scarman Inquiry', 2 November 1981, National Archives reference PREM-19–1521_150.jpg.
61. *Hansard*, House of Commons, 23 October 1985, column 355.
62. *Inquiries Act 2005* (London: The Stationery Office), paragraph 21.
63. Riots Communities and Victims Panel, *After the Riots: The Final Report of the Riots Communities and Victims Panel* (London, 2012), 6.
64. Home Affairs Committee, *Policing Large Scale Disorder*, paragraph 18.
65. Home Office Statistical Bulletin, *The Outcome of Arrests*.
66. Brian Bell, Laura Jaitman and Stephen Machin, 'Crime deterrence: evidence from the London 2011 riots', *Economic Journal*, 124, no. 576 (2014): 480–506.

4 The Algerian War is Not Over in France

1. Mustafa Dikeç, *Badlands of the Republic: Space, Politics and Urban Policy* (London: Blackwell, 2007), 144.
2. Derek Gregory, *The Colonial Present: Afghanistan, Palestine, Iraq* (London: Blackwell, 2004). This is also the interpretation of some of the activists in the *banlieues*.
3. Pierre-Yves Cusset et al., 'Jeunes issus de l'immigration: quels obstacles à leur insertion économique?', Note d'analyse, France Stratégie, March 2015; INSEE, *Données sociales. La société française* (Paris: INSEE, 2006). France Stratégie is an economic research and strategy unit that reports to the prime minister. INSEE is the national statistics bureau.
4. For BAC, see Mathieu Rigouste, *La domination policière: une violence industrielle* (Paris: La fabrique, 2012). For an account of what happened that day, see Ariane Chemin, 'Le dernier jour de Bouna Traoré et Zyed Benna', *Le Monde*, 7 December 2005.
5. Michel Kokoreff, *Sociologie des émeutes* (Paris: Payot, 2008).
6. Jean-Pierre Mignard and Emmanuel Tordjman, *L'affaire Clichy* (Paris: Stock, 2006).
7. See Muhittin's account in *Libération*, 'Muhittin, rescapé de Clichy, donne sa version', 16 December 2005.
8. For Mechmache's account, see Almamy Kanouté et al., '2005, pour rien? Analyses d'acteurs', *Mouvements*, 83 (2015): 50–62; and Mohamed Mechmache, 'Les révoltes de 2005, une prise de conscience politique', *Mouvements*, 83 (2015): 17–21. See also the eyewitness account provided by Antoine Germa, 'Clichy-sous-Bois: zone de non-droits ou zone d'injustices?' (2005), available at http://lmsi.net/Clichy-sous-Bois-zone-de-non (last accessed 11 March 2016).
9. Laurent Mucchielli and Abderrahim Aït-Omar, 'Les émeutes de novembre 2005: les raisons de la colère', in Véronique Le Goaziou and Laurent Mucchielli, eds, *Quand les banlieues brûlent . . .* (Paris: La Découverte, 2006), 5–30.
10. Michel Mazars, *Le traitement judicaire des « violences urbaines » de l'automne 2005: le cas de la Seine-Saint-Denis* (Document de travail, Centre d'analyse stratégique, 2007).
11. 'Le rapport qui contredit Sarkozy', *Libération*, 8 December 2005.
12. 'Nouveaux incidents à Montfermeil et Clichy-sous-Bois, en Seine-Saint-Denis', *Le Monde*, 31 May 2006.

13. Lorraine Millot, 'Beaucoup de ces Africains sont polygames …', *Libération*, 15 November 2005.
14. Martin Arnold, 'French minister says polygamy to blame for riots', *Financial Times*, 15 November 2005; Luc Bronner, 'M. Larcher fait le lien entre polygamie et violences urbaines', *Le Monde*, 16 November 2005; Denis Jeambar, 'Nicolas Sarkozy contre-attaque', *L'Express*, 17 November 2005.
15. Achille Mbembe, 'The Republic and its beast: on the riots in the French *banlieues*', in Charles Tshimanga et al., eds, *Frenchness and the African Diaspora: Identity and Uprisings in Contemporary France* (Bloomington: Indiana University Press, 2009), 49.
16. Pierre Tévanian, 'A conservative revolution within secularism: the ideological premises and social effects of the March 15, 2004 "anti-headscarf" law', in Tshimanga et al., eds, *Frenchness and the African Diaspora*, 199; Pierre Tévanian, *Chronique du racisme républicain* (Paris: Editions Syllepse, 2013).
17. Houria Bouteldja, 'L'autonomie des minorités comme préalable et objectif politique' (interview), *Mouvements*, 83 (2015): 22–8.
18. Nicolas Bancel, 'The law of February 23, 2005: the uses made of the revival of France's "colonial grandeur"', in Tshimanga et al., eds, *Frenchness and the African Diaspora*, 167–83.
19. Saïd Bouamama, 'Base matérielle, fonction économique et enjeux politiques du racisme respectable', postface to Tévanian, *Chronique du racisme républicain*; Sadri Khiari, *La contre-révolution coloniale en France: de de Gaulle à Sarkozy* (Paris: La fabrique, 2009).
20. Saïd Bouamama, 'Transmettre l'histoire de nos luttes' (interview), *Mouvements*, 83 (2015): 154–65; Saïd Bouamama, 'L'expérience politique des Noirs et des Arabes en France: mutations, invariances et récurrences', in Rafik Chekkat and Emmanuel D. Hoch, eds, *Race Rebelle: Luttes des quartiers populaires des années 1980 à nos jours* (Paris: Editions Syllepse, 2011), 29–45.
21. Saïd Bouamama, *Les classes et quartiers populaires: paupérisation, ethnicisation et discrimination* (Paris: Editions du Cygne, 2009); Sadri Khiari, *Pour une politique de la racaille: immigré-e-s, indigènes et jeunes de banlieues* (Paris: Textuel, 2006); Pierre Tévanian, *Le ministère de la peur* (Paris: L'esprit frappeur, 2003). The quote is from Mogniss H. Abdallah, *Rengainez, on arrive!* (Paris: Libertalia, 2012), 15.
22. Stefan Kipfer, 'Neocolonial urbanism? La rénovation urbaine in Paris', *Antipode*, 48, no. 3 (2016): 603–25.
23. Dikeç, *Badlands of the Republic*.
24. Mbembe, 'The Republic and its beast', 53.
25. Alec Hargreaves, 'An emperor with no clothes?', http://riotsfrance.ssrc.org/Hargreaves/ (2005) (last accessed 16 March 2016).
26. Michelle Zancarini-Fournel, 'Généalogie des rébellions urbaines en temps de crise (1971–1981)', *Vingtième Siècle. Revue d'histoire*, 84 (2004): 119–27. Unless otherwise stated, my account of the 1970s is based on this article, from where the epigraphs are also taken. See also Abdellali Hajjat, 'Rébellions urbaines et déviances policières', *Cultures & Conflits*, 93 (2014): 11–34.
27. Abdelkader Belbahri, 'Les Minguettes ou la surlocalisation du social', *Espaces et sociétés*, 45 (1984): 101–8; Adil Jazouli, *Les années banlieues* (Paris: Seuil, 1992).
28. For more on this policy, see Dikeç, *Badlands of the Republic*.
29. Zancarini-Fournel, 'Généalogie des rébellions urbaines'.
30. Laurent Bonelli, *La France a peur* (Paris: La Découverte, 2008); Laurent Mucchielli, *Violences et insécurité: fantasmes et réalités dans le débat français* (Paris: La Découverte, 2001).
31. 'Chère répression', *Libération*, 11 July 2002.
32. 'Le plus grand recul des droits de l'homme depuis l'Algérie', *Libération*, 25 May 2004.
33. Henri Leclerc, 'Libertés publiques: l'année horrible', in Ligue des droits de l'Homme, *L'état des droits de l'Homme en France* (Paris: La Découverte, 2004), 27.

34. Emmanuel Davidenkoff, 'Trois mesures phares', *Libération*, 8 November 2005.
35. Hugues Lagrange, 'Emeutes, ségrégation urbaines et aliénation politique', *Revue française de science politique*, 58, no. 3 (2008): 377–401.
36. 'Politique de la ville: Borloo vend ses maisons', *Libération*, 24 February 2005.
37. Kipfer, 'Neocolonial urbanism?'; Stefan Kipfer, 'Tackling urban apartheid: report from the Social Forum of Popular Neighbourhoods in Paris', *International Journal of Urban and Regional Research*, 33, no. 4 (2009): 1058–66. The programme is called Programme Nationale de Rénovation Urbaine, and the government agency that oversees it is the Agence Nationale pour la Rénovation Urbaine (ANRU).
38. INSEE, *Données sociales* (2006). Both epigraphs are from complaints filed with HALDE (*Haute autorité de lutte contre les discriminations*), included in its 2010 report, *Rapport annuel HALDE 2010* (Paris: La Documentation française), 38. HALDE was the Anti-discrimination and Equality Commission, created in 2004, dissolved in 2011.
39. Cusset et al., 'Jeunes issus de l'immigration'.
40. For an overview, see Dikeç, *Badlands of the Republic*.
41. Laurent Mucchielli, 'Autumn 2005: a review of the most important riot in the history of French contemporary society', *Journal of Ethnic and Migration Studies*, 35, no. 5 (2009): 731–51.
42. INSEE-DIV, no date, *Fiches Profil – Quartiers de la politique de la ville: Données des recensements de la population de 1990 et 1999* (CD-ROM); Observatoire national des zones urbaines sensibles (ONZUS), *Rapport 2009* and *Rapport 2013* (Saint-Denis: CIV); Agnès Jeannet, Laurent Caillot and Yves Calvez, *L'accès à l'emploi des jeunes de quartiers prioritaires de la politique de la ville* (Inspection générale des affaires sociales, 2010).
43. INSEE, *Immigrés et descendants d'immigrés en France* (Paris: INSEE, 2012).
44. Cusset et al., 'Jeunes issus de l'immigration'.
45. 'Les contrôles d'identité abusifs aggravent les tensions dans les cités', *Le Monde*, 20 April 2002.
46. Human Rights Watch, *'The Root of Humiliation': Abusive Identity Checks in France* (2012). The epigraphs that open this section are from this report, pages 1 and 10 respectively.
47. Dikeç, *Badlands of the Republic*.
48. Maurice Rajsfus, *La police et la peine de mort: 1977–2001=196 morts* (Paris: L'Esprit frappeur, 2002); Ivan du Roy and Ludo Simbille, *Homicides, accidents, « malaise », légitime défense: 50 ans de morts par la police*, www.bastamag.net, 13 March 2014.
49. Collectif Angles Morts, 'Permis de tuer', in *Permis de tuer: chronique de l'impunité policière* (Paris: Editions Syllepse, 2014), 7–17.
50. Amnesty International, *France: The Search for Justice* (London: Amnesty International Publications, 2005), 3.
51. Report by Mr Alvaro Gil-Robles, commissioner for human rights, *On the Effective Respect for Human Rights in France*, following his visit from 5 to 21 September 2005, paragraph 180
52. Lucie Bony, 'La prison, "une cité avec des barreaux"' (2016), interview, available at https://blogs.mediapart.fr/observatoire-international-des-prisons-section-francaise/blog/180816/la-prison-une-cite-avec-des-barreaux.
53. Iman Amrani and Angelique Chrisafis, 'Adama Traoré's death in police custody casts long shadow over French society', *The Guardian*, 17 February 2017; Angelique Chrisafis, 'French police brutality in spotlight again after officer charged with rape', *The Guardian*, 6 February 2017.
54. Amnesty International, *France: The Search for Justice*, 3.
55. Bouamama, 'Transmettre l'histoire de nos luttes'.

56. Amnesty International, *Public Outrage: Police Officers Above the Law in France* (London: Amnesty International Publications, 2009).
57. Collectif Angles Morts, *Vengeance d'Etat: Villiers-le-Bel* (Paris: Editions Syllepse, 2011).
58. 'Sarkozy, à droite dans ses bottes', *Libération*, 21 November 2005.
59. 'Parfois, la violence a du bon', *Le Canard enchaîné*, 11 April 2007, 8.
60. Amnesty International, *Upturned Lives: The Disproportionate Impact of France's State of Emergency* (London: Amnesty International Publications, 2016); Human Rights Watch, 'France: abuses under state of emergency' (2016), available at https://www.hrw.org/news/2016/02/03/france-abuses-under-state-emergency.

5 Even in Sweden

1. Cited in Allan Pred, *Even in Sweden: Racisms, Racialized Spaces, and the Popular Geographical Imagination* (Berkeley: University of California Press, 2000), 2.
2. Polly Toynbee, 'The most successful society the world has ever known', *The Guardian*, 25 October 2005.
3. Johan Ehrenberg and Sten Ljunggren, *Ekonomihandboken*, available at http://ekonomi-handboken.se; Bengt Larsson, Martin Letell and Håkan Thörn, eds, *Transformations of the Swedish Welfare State: From Social Engineering to Governance?* (London: Palgrave, 2012); Catharina Thörn, 'The Stockholm uprising and the myth of Swedish social democracy', *New Left Project*, 30 May 2013; 'The challenges of the Swedish model', *Financial Times*, 26 May 2013.
4. Parents are theoretically free to send their children to schools of their choice rather than strictly to local ones. This, however, requires resources (for example, time and money to drive children to school and back) and networks, which puts poorer families, especially if they are immigrants, at a disadvantage. Moreover, the private school sector, like the labour and housing markets in Sweden, is not immune from discrimination on a class or racial basis.
5. 'Sweden: The new model', *The Economist*, 13 October 2012.
6. 'A Nordic pyramid', *The Economist*, 12 March 2016.
7. OECD, *Divided We Stand: Why Inequality Keeps Rising* (Paris: OECD, 2011), including January 2015 update.
8. Eurostat; http://www.unric.org/en/youth-unemployment/27411–sweden-highest-ratio-of-youth-unemployment (accessed 10 July 2016).
9. Sally Weale, '"It's a political failure": how Sweden's celebrated schools system fell into crisis', *The Guardian*, 10 June 2015.
10. http://www.oecd.org/sweden/sweden-should-urgently-reform-its-school-system-to-improve-quality-and-equity.htm (accessed 10 July 2016); OECD, *Improving Schools in Sweden: An OECD Perspective* (Paris: OECD, 2015).
11. Lisa Kings, Aleksandra Ålund and Carl-Ulrik Schierup, 'Revolt of the urban periphery: Sweden's riots in context', *New Left Project*, 2 June 2013.
12. The scale of investment was huge, which led some scholars to argue that the programme was not merely a response to the housing shortage, but also a way to channel the post-war accumulation of capital to avoid a possible crisis. See Karin Grundström and Irene Molina, 'From Folkhem to lifestyle housing in Sweden: segregation and urban form, 1930s–2010s', *International Journal of Housing Policy*, 16, no. 3 (2016): 316–36.
13. Per-Markku Ristilammi, 'Alterity in modern Sweden', *Pro Ethnologia*, 4 (1996): 74.
14. Pred, *Even in Sweden*; Joachim Vogel, 'Urban segregation in Sweden', *Social Indicators Research*, 27, no. 2 (1992): 139–55.
15. Roger Andersson, 'Reproducing and reshaping ethnic residential segregation in Stockholm: the role of selective migration moves', *Geografiska Annaler: Series B. Human Geography*, 95, no. 2 (2013): 165.

16. Vanessa Barker, 'Policing difference', in Ben Bradford et al., eds, *The SAGE Handbook of Global Policing* (London: SAGE, 2016), 211–25; Andersson, 'Reproducing and reshaping ethnic residential segregation in Stockholm'.

17. Irene Molina, *Stadens rasifiering: Etnisk boendesegregation i folkhemmet*, Geografiska regionstudier, 32 (Uppsala, 1997).

18. For Rosengård, see Ristilammi, 'Alterity in modern Sweden'; for Gottsunda, see Molina, *Stadens rasifiering*.

19. Karin Hedin et al., 'Neoliberalisation of housing in Sweden: gentrification, filtering, and social polarisation', *Annals of the Association of American Geographers*, 102, no. 2 (2012): 443–63.

20. Brett Christophers, 'A monstrous hybrid: the political economy of housing in early twenty-first century Sweden', *New Political Economy*, 18, no. 6 (2013): 885–911; Ove Sernhede, Catharina Thörn and Håkan Thörn, 'The Stockholm uprising in context: urban social movements in the rise and demise of the Swedish welfare-state city', in Margit Mayer et al., eds, *Urban Uprisings: Challenging Neoliberal Urbanism in Europe* (Palgrave: London, 2016), 149–73.

21. Christophers, 'A monstrous hybrid'.

22. Roger Andersson and Anneli Kährik, 'Widening gaps: segregation dynamics during two decades of economic and institutional change in Stockholm', in Tiit Tammaru et al., eds, *Socio-economic Segregation in European Capital Cities: East Meets West* (London: Routledge, 2016), 110–31.

23. Hedin et al., 'Neoliberalisation of housing in Sweden'.

24. Anders Lindbom, 'Dismantling Swedish housing policy', *Governance: An International Journal of Policy and Administration*, 14, no. 4 (2001): 503–26.

25. Irene Molina and Sara Westin, 'Renoviction – even in Sweden', paper presented at the Association of American Geographers annual conference, 24–28 February 2012, New York.

26. 'House of horrors, part 2', *The Economist*, 26 November 2011.

27. 'Special report: the Nordic countries', *The Economist*, 2 February 2013.

28. Vogel, 'Urban segregation in Sweden'.

29. Ristilammi, 'Alterity in modern Sweden'; for Gottsunda, see Molina, *Stadens rasifiering*.

30. Pred, *Even in Sweden*.

31. For a detailed account that also includes extensive interviews with the perpetrator of these crimes, see Mattias Gardell, *Ras-Krigaren: Seriemördaren Peter Mangs* (Stockholm: Leopard förlag, 2015).

32. Per Olof Hallin, Alban Jashari, Carina Listerborn and Margareta Popoola, *Det är inte stenarna som gör ont. Röster från Herrgården, Rosengård – om konflikter och erkännande* (Malmö: Malmö Publikationer i Urbana Studier, 2010).

33. 'Another side of Malmö's infamous Rosengård', *The Local*, 2 March 2012, http://www.thelocal.se/20120302/39450.

34. Carl-Ulrik Schierup and Aleksandra Ålund, 'The end of Swedish exceptionalism? Citizenship, neoliberalism and the politics of exclusion', *Race & Class*, 53, no. 1 (2011): 45–64.

35. Ristilammi, 'Alterity in modern Sweden'.

36. http://megafonen.com/ayna-varfor-dom-finns-lognen-om-husby-mordet-igar/ (accessed 10 July 2016).

37. Ove Sernhede, 'Youth rebellion and social mobilisation in Sweden', *Soundings*, 56 (2014): 81–91. For food riots during the First World War, see, for example, 'Food riots in Sweden', *New York Times*, 7 May 1917.

38. Statistik om Stockholm, available at http://www.statistikomstockholm.se (accessed 10 July 2016).

39. I use a slightly modified version of the translation by Carl-Ulrik Schierup, Aleksandra Ålund and Lisa Kings, 'Reading the Stockholm riots – a moment for social justice?', *Race & Class*, 55, no. 3 (2014): 4. The original is available at http://megafonen.com/ayna-varfor-dom-finns-lognen-om-husby-mordet-igar/.

40. Ove Sernhede, 'School, youth culture and territorial stigmatisation in Swedish metropolitan districts', *Young*, 19, no. 2 (2011): 170.

41. Dennis Beach and Ove Sernhede, 'From learning to labour to learning for marginality: school segregation and marginalisation in Swedish suburbs', *British Journal of Sociology of Education*, 32, no. 2 (2011), 269.

42. Roger Andersson et al., *Large Housing Estates in Sweden*, RESTATE report (Utrecht University: Faculty of Geosciences, 2003).

43. Regeringskansliet, *Urbana utvecklingsområden. Statistisk uppföljning utifrån 7 indikationer* (Stockholm: Arbetsmarknadsdepartementet, 2013).

44. Guy Baeten et al., 'Pressure and violence: housing renovation and displacement in Sweden', *Environment and Planning A* (forthcoming); CRUSH, *Tretton myter om bostadsfrågan* (Årsta: Dokument press, 2016).

45. Stockholms stad, *Skillnadernas Stockholm* (Stockholm: Kommissionen för ett socialt hållbart Stockholm, 2015).

46. Grundström and Molina, 'From Folkhem to lifestyle housing in Sweden'.

47. Paulina de los Reyes et al., *Bilen brinner . . . men problemen är kvar. Berättelser om Husbyhändelserna i maj 2013* (Stockholm: Stockholmia, 2014).

48. Stefan Lisinski, 'Varannan polis som åtalas för våld går fri', *Dagens Nyheter*, 18 July 2013.

49. The text was originally published in the Stockholm paper *Dagens Nyheter* on 13 March 2013. It was translated into English by Rachel Willson-Broyles, and is available at http://www.asymptotejournal.com/nonfiction/jonas-hassen-khemiri-an-open-letter-to-beatrice-ask/. A version of the text was also published in 'Sweden's closet racists', *New York Times*, 20 April 2013.

50. Vanessa Barker, 'On Bauman's moral duty: population registries, REVA and eviction from the Nordic realm', in Anna Eriksson, ed., *Punishing the Other: The Social Production of Immorality Revisited* (London: Routledge, 2015), 184–207.

51. Pär Karlsson, 'Ny kritik mot Reva-projektet', *Aftonbladet*, 1 March 2013, http://www.aftonbladet.se/nyheter/article16337183.ab.

52. Frida Sundkvist, '9 av 10 i polisens id-jakt har rätt att vistas här', 25 February 2013, http://www.metro.se/nyheter/9–av–10–i–polisens–id–jakt–har–ratt–att–vistas–har/EVHmby!PMA3fueKtO7g2/.

53. Johanna Langhorst, 'Husby: polisen håller i nyckeln', 21 May 2013, https://feministisktperspektiv.se/2013/05/21/husby-polisen-haller-i-nyckeln/.

54. Brottsförebyggande rådet (Brå), *Diskriminering i rättprocessen. Om missgynnande av personer med utländsk bakgrund* (Stockholm: Brottsförebyggande rådet, 2008).

55. Carlos Rojas and Marlena Batist, *Förtroendet för polisen i Sveriges miljonprogram* (Stockholm: MIKLO, 2013).

56. Maria Ferm, *En stärkt polis*, Motion till riksdagen, 2014/15:1376, 7 November 2014.

57. Masoud Kamali, *Sverige inifrån. Röster om etnisk diskriminering* (Stockholm: Statens Offentliga Utredningar, 2005).

58. Les Back et al., 'Husby and territorial stigma in Sweden', *openDemocracy*, 10 June 2013; Baeten et al., 'Pressure and violence'.

6 Days of Rage in Greece

1 . John Karamichas, 'The December 2008 riots in Greece', *Social Movement Studies*, 8, no. 3 (2009): 289–93; Peter Bratsis, 'Legitimation crisis and the Greek explosion',

International Journal of Urban and Regional Research, 34, no. 1 (2010): 190–96; Panagiotis Sotiris, 'Reading revolt as deviance: Greek intellectuals and the December 2008 revolt of Greek youth', *Interface*, 5, no. 2 (2013): 47–77; Ed Vulliamy and Helena Smith, 'Children of the revolution', *The Guardian*, 22 February 2009.

2. Bratsis, 'Legitimation crisis and the Greek explosion', 193.
3. Stathis Kouvelakis, 'La Grèce en révolte' (2008), http://www.contretemps.eu/interventions/stathis-kouvelakis-grece-en-revolte (accessed 12 February 2016).
4. Yiannis Kaplanis, 'An economy that excludes the many and an "accidental" revolt', in Antonis Vradis and Dimitris Dalakoglou, eds, *Revolt and Crisis in Greece* (Oakland: AK Press & Occupied London, 2011), 215–28.
5. Kouvelakis, 'La Grèce en révolte'.
6. Eleni Portaliou, 'Social resistance movements against the Olympic Games 2004 in Athens', paper presented at Annual Meeting of International Network of Urban Research and Action, 2008.
7. Vaso Makrygianni and Haris Tsavdaroglou, 'Urban planning and revolt: a spatial analysis of the December 2008 uprising in Athens', in Vradis and Dalakoglou, eds, *Revolt and Crisis in Greece*, 29–57; Athina Arampatzi and Walter Nicholls, 'The urban roots of anti-neoliberal social movements: the case of Athens, Greece', *Environment and Planning A*, 44, no. 11 (2012): 2591–610.
8. Portaliou, 'Social resistance movements against the Olympic Games 2004 in Athens'; Josephine Iakovidou, Kostas Kanellopoulos and Loukia Kotronaki, 'The Greek uprising of December 2008', *Situations*, 3, no. 2 (2010): 145–57; Rania Astrinaki, "'(Un)hooding a rebellion', *Social Text*, 27, no. 4 (2009): 97–107.
9. Eurostat, accessed 12 February 2016.
10. Police could not enter universities in Greece. The 'university asylum' law was introduced in 1982, eight years after the fall of military dictatorship, to protect freedom of thought and expression. In 2011, however, this law was scrapped, and many of the reforms proposed in 2006 were approved by the parliament.
11. Spyros Dritsas and Giorgos Kalampokas, 'The first big wave: 2006–07', in Clare Solomon and Tania Palmieri, eds, *Springtime: The New Student Rebellions* (London: Verso, 2011), 213–18; Amnesty International, *Police Violence in Greece: Not Just 'Isolated Incidents'* (London: Amnesty International, 2012).
12. Bratsis, 'Legitimation crisis and the Greek explosion'.
13. Iakovidou, Kanellopoulos and Kotronaki, 'The Greek uprising of December 2008'. *Koukouloforoi* are those wearing hoods or balaclavas during demonstrations, and the term was used pejoratively by mainstream media to evoke an archetypal image of violent protestors.
14. Vulliamy and Smith, 'Children of the revolution'.
15. Iakovidou, Kanellopoulos and Kotronaki, 'The Greek uprising of December 2008'.
16. Andreas Kalyvas, 'An anomaly? Some reflections on the Greek December 2008', *Constellations*, 17, no. 2 (2010): 351–65; Loukia Kotronaki and Seraphim Seferiades, 'Sur les sentiers de la colère: l'espace-temps d'une révolte', *Actuel Marx*, 48 (2010): 152–65.
17. Stavros Stavrides, 'The December 2008 youth uprising in Athens: spatial justice in an emergent city of thresholds', *justice spatiale | spatial justice*, 2 (2010), http://www.jssj.org.
18. Reproduced in Solomon and Palmieri, *Springtime*, 235–6.
19. Kalyvas, 'An anomaly?', 356.
20. Amnesty International, *Greece: Alleged Abuses in the Policing of Demonstrations* (London: Amnesty International, 2009).
21. Sotiris, 'Reading revolt as deviance'; Costas Douzinas, *Philosophy and Resistance in the Crisis* (Cambridge: Polity, 2013).

22. Kalyvas, 'An anomaly?', 353.
23. Reproduced in Solomon and Palmieri, *Springtime*, 237–8.
24. Douzinas, *Philosophy and Resistance in the Crisis*, 151.
25. Eirini Gaitanou, 'The December explosion', in Solomon and Palmieri, *Springtime*, 222 and 224.
26. Albanian Migrants' Haunt (2008), 'Our share of these days!', https://clandestinenglish. wordpress.com/2008/12/19/our-share-of-these-days/#more-239 (accessed 19 February 2016).
27. Kalyvas, 'An anomaly?'
28. Cited in Vulliamy and Smith, 'Children of the revolution'.
29. Cited in ibid.
30. Cited in Vradis and Dalakoglou, eds, *Revolt and Crisis in Greece*.

7 Young Turks Find Peace in Revolt

1. Jean-François Pérouse, 'Hybristanbul: Turkey's urban development boom', *booksandideas*, 3 February 2014, available at http://www.booksandideas.net/Hybristanbul-2560. html; Bülent Diken, 'The emancipated city: notes on Gezi revolts', *Journal for Cultural Research*, 18, no. 4 (2014): 315–28.
2. *Milliyet*, 'İşte Erdoğan'ın çılgın projesi', 27 April 2011, http://www.milliyet.com.tr/iste-erdogan-in-cilgin-projesi/siyaset/siyasetdetay/27.04.2011/1382967/default.htm; 'Bir toplantı 22 çılgın proje', *Sabah*, 2 June 2011, http://www.sabah.com.tr/ekonomi/2011/06/02/bir-toplanti-22-cilgin-proje.
3. 'Le nouveau palais présidentiel d'Erdogan « le grand »', *Le Figaro*, 29 October 2014, http://www.lefigaro.fr/international/2014/10/29/01003-20141029ARTFIG00306-le-nouveau-palais-presidentiel-d-erdogan-le-grand.php (last accessed 28 April 2017).
4. '3. Boğaz Köprüsü'nün temeli atildi', *Sabah*, 29 May 2013, http://www.sabah.com.tr/ekonomi/2013/05/29/3-bogaz-koprusunun-temeli-atiliyor.
5. 'Abbas welcomed at Turkish presidential palace by Erdoğan – and 16 warriors', *The Guardian*, 12 January 2015, https://www.theguardian.com/world/2015/jan/12/abbas-erdogan-16-warriors-turkish-presidential-palace (last accessed 28 April 2017).
6. Pérouse, 'Hybristanbul'.
7. For the Viaport Venezia project, see the promotional video here: https://www.youtube.com/watch?v=54d4L_7SQtU (last accessed 30 June 2016).
8. Ozan Karaman, 'Urban neoliberalism with Islamic characteristics', *Urban Studies*, 50, no. 16 (2013): 3412–27; Erbatur Çavuşoğlu and Julia Strutz, '"We'll come and demolish your house!" The role of spatial (re-)production in the neoliberal hegemonic politics of Turkey', in Ismet Akça, Ahmet Bekmen and Baris Alp Özden, eds, *Turkey Reframed: Constituting Neoliberal Hegemony* (London: Pluto Press, 2014), 141–53.
9. Seltem Iyigun, 'As Turkey's economy booms, deep inequality persists', *Reuters*, 28 November 2012, http://www.reuters.com/article/turkey-unemployment-idUSL5E8MGBB420121128.
10. Erdem Yörük and Murat Yüksel, 'Class and politics in Turkey's Gezi protests', *New Left Review*, 89 (2014): 103–23.
11. Fercan Yalınkılıç, 'İnsaat sektörünün kredileri bankalar için risk yaratabilir', *Wall Street Journal*, 28 February 2014.
12. Efe Can Gürcan and Efe Peker, *Challenging Neoliberalism at Turkey's Gezi Park: From Private Discontent to Collective Class Action* (London: Palgrave, 2015).
13. Çavuşoğlu and Strutz, '"We'll come and demolish your house!"'; Sinan Erensü and Ozan Karaman, 'The work of a few trees: Gezi, politics and space', *International Journal of Urban and Regional Research* (forthcoming).

14. Başbakan Erdoğan'in Milli İradeye Saygı Ankara Miting'inde yaptığı konuşmanın tam metni, 16 June 2013.
15. https://twitter.com/RT_Erdogan/status/348058441094406144 (last accessed 30 June 2016).
16. Ethemcan Turhan, 'What is in a park?', *Centre for Policy and Research on Turkey* (2013), available at http://researchturkey.org/?p=3337.
17. Erdoğan Bayraktar, 2 September 2013, http://www.haberturk.com/gundem/haber/874181–rant-olmazsa-ulke-kalkinmaz.
18. Konutder (2013), *Konut Sektörü Değerlendirme Sunumu*, available at http://konutder.org.tr/upload/raporlar/da34e3a5574e29e97e04d5d902b99572.pdf.
19. This account is based on Çavuşoğlu and Strutz, ' "We'll come and demolish your house!" ', and Ozan Karaman, 'Urban renewal in İstanbul: reconfigured spaces, robotic lives', *International Journal of Urban and Regional Research*, 37, no. 2 (2013): 715–33.
20. Harun Gürek, *AKP'nin Müteahhitleri* (Istanbul: Güncel Yayıncılık, 2008).
21. John Lovering and Hade Türkmen, 'Bulldozer neo-liberalism in İstanbul: the state-led construction of property markets, and the displacement of the urban poor', *International Planning Studies*, 16, no. 1 (2011): 73–96; Karaman, 'Urban renewal in İstanbul'.
22. Erdogan Bayraktar, 13 November 2007, 'Kentsel dönüşümü tamamlayamazsak terörü de bitiremeyiz', http://www.mimdap.org/?p=2114.
23. Cited in Lovering and Türkmen, 'Bulldozer neo-liberalism in İstanbul', 84. PKK is the Kurdistan Workers' Party, currently in armed opposition to the Turkish state, which considers it a terrorist organization.
24. Çağlar Keyder, 'Globalisation and social exclusion in Istanbul', *International Journal of Urban and Regional Research*, 29, no. 1 (2005): 124–34.
25. Cited in Lovering and Türkmen, 'Bulldozer neo-liberalism in İstanbul', 88.
26. Gülçin Erdi Lelandais, 'Gezi protests and beyond: urban resistance under neoliberal urbanism in Turkey', in Margit Mayer, Catharina Thörn and Håkan Thörn, eds, *Urban Uprisings: Challenging Neoliberal Urbanism in Europe* (London: Palgrave, 2016), 283–308.
27. Osman Balaban, 'İnşaat sektörü neyin lokomotifi?', *Birikim*, 270 (2011): 19–26.
28. 'TOKI kentsel dönüşüme girdi', *Hürriyet*, 23 February 2011, http://www.hurriyet.com.tr/toki-kentsel-donusume-girdi-17088101.
29. '3. Boğaz Köprüsü'nün temeli atildi', *Sabah*, 29 May 2013, http://www.sabah.com.tr/ekonomi/2013/05/29/3–bogaz-koprusunun-temeli-atiliyor.
30. '1,845 Erdoğan insult cases opened in Turkey since 2014', *The Guardian*, 2 March 2016; 'Turkish court "orders Gollum study" in Erdogan case', *BBC News*, 1 December 2015; Melissa Eddy, 'Erdogan's attempt to suppress German satire has the opposite effect', *New York Times*, 30 March 2016.
31. Yörük and Yüksel, 'Class and politics in Turkey's Gezi protests'.
32. Fulya Ozerkan (2012), 'Turkey PM Recep Tayyip Erdogan sparks furor by saying he wants to "raise a religious youth"', http://news.nationalpost.com/news/turkey-pm-recep-tayyip-erdogan-sparks-furor-by-saying-he-wants-to-raise-a-religious-youth.
33. Efe Can Gürcan and Efe Peker, 'A class analytic approach to the Gezi Park events: challenging the "middle class" myth', *Capital & Class*, 39, no. 2 (2015): 321–43.
34. Eren Buğlalılar (2012), 'The prisoners of democracy AKP style in Turkey', http://mrzine.monthlyreview.org/2012/buglalilar030812.html; Eren Buğlalılar (2011), 'The epidemic of terrorism under Turkey's Mubarak', http://mrzine.monthlyreview.org/2011/buglalilar271211.html; Martha Mendoza (2011), 'AP IMPACT: 35,000 worldwide convicted for terror', http://www.cnsnews.com/news/article/ap-impact-35000-worldwide-convicted-terror-0 (last accessed 28 April 2017).

35. 'Egemen Bağış'tan Taksim protestolarıyla ilgili açıklama', *Hürriyet*, 16 June 2013, http://www.hurriyet.com.tr/egemen-bagistan-taksim-protestolariyla-ilgili-aciklama-23517868.
36. For data, see the websites of CPJ (Committee to Protect Journalists) and Reporters Without Borders Press Freedom Index, in particular the following: https://cpj.org/imprisoned/2013.php; https://cpj.org/reports/2015/12/china-egypt-imprison-record-numbers-of-journalists-jail.php; https://index.rsf.org/#!/index-details/TUR; Roy Greenslade, 'Record number of journalists in jail globally after Turkey crackdown', *The Guardian*, 13 December 2016.
37. Some of the most tweeted photographs can be seen here: http://onedio.com/haber/direnisin-sembolu-penguenler-119343 (last accessed 30 June 2016).
38. Amnesty International, *Gezi Park Protests: Brutal Denial of the Right to Peaceful Assembly in Turkey* (London: Amnesty International, 2013).
39. Amnesty International, *Adding Injustice to Injury: One Year on from the Gezi Park Protests in Turkey* (London: Amnesty International, 2014).
40. Cited in Amnesty International, *Gezi Park Protests*, 47.
41. Press release of the association dated 13 June 2013 is available here: http://www.ttb.org.tr/index.php/Haberler/hukuki-3862.html (last accessed 30 June 2016).
42. Amnesty International, *Gezi Park Protests*, 35.
43. Ayfer Karakaya-Stump (2014), 'Alevizing Gezi', *Jadaliyya*, http://www.jadaliyya.com/pages/index/17087/alevizing-gezi.
44. Erensü and Karaman, 'The work of a few trees'; Yaşar Adanalı, 'Tophane hızla dönüşüyor', 1 June 2015, http://t24.com.tr/haber/tophane-hizla-donusuyor,298369; Aslı Zengin, 'What is queer about Gezi?', *Cultural Anthropology*, 31 October 2013, http://www.culanth.org/fieldsights/407–what-is-queer-about-gezi.
45. 'Erdoğan: AKM yıkılacak, Taksim'e cami de yapılacak', *Radikal*, 2 June 2013.
46. 'Anti-capitalist Muslims' (*Antikapitalist Müslümanlar*) is a movement of devout Muslims who are outraged by the government's manipulation of Islam for its capitalist agenda.
47. Mehmet Barış Kuymulu, 'Reclaiming the right to the city: reflections on the urban uprisings in Turkey', *City*, 17, no. 3 (2013): 274–8; Yörük and Yüksel, 'Class and politics in Turkey's Gezi protests'; Gürcan and Peker, 'A class analytic approach to the Gezi Park events'; Ali Rıza Taşkale, 'There is another Turkey out there', *Third Text*, 30, nos 1–2 (2016): 138–46.
48. Amnesty International, *Gezi Park Protests*, 7.
49. Amnesty International, *Gezi Park Protests* and *Adding Injustice to Injury*.
50. 'Vali Mutlu: İlaçlı su, kimyasal değil', *NTV*, 16 June 2013, http://www.ntv.com.tr/turkiye/vali-mutlu-ilacli-su-kimyasal-degil,k91uUagIZ0i6ihzVcXIylg.
51. Cited in Lovering and Türkmen, 'Bulldozer neo-liberalism in İstanbul', 91.

8 Ghosts of Stories

1. Cited in *Handsworth Songs*, directed by John Akomfrah (1986). I am grateful to LUX Distribution for providing me access to this documentary.
2. John Benyon, 'Interpretations of civil disorder', in John Benyon and John Solomos, eds, *The Roots of Urban Unrest* (Oxford: Pergamon Press, 1987), 23–41.
3. *Hansard*, House of Commons, 23 October 1985, column 356.
4. Reverend Heber Brown, III, community activist in Baltimore, cited in Anjali Kamat, 'The Baltimore uprising', in Jordan T. Camp and Christina Heatherton, eds, *Policing the Planet: Why the Policing Crisis Led to Black Lives Matter* (London: Verso, 2016), 76.

Bibliography

The bibliography contains the main sources used in the writing of this book, as well as additional sources on urban politics and protest in general.

Abdallah, Mogniss H., *Rengainez, on arrive!* (Paris: Libertalia, 2012)

Abramsky, Sasha, *The American Way of Poverty: How the Other Half Still Lives* (New York: Nation Books, 2013)

Abu-Lughod, Janet, *Race, Space, and Riots in Chicago, New York, and Los Angeles* (Oxford: Oxford University Press, 2007)

Amnesty International, *Torture, Ill-Treatment and Excessive Force by Police in Los Angeles, California* (New York: Amnesty International, 1992)

—, *France: The Search for Justice* (London: Amnesty International, 2005)

—, *Greece: Alleged Abuses in the Policing of Demonstrations* (London: Amnesty International, 2009)

—, *Public Outrage: Police Officers Above the Law in France* (London: Amnesty International, 2009)

—, *Police Violence in Greece: Not Just 'Isolated Incidents'* (London: Amnesty International, 2012)

—, *Gezi Park Protests: Brutal Denial of the Right to Peaceful Assembly in Turkey* (London: Amnesty International, 2013)

—, *Adding Injustice to Injury: One Year on from the Gezi Park Protests in Turkey* (London: Amnesty International, 2014)

—, *Upturned Lives: The Disproportionate Impact of France's State of Emergency* (London: Amnesty International, 2016)

Andersson, Roger, 'Reproducing and reshaping ethnic residential segregation in Stockholm: the role of selective migration moves', *Geografiska Annaler: Series B. Human Geography*, 95, no. 2 (2013): 163–87

Andersson, Roger, et al., *Large Housing Estates in Sweden*, RESTATE report (Utrecht University: Faculty of Geosciences, 2003)

Andersson, Roger, and Anneli Kährik, 'Widening gaps: segregation dynamics during two decades of economic and institutional change in Stockholm', in Tiit Tammaru et al., eds, *Socio-economic Segregation in European Capital Cities: East Meets West* (London: Routledge, 2016), 110–31

Arampatzi, Athina, and Walter J. Nicholls, 'The urban roots of anti-neoliberal social movements: the case of Athens, Greece', *Environment and Planning A*, 44, no. 11 (2012): 2591–610

ArchCity Defenders, *Municipal Courts White Paper* (St Louis, 2014)

Arendt, Hannah, *The Life of the Mind*, vol. I *Thinking*, vol. II *Willing* (New York: Harcourt Brace Jovanovich, 1978)

Astrinaki, Rania, '(Un)hooding a rebellion', *Social Text*, 27, no. 4 (2009): 97–107

Back, Les, et al., 'Husby and territorial stigma in Sweden', *openDemocracy*, 10 June 2013

Baeten, Guy, et al., 'Pressure and violence: housing renovation and displacement in Sweden', *Environment and Planning A* (forthcoming)

Balaban, Osman, 'İnşaat sektörü neyin lokomotifi?', *Birikim*, 270 (2011): 19–26

Baldwin, James, 'A report from occupied territory', *The Nation*, 11 July 1966

Bancel, Nicolas, 'The law of February 23, 2005: the uses made of the revival of France's "colonial grandeur"', in Charles Tshimanga et al., eds, *Frenchness and the African Diaspora: Identity and Uprisings in Contemporary France* (Bloomington: Indiana University Press, 2009), 167–83

Barker, Vanessa, 'On Bauman's moral duty: population registries, REVA and eviction from the Nordic realm', in Anna Eriksson, ed., *Punishing the Other: The Social Production of Immorality Revisited* (London: Routledge, 2015), 184–207

—, 'Policing difference', in Ben Bradford et al., eds, *The SAGE Handbook of Global Policing* (London: SAGE, 2016), 211–25

Beach, Dennis, and Ove Sernhede, 'From learning to labour to learning for marginality: school segregation and marginalisation in Swedish suburbs', *British Journal of Sociology of Education*, 32, no. 2 (2011): 257–74

Belbahri, Abdelkader, 'Les Minguettes ou la surlocalisation du social', *Espaces et sociétés*, 45 (1984): 101–8

Bell, Brian, Laura Jaitman and Stephen Machin, 'Crime deterrence: evidence from the London 2011 riots', *Economic Journal*, 124, no. 576 (2014): 480–506

Benyon, John, ed., *Scarman and After: Essays Reflecting on Lord Scarman's Report, the Riots and Their Aftermath* (Oxford: Pergamon Press, 1984)

Benyon, John, and John Solomos, eds, *The Roots of Urban Unrest* (Oxford: Pergamon Press, 1987)

Bonelli, Laurent, *La France a peur* (Paris: La Découverte, 2008)

Bony, Lucie, 'La prison, "une cité avec des barreaux"' (2016), interview, available at https://blogs.mediapart.fr/observatoire-international-des-prisons-section-francaise/blog/180816/la-prison-une-cite-avec-des-barreaux (accessed 16 June 2016)

Bouamama, Saïd, *Les classes et quartiers populaires: paupérisation, ethnicisation et discrimination* (Paris: Editions du Cygne, 2009)

—, 'L'expérience politique des Noirs et des Arabes en France: mutations, invariances et récurrences', in Rafik Chekkat and Emmanuel D. Hoch, eds, *Race Rebelle: Luttes des quartiers populaires des années 1980 à nos jours* (Paris: Editions Syllepse, 2011), 29–45

—, 'Base matérielle, fonction économique et enjeux politiques du racisme respectable', postface to Pierre Tévanian, *Chronique du racisme républicain* (Paris: Editions Syllepse, 2013), 145–59

—, 'Transmettre l'histoire de nos luttes' (interview), *Mouvements*, 83 (2015): 154–65

Boudreau, Julie-Anne, *Global Urban Politics* (Cambridge: Polity Press, 2016)

Bouteldja, Houria, 'L'autonomie des minorités comme préalable et objectif politique' (interview), *Mouvements*, 83 (2015): 22–8

Bowling, Ben, and Coretta Phillips, 'Disproportionate and discriminatory: reviewing the evidence on police stop and search', *Modern Law Review*, 70, no. 6 (2007): 936–61

BIBLIOGRAPHY

Bratsis, Peter, 'Legitimation crisis and the Greek explosion', *International Journal of Urban and Regional Research*, 34, no. 1 (2010): 190–96

Brown, Colin, *Black and White Britain: The Third PSI Survey* (Aldershot: Gower, 1984)

Çavuşoğlu, Erbatur, and Julia Strutz, '"We'll come and demolish your house!" The role of spatial (re-)production in the neoliberal hegemonic politics of Turkey', in Ismet Akça, Ahmet Bekmen and Baris Alp Özden, eds, *Turkey Reframed: Constituting Neoliberal Hegemony* (London: Pluto Press, 2014), 141–53

Chaddha, Anmol, and William J. Wilson, '"Way down in the hole": systemic urban inequality and The Wire', *Critical Inquiry*, 38, no. 1 (2011): 164–88

Christophers, Brett, 'A monstrous hybrid: the political economy of housing in early twenty-first century Sweden', *New Political Economy*, 18, no. 6 (2013): 885–911

Clancy, Anna, et al., *Crime, Policing and Justice: The Experience of Ethnic Minorities: Findings from the 2000 British Crime Survey* (London: Home Office, 2001)

Coleman, Mat, 'State power in blue', *Political Geography*, 51, no. 1 (2016): 76–86

Collectif Angles Morts, *Vengeance d'Etat: Villiers-le-Bel* (Paris: Editions Syllepse, 2011)

—, *Permis de tuer: chronique de l'impunité policière* (Paris: Editions Syllepse, 2014)

Conde, Maite, and Tariq Jazeel, 'Kicking off in Brazil: manifesting democracy', *Journal of Latin American Cultural Studies*, 22, no. 4 (2013): 437–50

Conot, Robert, *Rivers of Blood, Years of Darkness* (New York: Bantam Books, 1967)

Cooper, Niall, Sarah Purcell and Sarah Jackson, *Below the Breadline: The Relentless Rise of Food Poverty in Britain* (London: Church Action on Poverty, Oxfam, The Trussell Trust, 2014)

Cottle, Michelle, 'Did integration cause the Cincinnati riots?', *New Republic*, 7 May 2001: 26–9

CRUSH, *Tretton myter om bostadsfrågan* (Årsta: Dokument Press, 2016)

Cusset, Pierre-Yves, et al., 'Jeunes issus de l'immigration: quels obstacles à leur insertion économique?', Note d'analyse, France Stratégie (March 2015)

Davis, Mike, *City of Quartz: Excavating the Future in Los Angeles* (New York: Vintage, 1992)

de los Reyes, Paulina, et al., *Bilen brinner ... men problemen är kvar. Berättelser om Husbyhändelserna i maj 2013* (Stockholm: Stockholmia, 2014)

Department of Justice, *Investigation of the Ferguson Police Department*, United States Department of Justice, Civil Rights Division, 4 March 2015

Deranty, Jean-Philippe, and Emmanuel Renault, 'Democratic agon: striving for distinction or struggle against domination and injustice?', in Andrew Schaap, ed., *Law and Agonistic Politics* (Farnham: Ashgate, 2009), 43–56

Derickson, Kate D., 'The racial state and resistance in Ferguson and beyond', *Urban Studies*, 53, no. 11 (2016): 2223–37

Dikeç, Mustafa, *Badlands of the Republic: Space, Politics and Urban Policy* (London: Blackwell, 2007)

—, *Space, Politics and Aesthetics* (Edinburgh: Edinburgh University Press, 2015)

Dikeç, Mustafa, and Erik Swyngedouw, 'Theorizing the politicizing city', *International Journal of Urban and Regional Research*, 41, no. 1 (2017)

Diken, Bülent, 'The emancipated city: notes on Gezi revolts', *Journal for Cultural Research*, 18, no. 4 (2014): 315–28

Douzinas, Costas, *Philosophy and Resistance in the Crisis* (Cambridge: Polity, 2013)

Downing, Emma, and Steven Kennedy, *Food Banks and Food Poverty* (House of Commons Library, 2014)

Dritsas, Spyros, and Giorgos Kalampokas, 'The first big wave: 2006–07', in Clare Solomon and Tania Palmieri, eds, *Springtime: The New Student Rebellions* (London: Verso, 2011), 213–18

du Roy, Ivan, and Ludo Simbille, *Homicides, accidents, « malaise », légitime défense: 50 ans de morts par la police*, www.bastamag.net, 13 March 2014

BIBLIOGRAPHY

Dutton, Thomas A., '"Violence": in Cincinnati', *The Nation*, 18 June 2001

Edelman, Peter, *So Rich, So Poor: Why It's So Hard to End Poverty in America* (New York: The New Press, 2012)

Erdi-Lelandais, Gülçin, 'Gezi protests and beyond: urban resistance under neoliberal urbanism in Turkey', in Margit Mayer, Catharina Thörn and Håkan Thörn, eds, *Urban Uprisings: Challenging Neoliberal Urbanism in Europe* (London: Palgrave, 2016), 283–308

Erensü, Sinan, and Ozan Karaman, 'The work of a few trees: Gezi, politics and space', *International Journal of Urban and Regional Research* (forthcoming)

Fogelson, Robert M., 'White on black: a critique of the McCone Commission report on the Los Angeles riots', *Political Science Quarterly*, 82, no. 3 (1967): 337–67

—, 'Violence and grievances: reflections on the 1960s', *Journal of Social Forces*, 26, no. 1 (1970): 157

Fraser, Nancy, *Justice Interruptus: Critical Reflections on the 'Postsocialist' Condition* (New York: Routledge, 1997)

Frye, Marilyn, *The Politics of Reality: Essays in Feminist Theory* (Berkeley: Crossing Press, 1983)

Gaitanou, Eirini, 'The December explosion', in Clare Solomon and Tania Palmieri, eds, *Springtime: The New Student Rebellions* (London: Verso, 2011), 222–6

Gilroy, Paul, *There Ain't No Black in the Union Jack: The Cultural Politics of Race and Nation* (London: Routledge, 1987)

Gooding-Williams, Robert, ed., *Reading Rodney King/Reading Urban Uprising* (New York: Routledge, 1993)

Gordon, Colin, *Mapping Decline: St. Louis and the Fate of the American City* (Philadelphia: University of Pennsylvania Press, 2008)

Graham, Stephen, *Cities under Siege: The New Military Urbanism* (London: Verso, 2010)

Gregory, Derek, *The Colonial Present: Afghanistan, Palestine, Iraq* (London: Blackwell, 2004)

Grundström, Karin, and Irene Molina, 'From Folkhem to lifestyle housing in Sweden: segregation and urban form, 1930s–2010s', *International Journal of Housing Policy*, 16, no. 3 (2016): 316–36

The Guardian/LSE, *Reading the Riots: Investigating England's Summer of Disorder* (London, 2011)

Gürcan, Efe C., and Efe Peker, 'A class analytic approach to the Gezi Park events: challenging the "middle class" myth', *Capital & Class*, 39, no. 2 (2015): 321–43

—, *Challenging Neoliberalism at Turkey's Gezi Park: From Private Discontent to Collective Class Action* (London: Palgrave, 2015)

Gürek, Harun, *AKP'nin Müteahhitleri* (Istanbul: Güncel Yayıncılık, 2008)

Haas, Michael, 'Metaphysics of paradigms in political science: theories of urban unrest', *Review of Politics*, 48, no. 4 (1986): 520–48

Hajjat, Abdellali, 'Rébellions urbaines et déviances policières', *Cultures & Conflits*, 93 (2014): 11–34

HALDE (*Haute autorité de lutte contre les discriminations*), *Rapport annuel HALDE 2010* (Paris: La Documentation française)

Hallin, Per Olof, Alban Jashari, Carina Listerborn and Margareta Popoola, *Det är inte stenarna som gör ont. Röster från Herrgården, Rosengård – om konflikter och erkännande* (Malmö: Malmö Publikationer i Urbana Studier, 2010)

Hamnett, Chris, 'The conditions in England's inner cities on the eve of the 1981 riots', *Area*, 15, no. 1 (1983): 7–13

Harvey, David, *The New Imperialism* (Oxford: Oxford University Press, 2003)

Hedin, Karin, et al., 'Neoliberalisation of housing in Sweden: gentrification, filtering, and social polarisation', *Annals of the Association of American Geographers*, 102, no. 2 (2012): 443–63

BIBLIOGRAPHY

Hennig, Benjamin, and Danny Dorling, 'The hollowing out of London: how poverty patterns are changing', *New Statesman*, 13 March 2015

Her Majesty's Inspectorate of Constabulary (HMIC), *Adapting to Protest: Nurturing the British Model of Policing* (London, 2009)

—, *Without Fear or Favour: A Review of Police Relationships* (London, 2011)

—, *Stop and Search Powers: Are the Police Using Them Effectively and Fairly?* (London, 2013)

Hinton, Elizabeth, *From the War on Poverty to the War on Crime: The Making of Mass Incarceration in America* (Cambridge, MA: Harvard University Press, 2016)

Home Affairs Committee, *Young Black People and the Criminal Justice System* (London: The Stationery Office, 2007)

—, *Policing Large Scale Disorder: Lessons from the Disturbances of August 2011* (London: The Stationery Office, 2011)

—, *Independent Police Complaints Commission* (London: The Stationery Office, 2013)

Home Office, *Stop and Search Manual* (London: Home Office, 2005)

—, *An Overview of Recorded Crimes and Arrests Resulting from Disorder Events in August 2011* (London: Home Office, 2011)

Home Office Statistical Bulletin, *The Outcome of Arrests during the Serious Incidents of Public Disorder in July and August 1981*, 13 October 1982 (available at the National Archives, reference HO 496/16)

Human Rights Watch, *'The Root of Humiliation': Abusive Identity Checks in France* (2012)

—, 'France: abuses under state of emergency' (2016), available at https://www.hrw.org/news/2016/02/03/france-abuses-under-state-emergency (accessed 16 June 2016)

Hurrell, Karen, *Race Disproportionality in Stops and Searches, 2011–12* (Manchester: Equality and Human Rights Commission, 2013)

Iakovidou, Josephine, Kostas Kanellopoulos and Loukia Kotronaki, 'The Greek uprising of December 2008', *Situations*, 3, no. 2 (2010): 145–57

INSEE, *Données sociales. La société française* (Paris: INSEE, 2006)

—, *Immigrés et descendants d'immigrés en France* (Paris: INSEE, 2012)

INSEE-DIV, n.d., *Fiches Profil – Quartiers de la politique de la ville: Données des recensements de la population de 1990 et 1999* (CD-ROM)

Jazouli, Adil, *Les années banlieues* (Paris: Seuil, 1992)

Jeannet, Agnès, Laurnet Caillot and Yves Calvez, *L'accès à l'emploi des jeunes de quartiers prioritaires de la politique de la ville* (Inspection générale des affaires sociales, 2010)

Kalyvas, Andreas, 'An anomaly? Some reflections on the Greek December 2008', *Constellations*, 17, no. 2 (2010): 351–65

Kamali, Masoud, *Sverige inifrån. Röster om etnisk diskriminering* (Stockholm: Statens Offentliga Utredningar, 2005)

Kamat, Anjali, 'The Baltimore uprising', in Jordan T. Camp and Christina Heatherton, eds, *Policing the Planet: Why the Policing Crisis Led to Black Lives Matter* (London: Verso, 2016), 73–82

Kanouté, Almamy, et al., '2005, pour rien? Analyses d'acteurs', *Mouvements*, 83 (2015): 50–62

Kaplanis, Yiannis, 'An economy that excludes the many and an "accidental" revolt', in Antonis Vradis and Dimitris Dalakoglou, eds, *Revolt and Crisis in Greece* (Oakland: AK Press & Occupied London, 2011), 215–28

Karakaya-Stump, Ayfer (2014), 'Alevizing Gezi', *Jadaliyya*, http://www.jadaliyya.com/pages/index/17087/alevizing-gezi (accessed 30 June 2016)

Karaman, Ozan, 'Urban renewal in İstanbul: reconfigured spaces, robotic lives', *International Journal of Urban and Regional Research*, 37, no. 2 (2013): 715–33

—, 'Urban neoliberalism with Islamic characteristics', *Urban Studies*, 50, no. 16 (2013): 3412–27

241

Karamichas, John, 'The December 2008 riots in Greece', *Social Movement Studies*, 8, no. 3 (2009): 289–93

Kawalerowicz, Juta, and Michael Biggs, 'Anarchy in the UK: economic deprivation, social disorganization, and political grievances in the London riot of 2011', *Social Forces*, 94, no. 2 (2015): 673–98

Keith, Michael, *Race, Riots and Policing: Lore and Disorder in a Multi-racist Society* (London: UCL Press, 1993)

Keyder, Çağlar, 'Globalisation and social exclusion in Istanbul', *International Journal of Urban and Regional Research*, 29, no. 1 (2005): 124–34

Khiari, Sadri, *Pour une politique de la racaille: immigré-e-s, indigènes et jeunes de banlieues* (Paris: Textuel, 2006)

—, *La contre-révolution coloniale en France: de de Gaulle à Sarkozy* (Paris: La fabrique, 2009)

Kings, Lisa, Aleksandra Ålund and Carl-Ulrik Schierup, 'Revolt of the urban periphery: Sweden's riots in context', *New Left Project*, 2 June 2013

Kipfer, Stefan, 'Tackling urban apartheid: report from the Social Forum of Popular Neighbourhoods in Paris', *International Journal of Urban and Regional Research*, 33, no. 4 (2009): 1058–66

—, 'Neocolonial urbanism? La rénovation urbaine in Paris', *Antipode*, 48, no. 3 (2016): 603–25

Kneebone, Elizabeth, and Emily Garr, *The Suburbanization of Poverty: Trends in Metropolitan America, 2000 to 2008* (Brookings Metropolitan Policy Program, 2010)

Kokoreff, Michel, *Sociologie des émeutes* (Paris: Payot, 2008)

Kotronaki, Loukia, and Seraphim Seferiades, 'Sur les sentiers de la colère: l'espace-temps d'une révolte', *Actuel Marx*, 48 (2010): 152–65

Kouvelakis, Stathis, 'La Grèce en révolte' (2008), http://www.contretemps.eu/interventions/stathis-kouvelakis-grece-en-revolte (accessed 12 February 2016)

Kuymulu, Mehmet B., 'Reclaiming the right to the city: reflections on the urban uprisings in Turkey', *City*, 17, no. 3 (2013): 274–8

Laclau, Ernesto, *On Populist Reason* (London: Verso, 2005)

Lagrange, Hugues, 'Emeutes, ségrégation urbaines et aliénation politique', *Revue française de science politique*, 58, no. 3 (2008): 377–401

Larsson, Bengt, Martin Letell and Håkan Thörn, eds, *Transformations of the Swedish Welfare State: From Social Engineering to Governance?* (London: Palgrave, 2012)

Leclerc, Henri, 'Libertés publiques: l'année horrible', in Ligue des droits de l'Homme, *L'état des droits de l'Homme en France* (Paris: La Découverte, 2004)

Lindbom, Anders, 'Dismantling Swedish housing policy', *Governance: An International Journal of Policy and Administration*, 14, no. 4 (2001): 503–26

Lindsey, Treva B., 'Post-Ferguson: A "herstorical" approach to black violability', *Feminist Studies*, 41, no. 1 (2015): 235

Locke, Alain, *The Works of Alain Locke*, ed. Charles Molesworth (Oxford: Oxford University Press, 2012)

Logan, John R., and Brian Stults, 'The persistence of segregation in the metropolis: new findings from the 2010 census', census brief prepared for Project US2010 (2011)

Lovering, John, and Hade Türkmen, 'Bulldozer neo-liberalism in İstanbul: the state-led construction of property markets, and the displacement of the urban poor', *International Planning Studies*, 16, no. 1 (2011): 73–96

Macpherson, William, *The Stephen Lawrence Inquiry* (London: Home Office, 1999)

Makrygianni, Vaso, and Haris Tsavdaroglou, 'Urban planning and revolt: a spatial analysis of the December 2008 uprising in Athens', in Antonis Vradis and Dimitris Dalakoglou, eds, *Revolt and Crisis in Greece* (Oakland: AK Press & Occupied London, 2011), 29–57

Marx, Gary, 'Issueless riots', *Annals of the American Academy of Political and Social Science*, 391, no. 1 (1970): 21–33

Mayer, Margit, Catharina Thörn and Håkan Thörn, eds, *Urban Uprisings: Challenging Neoliberal Urbanism in Europe* (London: Palgrave, 2016)

Mazars, Michel, *Le traitement judicaire des « violences urbaines » de l'automne 2005: le cas de la Seine-Saint-Denis* (Document de travail, Centre d'analyse stratégique, 2007)

Mbembe, Achille, 'The Republic and its beast: on the riots in the French *banlieues*', in Charles Tshimanga et al., eds, *Frenchness and the African Diaspora: Identity and Uprisings in Contemporary France* (Bloomington: Indiana University Press, 2009)

Mechmache, Mohamed, 'Les révoltes de 2005, une prise de conscience politique', *Mouvements*, 83 (2015): 17–21

Merrifield, Andy, *The Politics of the Encounter: Urban Theory and Protest under Planetary Urbanisation* (Athens, GA: University of Georgia Press, 2013)

Metropolitan Police Authority (MPA), *Report of the MPA Scrutiny on MPS Stop and Search Practice* (London: MPA, 2004)

Metzger, Molly W., *Section 8 in the St. Louis Region: Local Opportunities to Expand Housing Choice* (Washington University in St Louis: Center for Social Development, 2014)

Mignard, Jean-Pierre, and Emmanuel Tordjman, *L'affaire Clichy* (Paris: Stock, 2006)

Miller, Byron, and Walter J. Nicholls, 'Social movements in urban society: the city as a space of politicisation', *Urban Geography*, 34, no. 4 (2013): 452–73

Ministry of Justice, *Statistics on Race and the Criminal Justice System 2012* (London, 2013)

Mitchell, Don, 'Introduction: the lightning flash of revolt', in Neil Smith and Don Mitchell, eds, *Revolting New York* (Athens, GA: University of Georgia Press, forthcoming)

Mitchell, Don, Kafui Attoh and Lynn Staeheli, ' "Broken windows is not the panacea": common sense, good sense, and police accountability in American cities', in Jordan T. Camp and Christina Heatherton, eds, *Policing the Planet: Why the Policing Crisis Led to Black Lives Matter* (London: Verso, 2016), 237–57

Molina, Irene, *Stadens rasifiering: Etnisk boendesegregation i folkhemmet*, Geografiska region-studier, 32 (Uppsala, 1997)

Moore, Dan P., *Mark Twain was Right: The 2001 Cincinnati Riots* (Lansing, MI: Microcosm Publishing, 2012)

Mucchielli, Laurent, *Violences et insécurité: fantasmes et réalités dans le débat français* (Paris: La Découverte, 2001)

—, 'Autumn 2005: a review of the most important riot in the history of French contemporary society', *Journal of Ethnic and Migration Studies*, 35, no. 5 (2009): 731–51

Mucchielli, Laurent, and Abderrahim Aït-Omar, 'Les émeutes de novembre 2005: les raisons de la colère', in Véronique Le Goaziou and Laurent Mucchielli, eds, *Quand les banlieues brûlent . . .* (Paris: La Découverte, 2006), 5–30

MVA and Joel Miller, *Profiling Populations Available for Stops and Searches* (London: Home Office, 2000)

Nicholls, Walter J., Byron Miller and Justin Beaumont, eds, *Spaces of Contention: Spatialities and Social Movements* (London: Routledge, 2013)

Nicholls, Walter J., and Justus Uitermark, *Cities and Social Movements: Immigrant Rights Activism in the US, France, and the Netherlands, 1970–2015* (London: Wiley-Blackwell, 2016)

Nwabuzo, Ojeaku, *The Riot Roundtables: Race and the Riots of August 2011* (London: Runnymede Trust, 2012)

Observatoire national des zones urbaines sensibles (ONZUS), *Rapport 2009* and *Rapport 2013* (Saint-Denis: CIV)

OECD, *Divided We Stand: Why Inequality Keeps Rising* (Paris: OECD, 2011)

Office for National Statistics, *Persistent Poverty in the UK and EU, 2008–2013*

Oppenheimer, David B., 'California's anti-discrimination legislation, Proposition 14, and the constitutional protection of minority rights', *Golden Gate University Law Review*, 40 (2010): 117–27

Parmar, Alpa, 'Stop and search in London: counter-terrorist or counter-productive?', *Policing & Society*, 21, no. 4 (2011): 369–82

Pérouse, Jean-François, 'Hybristanbul: Turkey's urban development boom', *booksandideas*, 3 February 2014, available at http://www.booksandideas.net/Hybristanbul-2560.html (accessed 16 June 2016)

Piketty, Thomas, *Capital in the Twenty-first Century* (Cambridge, MA: Harvard University Press, 2014)

Portaliou, Eleni, 'Social resistance movements against the Olympic Games 2004 in Athens', paper presented at Annual Meeting of International Network of Urban Research and Action, 2008

Pred, Allan, *Even in Sweden: Racisms, Racialized Spaces, and the Popular Geographical Imagination* (Berkeley: University of California Press, 2000)

Prime Minister, 'Scarman Inquiry', 2 November 1981, National Archives reference PREM-19–1521_150.jpg

PSE, *The Impoverishment of the UK: PSE UK First Results* (2013; see PSE website: www.poverty.ac.uk)

Rajsfus, Maurice, *La police et la peine de mort: 1977–2001=196 morts* (Paris: L'Esprit frappeur, 2002)

Rankine, Claudia, *Citizen: An American Lyric* (London: Penguin Books, 2015)

Reardon, Sean F., and Kendra Bischoff, 'Growth in the residential segregation of families by income, 1970–2009', report prepared for Project US2010 (2011)

Regeringskansliet, *Urbana utvecklingsområden. Statistisk uppföljning utifrån 7 indikationer* (Stockholm: Arbetsmarknadsdepartementet, 2013)

Reicher, S., 'The St. Pauls' riot: an explanation of the limits of crowd action in terms of a social identity model', *European Journal of Social Psychology*, 14 (1984): 1–21

Report of the Independent Commission on the Los Angeles Police Department, 1991 (the 'Christopher Commission report')

Rigouste, Mathieu, *La domination policière: une violence industrielle* (Paris: La fabrique, 2012)

Riots Communities and Victims Panel, *After the Riots: The Final Report of the Riots Communities and Victims Panel* (London, 2012)

Ristilammi, Per-Markku, 'Alterity in modern Sweden', *Pro Ethnologia*, 4 (1996): 71–80

Rothstein, Richard, *The Making of Ferguson: Public Policies at the Root of its Troubles* (Washington DC: Economic Policy Institute, 2014)

Routledge, Paul, 'Introduction: cities, justice and conflict', *Urban Studies*, 47, no. 6 (2010): 1165–77

Rudé, George, *The Crowd in History* (London: Serif, 2005 [1964])

Sakizlioglu, Nur B., and Justus Uitermark, 'The symbolic politics of gentrification: the restructuring of stigmatized neighbourhoods in Amsterdam and Istanbul', *Environment and Planning A*, 46, no. 6 (2014): 1369–85

Scarman, Lord, *The Scarman Report: The Brixton Disorders 10–12 April 1981* (Harmondsworth: Penguin, 1982)

Schierup, Carl-Ulrik, and Aleksandra Ålund, 'The end of Swedish exceptionalism? Citizenship, neoliberalism and the politics of exclusion', *Race & Class*, 53, no. 1 (2011): 45–64

Schierup, Carl-Ulrik, Aleksandra Ålund and Lisa Kings, 'Reading the Stockholm riots – a moment for social justice?', *Race & Class*, 55, no. 3 (2014): 1–21

Scott, Allen, ed., *The City: Los Angeles and Urban Theory at the End of the Twentieth Century* (Berkeley: University of California Press, 1998), 311–35

Sernhede, Ove, 'School, youth culture and territorial stigmatisation in Swedish metropol-itan districts', *Young*, 19, no. 2 (2011): 159–80

—, 'Youth rebellion and social mobilisation in Sweden', *Soundings*, 56 (2014): 81–91

Sernhede, Ove, Catharina Thörn and Håkan Thörn, 'The Stockholm uprising in context: urban social movements in the rise and demise of the Swedish welfare-state city', in Margit Mayer et al., eds, *Urban Uprisings: Challenging Neoliberal Urbanism in Europe* (Palgrave: London, 2016), 149–73

Shklar, Judith, *The Faces of Injustice* (New Haven, CT: Yale University Press, 1990)

Skirtz, Alice, *Econocide: Elimination of the Urban Poor* (Washington DC: NASW Press, 2012)

Slater, Tom, 'From "criminality" to marginality: rioting against a broken state', *Human Geography*, 4, no. 3 (2011): 106–15

Smith, David, and Jeremy Gray, *Police and People in London IV: The Police in Action* (London: Policy Studies Institute, 1983)

Smith, Neil, and Don Mitchell, eds, *Revolting New York* (Athens, GA: University of Georgia Press, forthcoming)

Sotiris, Panagiotis, 'Reading revolt as deviance: Greek intellectuals and the December 2008 revolt of Greek youth', *Interface*, 5, no. 2 (2013): 47–77

Stavrides, Stavros, 'The December 2008 youth uprising in Athens: spatial justice in an emergent city of thresholds', *justice spatiale | spatial justice*, 2 (2010), http://www.jssj.org

Stevens, Philip, and Carole Willis, *Race, Crime and Arrests* (London: Her Majesty's Stationery Office, 1979)

Stockholms stad, *Skillnadernas Stockholm* (Stockholm: Kommissionen för ett socialt hållbart Stockholm, 2015)

Sutterlüty, Ferdinand, 'The hidden morale of the 2005 French and 2011 English riots', *Thesis Eleven*, 121, no. 1 (2014): 38–56

Swyngedouw, Erik, *The Promises of the Political: Post-Democratization, Apocalyptic Environments, and Insurgent Cities* (Boston: MIT Press, 2018 forthcoming)

Taşkale, Ali R., 'There is another Turkey out there', *Third Text*, 30, nos 1–2 (2016): 138–46

Tévanian, Pierre, *Le ministère de la peur* (Paris: L'esprit frappeur, 2003)

—, 'A conservative revolution within secularism: the ideological premises and social effects of the March 15, 2004 "anti-headscarf" law', in Charles Tshimanga et al., eds, *Frenchness and the African Diaspora: Identity and Uprisings in Contemporary France* (Bloomington: Indiana University Press, 2009): 187–204

—, *Chronique du racisme républicain* (Paris: Editions Syllepse, 2013)

Thörn, Catharina, 'The Stockholm uprising and the myth of Swedish social democracy', *New Left Project*, 30 May 2013

Travis, Jeremy, Bruce Western and Steve Redburn, eds, *The Growth of Incarceration in the United States* (Washington DC: National Research Council, 2014)

Turam, Berna, *Gaining Freedoms: Claiming Space in Istanbul and Berlin* (Stanford: Stanford University Press, 2015)

UN-Habitat, *State of the World's Cities 2012/2013*

Violence in the City – An End or A Beginning? A Report by the Governor's Commission on the Los Angeles Riots, 2 December 1965 (the 'McCone Report')

Vogel, Joachim, 'Urban segregation in Sweden', *Social Indicators Research*, 27, no. 2 (1992): 139–55

Wilkinson, Steven I., 'Riots', *Annual Review of Political Science*, 12 (2009): 329–43

Wilson, William J., *The Truly Disadvantaged: The Inner City, the Underclass, and Public Policy*, 2nd edn (Chicago: University of Chicago Press, 2012)

Winlow, Simon, et al., *Riots and Political Protest: Notes From the Post-political Present* (New York: Routledge, 2015)

BIBLIOGRAPHY

Wolf, Martin, *The Shifts and the Shocks* (London: Allen Lane, 2014)

Yörük, Erdem, and Murat Yüksel, 'Class and politics in Turkey's Gezi protests', *New Left Review*, 89 (2014): 103–23

Young, Iris M., *Inclusion and Democracy* (Oxford: Oxford University Press, 2000)

Zancarini-Fournel, Michelle, 'Généalogie des rébellions urbaines en temps de crise (1971–1981)', *Vingtième Siècle. Revue d'histoire*, 84 (2004): 119–27

Illustration Credits

Index

248

INDEX